Dorothy S. Strickland
Richard F. Abrahamson
Roger C. Farr
Nancy R. McGee
Nancy L. Roser

2

Karen S. Kutiper
Patricia Smith

HBJ LANGUAGE

HBJ HARCOURT BRACE JOVANOVICH, PUBLISHERS
Orlando   San Diego   Chicago   Dallas

Copyright © 1990 by Harcourt Brace Jovanovich, Inc.

All rights reserved. No part of this publication may be reproduced or transmitted in any form or by any means, electronic or mechanical, including photocopy, recording, or any information storage and retrieval system, without permission in writing from the publisher.

Requests for permission to make copies of any part of the work should be mailed to: Copyrights and Permissions Department, Harcourt Brace Jovanovich, Publishers, Orlando, Florida 32887

Printed in the United States of America

ISBN 0-15-316411-5

Acknowledgments

For permission to reprint copyrighted material, grateful acknowledgment is made to the following sources:

Clarion Books/Ticknor & Fields, a Houghton Mifflin Company: "The Cheerful Child's Week" from *The Way I Feel . . . Sometimes* by Beatrice Schenk de Regniers. Copyright © 1988 by Beatrice Schenk de Regniers.

William Cole: "Just for a Change" by William Cole from *The Second Poetry Drawing Book* by William Cole and Julia Colmore. Copyright © 1962 by William Cole.

Beatrice Schenk de Regniers: "Sing a Song of Pockets" from *Something Special* by Beatrice Schenk de Regniers. © 1958, 1986 by Beatrice Schenk de Regniers.

Dial Books for Young Readers: Text and illustrations from *Cat & Canary* (Titled: "Cat and Canary") by Michael Foreman. Copyright © 1984 by Michael Foreman.

Houghton Mifflin Company: "The Man That Had Little to Say" from *I Met a Man* by John Ciardi. Copyright © 1961 by John Ciardi.

Little, Brown and Company: Text and illustrations from *Under the Lemon Tree* by Edith Thacher Hurd, illustrated by Clement Hurd. Text copyright © 1980 by Edith Thacher Hurd; illustrations copyright © 1980 by Clement Hurd.

S. Robert Ramsey, on behalf of James Ramsey: Abridged and adapted from *Going to the Museum* by James Ramsey. Copyright © 1985 by James Ramsey.

Marian Reiner, on behalf of Eve Merriam: "Left Foot, Right Foot" from *Blackberry Ink* by Eve Merriam. Copyright © 1985 by Eve Merriam. All rights reserved.

Karen Solomon: "Shoes Have Tongues" from *Funday and Father Gander* by Ilo Orleans. "The Wind" from *I Watch the World Go By* by Ilo Orleans.

Art Acknowledgments

Michael Adams: 27; Alex Bloch: 186, 240, 286, 300; Deborah Borgo: 236, 304; Ray Burns: 24, 143, 193; Suzanne Clee: 99, 140, 272, 273, 275, 276, 288, 303, EP16, EP24; Olivia Cole: 180, 181, 244; Eulala Connor: 130, 188; Terri Cowgill: 332; Wendy Crockett: 63, 77, 148, 196, 219, 230, 306, EP48; Diane Dawson-Hearn: 246; Marlene Ekman: 38, 242, 289; Michael Foreman: 206, 207, 208, 209, 210, 211, 212, 213; Llyn Hunter: 32, 40, 41, 48, 78, 80, 94, 95, 104, 115, 135, 138, 182, 195, 254, 280, 281, 290; Clement Hurd: 152, 153, 154, 155, 156, 157, 158, 159; Susan Jaekel: 28, 29; Loretta Lustig: 30, 31, 184, 294; Laurie Marks: 35, 47, 131, 141, 224, 226, 227, 298; Jane McCreary: 11, 25, 61, 64, 86, 98, 100, 232, G2, G7; Dana McMahan: 194; Christine McNamara: 36, G5, G6; Sharron O'Neil: 45, 75, 82, 83, 92, 129, 174, 176, 191, 233, 248, 253, 282, 283; Rik Olson: 8–9, 26, 76, 98, 101, 130, 176; Sue Parnell: 66, 69, 71, 238; Jan Pyk: 134, 136, 144, 145, 284; Sandy Rabinowitz: 122; James Ramsey: 54, 55, 56, 57, 58, 59; Doug Roy: 101; Ed Sauk: 67, 116; Dennis Schofield: 177; Mira Shallcross: 17, 20, 112, 113, 118, 192, 254, 292, 334, 335, EP4, WH16, WH31; D. J. Simison: 34, 84, 90, 142, 234, 260–265; Rosiland Solomon: 37, 46, 178, 183, 185, 190, 250–252, 302; Wayne Still: 128; Tom Vroman: 18, 69, 121, 168, 224, 273.

Cover: Tom Vroman

Production and Layout: The Hampton Brown Company

Photo Acknowledgments

PHOTOGRAPHS: Pages 2 (b), HBJ Photo/Rob Downey; 3, HBJ Photo/Rob Downey; 4 (t), HBJ Photo/Rob Downey; (b) HBJ Photo/Rob Downey; 5 (t), HBJ Photo/Rob Downey; (b) HBJ Photo/Rob Downey.

UNIT 1: 6, HBJ Photo/Tom G. O'Neal; 7 (l), HBJ Photo/Tom G. O'Neal; (c), HBJ Photo/Tom G. O'Neal; (r), HBJ Photo/Tom G. O'Neal; 14 (b), HBJ Photo/Tom G. O'Neal; 19 (b), HBJ Photo/Tom G. O'Neal; 23 (t), HBJ Photo/Tom G. O'Neal; (b), HBJ Photo/Tom G. O'Neal; 42 (t), HBJ Photo/Charlie Burton.

UNIT 2: 52, HBJ Photo/Tom G. O'Neal; 53, James Ramsey; 64, HBJ Photo/Rob Downey; 68, HBJ Photo/Rob Downey; 72, HBJ Photo/Rob Downey; 74 (l), HBJ Photo/Rob Downey; (r), HBJ Photo/Rob Downey; (b), HBJ Photo/Rob Downey; 88, HBJ Photo/Tom G. O'Neal; 96, HBJ Photo/Charlie Burton; 97, HBJ Photo/Charlie Burton.

UNIT 3: 110, HBJ Photo/Rob Downey; 111 (l), HBJ Photo/Tom G. O'Neal; (r), HBJ Photo/Tom G. O'Neal; 116, HBJ Photo/Tom G. O'Neal; 119, HBJ Photo/Terry McMenamy; 122, HBJ Photo/Terry McMenamy; 127 (l), HBJ Photo/Terry McMenamy; (r), HBJ Photo/Terry McMenamy; (b), HBJ Photo/Terry McMenamy; 132, HBJ Photo/Rob Downey.

UNIT 4: 150, W. Steinmetz/The Image Bank; 151, Jerry O'Day; 163, Steve McCutcheon/MONKMEYER PRESS; 164, Horizon Images, Inc./MONKMEYER PRESS; 165, HBJ Photo/Rob Downey; 173 (l), HBJ Photo/Rob Downey; (r), HBJ Photo/Rob Downey; (b), HBJ Photo/Rob Downey; 175, HBJ Photo/Rob Downey.

UNIT 5: 204, Lee Hocker; 205, Ron Sutherland; 220, HBJ Photo/Charlie Burton; 223, HBJ Photo/Charlie Burton; 225, HBJ Photo/Charlie Burton; 229 (l), HBJ Photo/Charlie Burton; (r), HBJ Photo/Charlie Burton; (b), HBJ Photo/Charlie Burton; 231, HBJ Photo/Charlie Burton.

continued at the back of the book

Contents

A Letter to the Student ... 1
Understanding the Writing Process ... 2

1 Telling About Pictures ... 6

Reading ↔ Writing Connection

Reading/Literature Model	Reading with a Writer's Eye: *Sentences About Pictures* by Nancy Muñoz, Lukas Badowski, and Evan Huber	8
Thinking Skills	Thinking As a Writer: Studying a Sentence About a Picture	10
	Using Details to Tell the Main Idea	12
Writer's Craft	Developing the Writer's Craft: Using Exact Words	13

Composition Focus: Sentence About a Picture

Writing Process	1 Prewriting	14
Listening/Speaking	How to Have a Class Talk	16
Writing Process	2 Drafting	17
Writing Process	3 Responding and Revising	19
Writing Process	4 Proofreading	22
Writing Process	5 Publishing	23
Listening/Speaking	How to Listen for the Main Idea	25
Cross-Curricular Writing	Writing in the Content Areas	26

Connecting **WRITING** and **LANGUAGE** ... 27

Language Focus: Sentences

Grammar	1 What Is a Sentence?	28
Grammar	2 Naming Part of a Sentence	30
Grammar	3 Telling Part of a Sentence	32
Grammar	4 Word Order in a Sentence	34
Grammar	5 Statements	36
Grammar	6 Questions	38
Grammar	7 Exclamations	40
Grammar/Usage	8 Kinds of Sentences	42
Vocabulary	Building Vocabulary: Rhyming Words	44
Listening/Speaking	Listening to a Poem: "Left Foot, Right Foot" by Eve Merriam	45
	Language Enrichment: Sentences	46

Connecting **LANGUAGE** and **WRITING** ... 47

Unit Checkup ... 48

v

2 Telling About Yourself — 52

Reading ↔ Writing Connection

Reading/Literature Model	Reading with a Writer's Eye: "Going to the Museum" by James Ramsey	54
Thinking Skills	Thinking As a Writer: Studying a Personal Story	60
	Grouping Ideas by Topic	62
Writer's Craft	Developing the Writer's Craft: Using Synonyms	63

Composition Focus: Personal Story

Writing Process	1 Prewriting	64
Listening/Speaking	How to Tell About Ideas in Order	67
Writing Process	2 Drafting	68
Writing Process	3 Responding and Revising	70
Listening/Speaking	How to Work in a Response Group	72
Writing Process	4 Proofreading	73
Writing Process	5 Publishing	74
Cross-Curricular Writing	Writing in the Content Areas	76
	Connecting WRITING and LANGUAGE	77

Language Focus: Nouns

Grammar	1 Naming Words for People and Animals	78
Grammar	2 Naming Words for Places and Things	80
Grammar/Spelling	3 Nouns That Name More Than One	82
Grammar/Spelling	4 More Nouns That Name More Than One	84
Grammar/Spelling	5 Other Nouns That Name More Than One	86
Grammar	6 Nouns That Name Special People and Animals	88
Grammar	7 Nouns That Name Special Places	90
Grammar	8 Days, Months, and Holidays	92
Grammar/Usage	9 Words That Take the Place of Nouns	94
Grammar/Usage	10 The Pronouns I and Me	96
Vocabulary	Building Vocabulary: Compound Words	98
Listening/Speaking	Listening to a Poem: "Sing a Song of Pockets" by Beatrice Schenk de Regniers	99
	Language Enrichment: Nouns	100
	Connecting LANGUAGE and WRITING	101
	Unit Checkup	102
	Cumulative Review	106

VI

 **Sharing Your News** 110

Reading ↔ Writing Connection

Reading/Literature Model	Reading with a Writer's Eye: Friendly Letters by Shannon Chamberlin and David Living	112
Thinking Skills	Thinking As a Writer: Studying a Friendly Letter	114
	Picturing Events	116
Writer's Craft	Developing the Writer's Craft: Writing for Your Reader	117

Composition Focus: Friendly Letter

Writing Process	1 Prewriting	118
Writing Process	2 Drafting	120
Writing Process	3 Responding and Revising	122
	Revising Workshop: Joining Sentences	125
Writing Process	4 Proofreading	126
Writing Process	5 Publishing	127
Listening/Speaking	How to Talk on the Telephone	129
Cross-Curricular Writing	Writing in the Content Areas	130
	Connecting WRITING and LANGUAGE	131

Language Focus: Verbs

Grammar	1 Action Verbs	132
Grammar/Usage	2 Verbs That Tell About Now	134
Grammar/Usage	3 Verbs That Tell About the Past	136
Grammar/Usage	4 The Verbs Is and Are	138
Grammar/Usage	5 The Verbs Was and Were	140
Vocabulary	Building Vocabulary: Words That Have More Than One Meaning	142
Listening/Speaking	Listening to a Poem: "Shoes Have Tongues" by Ilo Orleans	143
	Language Enrichment: Verbs	144
	Connecting LANGUAGE and WRITING	145
	Unit Checkup	146

VII

4 Telling What Things Are Like 150

Reading ↔ Writing Connection

Reading/Literature Model	Reading with a Writer's Eye: Under the Lemon Tree by Edith Thacher Hurd	152
Thinking Skills	Thinking As a Writer: Studying a Paragraph That Describes	160
	Paying Attention to Details	162
Writer's Craft	Developing the Writer's Craft: Using Colorful Words	163

Composition Focus: Paragraph That Describes

Writing Process	1 Prewriting	164
Writing Process	2 Drafting	167
Writing Process	3 Responding and Revising	169
	Revising Workshop: Adding Describing Words to Sentences	171
Writing Process	4 Proofreading	172
Writing Process	5 Publishing	173
Listening/Speaking	How to Give an Oral Description	175
Cross-Curricular Writing	Writing in the Content Areas	176
	Connecting WRITING and LANGUAGE	177

Language Focus: Describing Words

Grammar	1 Describing Words	178
Grammar	2 Describing Words for Shape and Color	180
Grammar	3 Describing Words for Size and Number	182
Grammar	4 Describing Words for Taste, Smell, Feel, and Sound	184
Grammar	5 Describing Words for Feelings	186
Grammar/Usage	6 Describing Words with er and est	188
Vocabulary	Building Vocabulary: Antonyms	190
Listening/Speaking	Listening to a Poem: "Just for a Change" by William Cole	191
	Language Enrichment: Describing Words	192
	Connecting LANGUAGE and WRITING	193
	Unit Checkup	194
	Cumulative Review	198

VIII

5 Telling Stories 204

Reading ↔ Writing Connection

Reading/Literature Model	Reading with a Writer's Eye: adapted from Cat and Canary by Michael Foreman	**206**
Thinking Skills	Thinking As a Writer: Studying a Story	**214**
	Thinking About What Might Happen	**217**
Writer's Craft	Developing the Writer's Craft: Using Enough Details	**218**

Composition Focus: Story

Writing Process	1 Prewriting	**220**
Writing Process	2 Drafting	**223**
Writing Process	3 Responding and Revising	**225**
Writing Process	4 Proofreading	**228**
Writing Process	5 Publishing	**229**
Listening/Speaking	How to Give Reasons	**231**
Cross-Curricular Writing	Writing in the Content Areas	**232**
	Connecting **WRITING** and **LANGUAGE**	**233**

Language Focus: Verbs

Grammar/Usage	1 Verbs That Tell About Now or the Past	**234**
Grammar/Usage	2 The Verbs Is, Are, Was, and Were	**236**
Grammar/Usage	3 The Verbs Has, Have, and Had	**238**
Grammar/Usage	4 Helping Verbs	**240**
Grammar/Usage/Spelling	5 The Verbs Come and Run	**242**
Grammar/Usage/Spelling	6 The Verbs Go and Do	**244**
Grammar/Usage/Spelling	7 The Verbs See and Give	**246**
Grammar/Spelling	8 Contractions	**248**
Vocabulary	Building Vocabulary: Prefixes	**250**
Listening/Speaking	Listening to a Poem: "The Wind" by Ilo Orleans	**251**
	Language Enrichment: Verbs	**252**
	Connecting **LANGUAGE** and **WRITING**	**253**
	Unit Checkup	**254**

6 Telling How to Do Something 258

Reading ⟷ Writing Connection

Reading/Literature Model	Reading with a Writer's Eye: "Carmen's Surprise" by Lorenca Rosal	260
Thinking Skills	Thinking As a Writer: Studying a How-to Paragraph	266
	Connecting Ideas in Sequence	268
Writer's Craft	Developing the Writer's Craft: Getting the Reader's Interest	269

Composition Focus: How-to Paragraph

Writing Process	1 Prewriting	270
Writing Process	2 Drafting	272
Writing Process	3 Responding and Revising	274
	Revising Workshop: Joining Sentences	277
Writing Process	4 Proofreading	278
Writing Process	5 Publishing	279
Listening/Speaking	How to Give Directions	280
Listening/Speaking	How to Follow Directions	281
Cross-Curricular Writing	Writing in the Content Areas	282

Connecting **WRITING** and **LANGUAGE**   283

Language Focus: Mechanics Wrap-up

Mechanics	1 Sentences	284
Mechanics	2 Names, Titles of People, I	286
Mechanics	3 Names of Special Places	288
Mechanics	4 Days of the Week	290
Mechanics	5 Months of the Year	292
Mechanics	6 Holidays	294
Mechanics	7 Titles of Books, Stories, and Poems	296
Mechanics	8 Friendly Letter	298
Mechanics	9 Envelope	300
Vocabulary	Building Vocabulary: Suffixes	302
Listening/Speaking	Listening to a Poem: "The Cheerful Child's Week" by Beatrice Schenk de Regniers	303
	Language Enrichment: Mechanics	304

Connecting **LANGUAGE** and **WRITING**   305

Unit Checkup   306
Cumulative Review   310

x

Study Skills — 317

1 Using ABC Order	319
2 Finding Words in a Dictionary	320
3 Using a Dictionary Entry	321
4 Using the Parts of a Book	323
5 Using an Index	324
6 Understanding Kinds of Books	325
7 Writing a Book Report	326
8 Taking a Test	327
9 Using Charts	328
10 Using Bar Graphs	330
11 Using Pictographs	332
12 Using Maps	334
13 Writing Telephone Messages	336
14 Filling Out Forms	337

Extra Practice — 1

Unit 1: Sentences	3
Unit 2: Nouns	11
Unit 3: Verbs	21
Unit 4: Describing Words	26
Unit 5: Verbs	32
Unit 6: Mechanics Wrap-up	40

Writer's Handbook — 1

Grammar	3
Mechanics	10
Usage	13
Composition	16
Vocabulary	32
Spelling	33

Glossary — 1

Composition Terms	2
Literary Terms	8

Word Book — 1

What Is a Word Book?	2
How to Use Your Word Book	3

Index

Dear Student,

    Do you know that you use English all day long? You use English when you listen to your teacher and when you tell a story to your class. You use English when you read a book and when you write a sentence.

    This book, <u>HBJ Language</u>, can help you learn to use English better when you listen and speak. It can also help you use English better when you read and write.

    We hope you have fun learning more about your language.

                                      Sincerely,
                                      The Editors

Understanding the Writing Process

Would you like to write a letter to someone? Would you like to write an exciting story? Guess what? You can! Find out how good writers do these things.

Good writers follow certain steps when they write. These steps are called the **writing process.** The Writing Process helps writers plan what to write about. It helps them make their writing clear and interesting. Here are the five stages of the Writing Process.

1. Prewriting
2. Drafting
3. Responding and Revising
4. Proofreading
5. Publishing

Name _____

1 Prewriting

Prewriting is a way to get ideas for writing. Turn on your imagination during prewriting! Here are some ways to get ideas.

- Talk to other people.
- Draw pictures.
- Think about things you have done.

Then choose an idea that you and your readers will like. Write everything you can think of about the idea. You may use lists, drawings, pictures, or charts to help you put your ideas in order.

Chart

My Favorite Pet	
What It Looks Like	What It Does
1. little	1. plays with me
2. fluffy	2. barks
3. big ears	3. does tricks

Understanding the Writing Process

Name _____

2 Drafting

Before you begin the **drafting** stage, think about your prewriting ideas. Do you still want to write about those ideas? If not, then go back to the prewriting stage and think of new ideas.

Then use the information in your list, drawing, picture, or chart to make a first try at writing. A first try is called a **first draft.**

Write quickly and do not worry about mistakes. Just try to get all of your ideas down on paper.

3 Responding and Revising

After writing a first draft, carefully read your work. Sometimes you may read your work to classmates and talk about it. This is called **responding.** Your classmates may have ideas for making your work better.

Then use some of your classmates' ideas, as well as your own. Make changes or add more to your writing. This is called **revising.**

Name _____

4 Proofreading

In the **proofreading** stage, you read your writing again. This time, check to make sure that you used capital letters and end marks correctly. Check your spelling.

5 Publishing

The last stage is called publishing. **Publishing** means sharing your work with other people. First, make a neat copy of your work. Then, share it in an interesting way. Here are some ways to share your work.

- Read it to your family or friends.
- Draw a picture or make a model to go with it.
- Act it out as a play.
- Make a tape recording of it.
- Put it on a bulletin board.
- Make a special stand for it.

Understanding the Writing Process

UNIT 1

Telling About Pictures

◆ **COMPOSITION FOCUS:** Sentence About a Picture
◆ **LANGUAGE FOCUS:** Sentences

Your family and close friends probably know a lot about you. They know your favorite food, a book you like, or a game you like to play.

How would you tell a new friend about yourself? Nancy, Lukas, and Evan drew pictures and wrote sentences to tell about themselves.

In this unit you will learn how to write a sentence that tells about a picture about yourself.

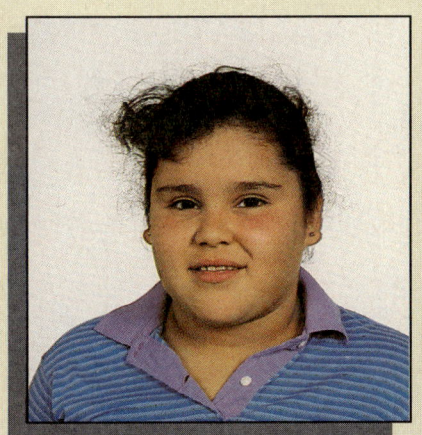  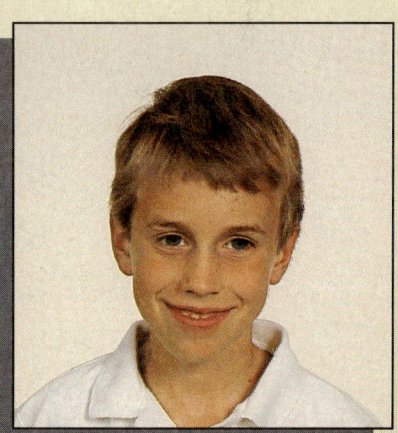

Nancy Muñoz, Lukas Badowski, and Evan Huber wrote sentences to tell about their pictures.

Name _____

Reading with a Writer's Eye
Sentence About a Picture

Here are the pictures and sentences that Nancy, Lukas, and Evan shared with their class. Read the sentences and look at the pictures. What do you find out about the children?

Nancy

Sometimes I invite my friends to a pizza party.

8 READING ◆ WRITING CONNECTION

Name _____

Lukas

I would like to go to China because some of my friends are there.

Evan

I like to play games with my little brother.

Respond

1. How did you feel when you read Evan's sentence?

Discuss

2. What did you learn about Lukas?
3. What did you learn about Nancy?

Name _____

Thinking As a Writer
Studying a Sentence About a Picture

> **Writer's Guide**
> ◆ A sentence tells a complete thought.
> ◆ It begins with a capital letter.
> ◆ It ends with a special mark.

Nancy, Lukas, and Evan wrote sentences to tell about their pictures. A **sentence** is a group of words that tells a complete thought. It tells what someone or something is or does.

Look at Nancy's picture and sentence.

A sentence begins with a capital letter. — Sometimes I invite my friends to a pizza party. — A sentence ends with a special mark.

Discuss

1. Does Nancy's sentence tell a complete thought? Tell why or why not.
2. How does the sentence begin and end?
3. How does Nancy's sentence tell about her picture?

10   READING ↔ WRITING CONNECTION

Name _____

Try Your Hand

A. Choose Sentences   Look at each picture. Draw a line to the group of words that tells a complete thought about the picture.

1.
   - I grew a beautiful flower.
   - a beautiful flower

2.
   - play basketball
   - I like to play basketball.

B. Say Complete Sentences   Look at the details in each picture. Think of the main idea. Then work with a partner. Say a sentence to tell the main idea.

3.

4.

READING ↔ WRITING CONNECTION   11

Name _____

Thinking As a Writer
Using Details to Tell the Main Idea

Kelly's sentence tells what her picture is mostly about. It tells the **main idea.** Before writing, she thought about the **details** in her picture. She used the details to tell the main idea.

Writer's Guide

- To write a sentence about a picture, good writers look at all the details first.
- Then they put the details together to tell the main idea.

Details
Kelly   plants
bone   mother
dog   chair

Main Idea

Discuss

1. Why do you think Kelly decided to write about playing with her dog?
2. Imagine Kelly's picture shows a cat instead of a dog. What should her sentence say? Why?

Try Your Hand

Use Details to Tell the Main Idea Look at Evan's picture again. What details did Evan use to write his sentence?

12   READING ↔ WRITING CONNECTION

Name _____

Developing the Writer's Craft
Using Exact Words

Writer's Guide

◆ Good writers use exact words to give a reader more information.

Good writers use exact words in their sentences. Exact words give more information.

1. At the grocery story I buy <u>food</u>.

2. At the grocery store I buy <u>corn</u>, <u>oatmeal</u>, <u>ham</u>, and <u>pancakes</u>.

Shawna wrote the second sentence to tell about her picture. The exact words <u>corn</u>, <u>oatmeal</u>, <u>ham</u>, and <u>pancakes</u> tell more than the word <u>food</u>.

Discuss

1. In each pair, which word is a more exact word?

    a. hammer—tool   **b.** speak—whisper   **c.** pet—kitten

2. Which sentence is clearer? Why?
    a. A bird goes away.   **b.** A goose flies away.

Try Your Hand

Use Exact Words   Write the sentences. Use exact words for the underlined words. Use the words in the box.

| doll | rabbit | Sara | hops |

1. Did <u>the</u> <u>girl</u> buy a <u>toy</u>?   2. The <u>pet</u> <u>moves</u>.

READING ↔ WRITING CONNECTION   13

Name _____

1 Prewriting
Sentence About a Picture

Look at what Roberto did to plan his picture and sentence.

Roberto followed the **Writer's Guide.** First Roberto talked with his classmates about what makes each of them special.

Roberto wrote a list of all his ideas. He decided to tell about riding his bike. He decided he would share his sentence with his classmates because they also liked to ride bikes. Roberto drew a line around that idea.

Writer's Guide

☑ Talk about ideas.
☑ Make a list of ideas.
☑ Decide who will read your sentence.
☑ Choose an idea that you and your readers will like.

1. (ride my bike)
2. look for rocks
3. play soccer

Name _____

Discuss

1. How did Roberto follow the **Writer's Guide**?

2. Roberto did not write ideas about what the people in his family like to do. Why not?

Try Your Hand

Now plan your picture and sentence.

A. Think of Ideas
Think about what makes you special. You may want to talk to others to get ideas.

Eagle Ideas

1. What do you like to do best?
2. What is your favorite food, book, or game?
3. What makes you happy?

B. Write Your Ideas
Make a list of your ideas.

C. Choose an Idea
Decide who will read your sentence. Decide which idea you like best. Draw a line around the idea.

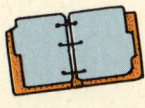 Put your plan in your **Writer's Notebook**. You will use it when you write your sentence.

COMPOSITION: PREWRITING   Sentence About a Picture

Name _____

Listening and Speaking
How to Have a Class Talk

A class talk can help you be a better writer.

When You Are the Speaker	**When You Are a Listener**
◆ Think about what you want to say before you speak. ◆ Speak clearly so that everyone can hear you. ◆ Explain your ideas carefully.	◆ Look at the speaker. Think about what the speaker is saying. ◆ Wait your turn to speak. ◆ Ask questions about things you do not understand.

Practice

Talk with your whole class or a group about ideas to write about. After you talk, follow these directions.

1. Write a new idea you learned.

_____
_____
_____
_____

2. Write an idea you shared.

_____
_____
_____
_____

Name _____

2 Drafting
Sentence About a Picture

Writer's Guide
- ☑ Draw a picture that shows your idea.
- ☑ Think about the details in your picture.
- ☑ Write a sentence to tell the main idea of your picture.

Roberto followed the **Writer's Guide** to draw a picture and write a sentence about it. Since he was telling about himself, Roberto put himself in the picture.

Then Roberto remembered that he liked to ride bikes with his best friend. He added his friend to the picture.

COMPOSITION: DRAFTING Sentence About a Picture **17**

Name _____

Next Roberto thought about the details in his picture. He wrote a sentence to tell the main idea of his picture.

> I am seven and I like to ride my bike with my friend.

Discuss

1. Why did Roberto add to his picture?
2. What does Roberto's sentence tell about him?

Try Your Hand

Now write your sentence.

A. Think About Your Idea   Do you like the idea you chose? If not, choose another idea.

B. Draw a Picture   Draw a picture that shows your idea.

C. Check Your Picture   Does your picture show your idea clearly? Add details if you need to.

D. Keep an Eagle Eye on Who, What, and Why   Remember that you are writing a sentence to tell your readers about your picture.

E. Write Your First Draft   On a clean sheet of paper, write a sentence that tells the main idea of your picture. Write quickly. You can fix any mistakes later.

 Put your picture and your first draft in your **Writer's Notebook.** You will check them in the next lesson.

Name _____

3 Responding and Revising
Sentence About a Picture

Roberto read his sentence to himself. Then he used the **Writer's Guide** to help him make his sentence better. He asked Lori to help him. Look at what they did.

Writer's Guide

☑ Talk about your work.
☑ Be sure your sentence tells the main idea of your picture.
☑ Be sure to tell what your readers might like to know.
☑ Make changes.

I like the way your sentence tells about your picture.

Thanks. Do you think the class will like my sentence?

Yes, but do you need the part about being seven years old?

No, I do not. I will take that part out.

COMPOSITION: RESPONDING/REVISING   Sentence About a Picture   19

Name _____

Roberto thought about what he and Lori had talked about. He took out some words that did not tell about his main idea. He used this mark ⌒ .

Take out [I am seven and I like to ride my bike with my friend.

Discuss

1. What did Roberto take out of his sentence?
2. How did this change make Roberto's sentence better?
3. How would you change Roberto's sentence to make it better?

Name _____

Try Your Hand

Check your sentence. Use the **Editor's Marks** to show your changes.

A. Think About Your Sentence Read your sentence to yourself or to a classmate. Does your sentence tell the main idea of your picture?

B. Make Changes
- Does everything in your sentence tell the main idea? Take out extra words. Use this mark ℮ .
- Does your sentence tell a complete thought? Add words if you need to.

Editor's Marks
∧ Add something.
℮ Take out something.
⌐∧ Change something.
↶ Move something.

C. Check Your Sentence Read your sentence again. Does your sentence say what you want it to say? Make changes until you are happy with your work.

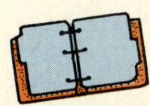 Put your picture and sentence in your **Writer's Notebook.** In the next lesson, you will fix any mistakes.

COMPOSITION: RESPONDING/REVISING   Sentence About a Picture   **21**

Name _____

4 Proofreading
Sentence About a Picture

Roberto drew another picture and wrote a sentence about it. He followed the **Writer's Guide** to correct the mistakes in his sentence. Look at what he did.

baseball is my favorite game⊙
≡

Writer's Guide

☑ Be sure your sentence begins with a capital letter.
☑ Be sure your sentence ends with a special mark.
⇨ Use the **Writer's Handbook** for help.

Discuss

1. Why did Roberto use this mark ≡ ?
2. How did Roberto end his sentence?

Try Your Hand

Now correct any mistakes in your sentence. Follow the **Writer's Guide**. Use the **Editor's Marks** to show your changes.

Editor's Marks

≡ Use a capital letter.
⊙ Add a period.
∧ Add something.
℮ Take out something.
⌒ Change something.
◯ Check the spelling.

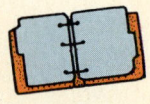
Put your sentence and picture in your **Writer's Notebook**. You will share it in the next lesson.

Name _____

5 Publishing
Sentence About a Picture

Before Roberto shared his picture and sentence, he followed the **Writer's Guide**. He copied his sentence neatly below his picture.

Roberto put his picture and sentence on the cover of his **Writer's Notebook.** He shared it with his classmates. You can find Roberto's picture and sentence on page 16 of the **Writer's Handbook.**

Writer's Guide

- ☑ Copy your sentence over neatly.
- ☑ Be sure nothing is left out.
- ☑ Be sure there are no mistakes.
- ☑ Share your sentence and picture in an interesting way.

Roberto put his picture and sentence on his **Writer's Notebook.**

Roberto shared his work with his class.

COMPOSITION: PUBLISHING   Sentence About a Picture

Name _____

Discuss

1. Why did Roberto check his sentence before sharing it?
2. How did Roberto share his picture and sentence?
3. Name other ways Roberto could share his work.

Try Your Hand

Share Your Picture and Sentence Follow the **Writer's Guide**. You may want to share your work in the way Roberto did. You may want to try one of these ideas.

- Put your picture and sentence in a big envelope. Mail it to someone special.
- Make a frame out of colored paper for your picture and sentence. Display your work in your classroom.
- Put your work with your classmates' work into a class book. Help make a special cover for the book. Share it with another class.

Name _____

Listening and Speaking
How to Listen for the Main Idea

A picture has a main idea. A story also has a main idea. The **main idea** is what the story is mostly about.

You can listen to a story to find out the main idea. A good listener can find out the main idea by following these steps.

- ◆ Listen carefully. Pay attention to the details.
- ◆ Think about what you hear. What one idea do all the details tell about?

Practice

1. Look at the picture. Listen for the main idea of the story.

2. Draw a line under the main idea.

   a. Kelly digs in the sandbox.

   b. Kelly enjoys playing in the park.

Name _____

Writing in the Content Areas

Now use what you have learned to draw pictures and write about them. Use these ideas or ideas of your own.

Writer's Guide

When you write, use the stages of the Writing Process.
- Plan your writing.
- Write what you want to say to your readers.
- Talk with your classmates about your writing.
- Make your writing clear. Change words if you need to.
- Fix any mistakes.
- Share your writing.

Music

Draw pictures of you and your classmates having a sing-along. Write sentences to go with the pictures. Keep the pictures and sentences in a folder to share with your friends. Add to the folder during the year.

Science

Make a display of Active Animals with your class. Draw a picture of your favorite animal. Show how it moves. Write a sentence for your picture. Share your work with your classmates. Then put your work on a bulletin board.

Name _____

CONNECTING
WRITING AND LANGUAGE

You can share information about yourself by drawing a picture and writing about it. Look at the pictures. Read what the children wrote about their pictures.

My grandpa plays checkers with me.

I like to read stories to my little sister.

◆ **Sentences About Pictures**   Each group of words above is called a **sentence.** Each sentence tells a complete thought. Writers can use sentences to tell the main idea of pictures.

◆ **Language Focus: Sentences**   You will learn more about sentences in the next lessons. You will also learn about different kinds of sentences.

Name _____

1 What Is a Sentence?

◆ **FOCUS**   A **sentence** is a group of words that tells a complete thought.

the children

The children sing.

Every sentence begins with a capital letter and ends with a special mark.

    Sentence   **1.** The girl plays the piano.

  Not a Sentence   **2.** the girl

Which group of words under the pictures is a sentence? How do you know?

Guided Practice

A. Which groups of words are sentences? Why?

  1. Mary plays the piano.   **2.** the music

  3. The children have fun.   **4.** play games

Write the sentences.

5. _____

6. _____

28 GRAMMAR Sentences

Name _____

THINK AND REMEMBER
♦ Use a sentence to tell a complete thought.

Independent Practice

B. Writing Sentences   Read each group of words. Add words to make a sentence. Use the picture for help.

7. _____The rain_____ pours down.

8. _____ stay inside.

9. They _____.

10. The music _____.

11. Mary and Tim _____.

12. _____ are happy.

Application—Writing

Journal Entry   Write a journal entry about what is important to you. Use page 22 of the **Writer's Handbook** for help.

GRAMMAR Sentences   **29**

Name _____

2 Naming Part of a Sentence

◆ **FOCUS** A sentence has a **naming part** that names <u>who</u> or <u>what</u>.

Beth reads her letter.   A book came in the mail, too.

Remember that a sentence tells a complete thought. Every sentence has a naming part that names <u>who</u> or <u>what</u> the sentence is about.

1. Beth opens a letter.   2. The book is a gift.

Look at the sentences in the picture. <u>Who</u> reads a letter? <u>What</u> came in the mail?

Guided Practice

A. Tell the naming part for each sentence. Then tell if it names <u>who</u> or <u>what</u>. Write each naming part.

1. Beth has a letter.   _____

2. The letter is funny.   _____

3. Grandma sent it.   _____

30   GRAMMAR   Naming Part of a Sentence

Name _____

THINK AND REMEMBER

◆ Use a **naming part** in a sentence to name <u>who</u> or <u>what</u>.

Independent Practice

B. Writing Naming Parts   Look at the picture. Write a naming part to begin each sentence.

4. 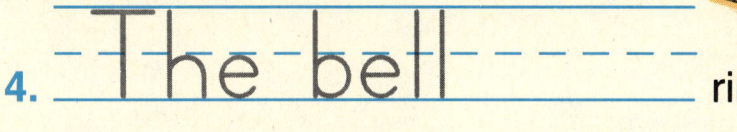 rings.

5. _____ goes to the door.

6. _____ comes in.

7. _____ shows him her book.

8. _____ is about dinosaurs.

9. _____ read the book.

Application—Writing and Speaking

Sentences   Write sentences to share with your class about a gift someone gave you. Be sure each sentence has a naming part.

GRAMMAR   Naming Part of a Sentence   **31**

Name _____

3 Telling Part of a Sentence

◆ **FOCUS**   A sentence has a **telling part** that tells what someone or something is or does.

The children act out a play.

Every sentence has a telling part. The telling part tells what someone or something is or does. The telling part works with the naming part to tell a complete thought.

1. John walks on stage.   2. The children are happy.

Guided Practice

A. Find the telling part in each sentence. Then write the telling part.

1. Ann speaks loudly.   _____

2. A teacher helps her.   _____

3. The curtains close.   _____

32   GRAMMAR   Telling Part of a Sentence

Name _____

THINK AND REMEMBER
◆ Use a **telling part** in a sentence to tell what someone or something is or does.

Independent Practice

B. Writing Telling Parts Write a telling part to finish each sentence. Use the words in the box.

> likes the story
> clap loudly
> pulls the ropes
> starts
> puts on his mask
> give a play

4. The children _give a play_____.

5. A girl _____.

6. John _____.

7. The play _____.

8. Everyone _____.

9. They _____.

Application—Writing

Report About a Play Imagine that you saw the play shown in the picture. Write sentences to tell a friend about it.

GRAMMAR Telling Part of a Sentence 33

Name _____

4 Word Order in a Sentence

◆ **FOCUS** The words in a sentence should be in an order that makes sense.

The words in a sentence should be in an order that makes sense. If the words are mixed up, the sentence does not make sense.

Sentence 1. I like my puzzle.
Not a Sentence 2. I puzzle like my.

Look at the picture. How should the sentences be written?

1. puzzle the Mix pieces.
2. together pieces the Put.

Guided Practice

A. Which groups of words are in the correct order?

1. has a Brad puzzle.
2. There are many pieces.
3. the What make puzzle will picture?
4. Brad likes puzzles.

Write the sentences that make sense.

5. _____

6. _____

34 GRAMMAR Word Order in a Sentence

Name _____

THINK AND REMEMBER
◆ Put the words in a sentence in an order that makes sense.

Independent Practice

B. Writing Sentences   Write each group of words in an order that makes sense.

game me Ruth a shows.

7. Ruth shows me a game.

is card game It a.

8. _____

play start We to.

9. _____

Our fun game is!

10. _____

Application—Writing and Speaking

Puzzle   Write a sentence about a game. Cut out each word. Mix up the words. Then ask a friend to put the words together to make a sentence.

Name _____

5 Statements

◆ **FOCUS**   A **statement** is a sentence that tells something.

The dancer leaps into the air.

One kind of sentence is called a statement. A statement tells something. It begins with a capital letter. It ends with a **period (.)**.

The man is a dancer**.**

Use statements to tell about the picture.

Guided Practice

A. Correct the mistakes in each sentence.

1. the children learn to dance

   _____ he children learn to dance _____

2. a dancer shows them how to move

   _____ dancer shows them how to move _____

36   GRAMMAR   Statements

Name _____

> **THINK AND REMEMBER**
> ◆ Use a **statement** to tell something.
> ◆ Begin a statement with a capital letter and end it with a **period (.)**.

Independent Practice

B. Writing Statements Write each statement correctly.

we make a mask

3. We make a mask.

i cut out whiskers

4. _____

pablo draws a mouth

5. _____

our mask looks great

6. _____

Application—Writing and Speaking

How-to Sentence Draw a picture of something you know how to make. Write a statement about your picture. Share your work with a younger student.

GRAMMAR Statements 37

Name _____

6 Questions

◆ **FOCUS** A **question** is a sentence that asks something.

Where are we going?

A sentence that asks something is a question. It begins with a capital letter. It ends with a **question mark (?)**.

What is the family doing?

What kind of sentences are the children in the picture using? How do you know?

How long will we stay?

Guided Practice

A. Find the sentences that are questions.

1. Are we going fishing?
2. I am ready to go!
3. The poles are in the car.
4. Where is the net?

Now write the questions.

5. _____

6. _____

Name _____

THINK AND REMEMBER
- Use a **question** to ask something.
- Begin a question with a capital letter and end it with a **question mark (?)**.

Independent Practice

B. Writing Questions Begin each question with a question word from the box. Use the correct end mark.

Are	When
What	How
Who	Do

7. **Do** you see the lake **?**

8. _____ kinds of fish are there __

9. _____ these fish good __

10. _____ big are the fish __

11. _____ do we begin fishing __

12. _____ has the net __

Application—Writing, Listening, and Speaking

Interview Write questions to ask the boy in the picture about his fishing trip. Ask a classmate to pretend to be the boy. Ask your questions.

GRAMMAR Questions 39

Name _____

7 Exclamations

◆ **FOCUS** An **exclamation** is a sentence that shows strong feeling.

A sentence that shows strong feeling is called an exclamation. It begins with a capital letter. It ends with an **exclamation point (!)**.

The fire is coming!

Exclamations tell about feelings. Which feelings do the sentences in the picture show?

Guided Practice

A. Which sentences are exclamations? Tell why.

1. How brave the fire fighters are!

2. They call for water.

3. How hot the fire is!

4. They did a good job.

Write the exclamations.

5. _____

6. _____

40 GRAMMAR Exclamations

Name _____

> **THINK AND REMEMBER**
> ◆ Use an **exclamation** to show strong feeling.
> ◆ Begin an exclamation with a capital letter and end it with an **exclamation point (!)**.

Independent Practice

B. Writing Exclamations   Look at the picture. Finish each exclamation.

7. An animal _is trapped!_ _____

8. The fire fighter _____

9. How happy _____

10. Now the deer _____

Application—Writing and Speaking

Sentences   Find a picture of someone showing strong feeling. Write exclamations about it. Share your work.

GRAMMAR Exclamations 41

Name _____

8 Kinds of Sentences

◆ **FOCUS** A sentence can tell something, ask something, or show strong feeling.

Remember that a statement tells something. A question asks something. An exclamation shows strong feeling.

Name the kinds of sentences in the picture.

Guided Practice

A. Tell whether each sentence is a statement, a question, or an exclamation. Then write the end mark.

1. I love my pet ___

2. What does your pet eat ___

3. Lizards eat bugs ___

4. How quick your lizard is ___

42 GRAMMAR/USAGE Kinds of Sentences

Name _____

THINK AND REMEMBER

- Use a **statement** to tell something.
- Use a **question** to ask something.
- Use an **exclamation** to show strong feeling.

Independent Practice

B. Writing Sentences   Finish each sentence. Make **6** and **7** statements. Make **8** and **9** questions. Make **10** an exclamation.

5. Sharing time is _really great!_____

6. I will share a _____

7. My friend shares a _____

8. What _____

9. Who _____

10. That is so _____

Application—Speaking

Sharing   Bring something to school to share. Tell your class about it. Use the three kinds of sentences.

GRAMMAR/USAGE   Kinds of Sentences

Name _____

Building Vocabulary
Rhyming Words

Rhyming words end with the same sound. man—pan

Reading Practice

Read the poem by John Ciardi. Draw a line under words that rhyme with the underlined words.

> **The Man That Had Little to Say**
>
> I met a man at one o'clock who said "Hello"
>   at two.
> At three o'clock he looked at me and said,
>   "How do you do?"
> At ten-to-four he said "Good-bye" And started
>   on his way.
> I'm glad he came to see me but he hadn't
>   much to say.

Writing Practice

Finish this poem. Make the lines rhyme.

| know | see |
| through | over |

I talk to you _____

And when I'm _____,

You talk to me. _____

We're friends, you _____.

Project

◆ Choose an ending sound like at, en, ip, an, or ug.
◆ List words that end with that sound.
◆ Use some of the words in a poem.

Listening and Speaking

Poetry

Listen to the poem. Then read aloud the poem with your classmates.

Left Foot, Right Foot
by Eve Merriam

Left foot,
Right foot,
Where are my slippers?

Left foot,
Right foot,
Where are my sneakers?

Left foot,
Right foot,
Where are my rain boots?

Left foot,
Right foot,
Where are my toes?

They're just where you left them—
On the end of your nose.

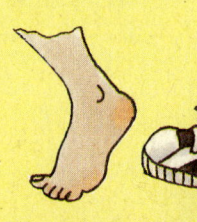

Language Enrichment
Sentences

Use what you know about sentences to do these activities.

 **Sense and Nonsense**

Make new sentences with your class.

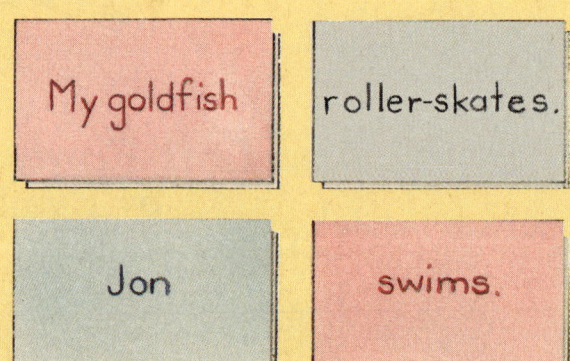

- Find two shoe boxes. Label one <u>Naming Part</u> and one <u>Telling Part</u>.
- Write a complete sentence on a card.
- Cut between the naming part and the telling part. Put each part in the right box.
- Take turns picking a card from each box. Put the cards together. Does the new sentence make sense?

 **Sounding It Out**

Here is how to read a story in a new way.

1. Make up a sound for each end mark in a story. For example, clap twice for an exclamation point. Tap your feet once for a period. Say "Hmmm?" for a question mark.
2. Make two teams. Team A reads the story. Team B makes the sounds.

Name _____

CONNECTING
LANGUAGE AND WRITING

In this unit you learned about sentences.

◆ **Using Sentences in Your Writing**   Using different kinds of sentences will help make your writing interesting.

Know and Tell

Ask a friend questions about himself or herself. You might ask questions like these.
- ◆ When is your birthday?
- ◆ What is your favorite book?

Use complete sentences to write the answers. Then tell your class about your friend.

I'm in a Rhyme!

Write a poem about yourself. Use rhyming words. Use different kinds of sentences. Share your poem at a class poetry reading.

CONNECTING LANGUAGE AND WRITING   47

Name _____

 Unit Checkup

Sentence About a Picture pages 10–11

Look at Ramon's picture and sentence. Then draw a line under the answer to each question.

1. Ramon's sentence tells a complete thought. How do you know?
   a. It tells what someone does.
   b. It begins with the word <u>On</u>.
2. How can you tell that Ramon wrote a sentence?
   a. It has many words in it.
   b. It begins with a capital letter and ends with a special mark.

Using Details to Tell the Main Idea page 12

Use the picture and details to write a sentence that tells the main idea.

Details
Sally	flowers
home	dirt
pots	bricks

3. _____

48 UNIT CHECKUP Unit 1

Name _____

Using Exact Words page 13
Write a more exact word from the box for each underlined word.

| races | oats |
| Ken | barn |

4. The little horse <u>runs</u> to the <u>building</u>.

   _____   _____

5. <u>The boy</u> has <u>food</u> for it to eat.

   _____   _____

The Writing Process pages 14-24
Draw a line under the answer to each question.

6. What should you do after you write the first draft of your sentence?

   a. Draw a picture that shows your idea.

   b. Talk about your sentence with a classmate.

7. What should you do if your sentence about your picture does not tell a complete thought?

   a. Add words to tell who the sentence is about or to tell what happens.

   b. Take out extra words.

What Is a Sentence? pages 28–29
Draw a line around each group of words that tells a complete thought.

8. The play is funny.   9. laughs loudly

10. the curtain   11. Sue wears a wig.

Naming Part of a Sentence pages 30–31
Write a naming part that tells who or what to finish each sentence. Use the word box.

> **Who**
> Tom
> The girl
> **What**
> Our computer
> Her story

12. _____ is new.

13. _____ plays a game on it.

14. _____ uses the computer to write a story.

15. _____ is about a pet snake.

Telling Part of a Sentence pages 32–33
Draw a line under each telling part.

16. Ben and I enjoy singing.   17. Ben sings a new song.
18. I listen to Ben's song.   19. The song makes me laugh.

Word Order in a Sentence pages 34–35
Write each group of words in order.

Wendy letter me writes a to .

20. _____

letter I Wendy's read .

21. _____

Name _____

Statements   pages 36–37
Draw a line around the statement that is written correctly.

22. we see a puppet show   We see a puppet show.

23. The puppets are silly.   the puppets are silly

Questions   pages 38–39
Draw a line under each question.

24. Do you like the zoo?   **25.** Are you ready?

26. Let's go see the animals.   **27.** Where are the zebras?

Exclamations   pages 40–41
Draw a line under each exclamation.

28. We are very hungry.   **29.** It smells so good!

30. Dad has a pizza for us!   **31.** Do you like pizza too?

Kinds of Sentences   pages 42–43
Draw a line under S, Q, or E to show what kind of sentence each is.

S—statement
Q—question
E—exclamation

32. I am reading a new book.   S Q E

33. It is so exciting!   S Q E

34. Have you read it?   S Q E

Rhyming Words   page 44
Choose a rhyming word from the box to finish this rhyme.

   A spider I think
   _____
   _ _ _ _ _ _ _ _ _ _

35. Crawled down my _____ .

leg
sink

UNIT CHECKUP   Unit 1   **51**

UNIT 2

Telling About Yourself

◆ **COMPOSITION FOCUS:** Personal Story
◆ **LANGUAGE FOCUS:** Nouns

A good way to get to know people is by reading what they write about themselves. People write to tell about things they have done. They write to tell how they feel about things.

A boy named James Ramsey spent a day at the museum with his dad. He wrote a story about that day. When he entered his story in a school contest, it won an award!

James likes to write stories about himself. In this unit you will learn to write a story about yourself.

James Ramsey wrote a story to tell about himself.

UNIT 2 53

Name _____

Reading with a Writer's Eye
Personal Story

Get to know James Ramsey. Read his story to find out how James tells about himself and the things he likes to do.

Going to the Museum
by James Ramsey

When I lived in New York, I would ask my dad, "Can we go to the Natural History Museum?"

He'd usually say, "I'm too busy!" and I'd say, "You're always busy."

Sometimes he'd say, "Okay, okay." Then my dad and I would go there.

We would get into the train and slowly go down into the ground. At 79th Street we would get off and run to the museum. The museum looked like a castle. It had towers and everything.

54 READING ↔ WRITING CONNECTION

I'd say, "Come on, Dad!" Then we'd run in. At the gate we'd get a badge with a Stegosaurus on it. The first thing I'd see was a part of a giant tree.

Then I'd see a giant spider. After that, we'd see a giant squid. Then I'd see fireflies.

Later, we'd go downstairs. We'd see a blue whale hanging from the ceiling and sea animals around it, like fish, sharks, whales, penguins, and seals.

Name _____

After looking at the whale, I'd go to the cafeteria and get a hot dog. Then we'd go up to the fourth floor and see my favorite part, the DINOSAURS! There were two rooms of dinosaurs. The first room had Cretaceous dinosaurs. We'd see Tyrannosaurus rex—my favorite.

We'd also see Triceratops and Styracosaurus. In that room I would always draw pictures of the dinosaurs.

Then we'd go to the next room. That's the room with the Triassic and Jurassic dinosaurs. I'd see Brontosaurus and Stegosaurus. Brontosaurus was big and long. Stegosaurus was small and short.

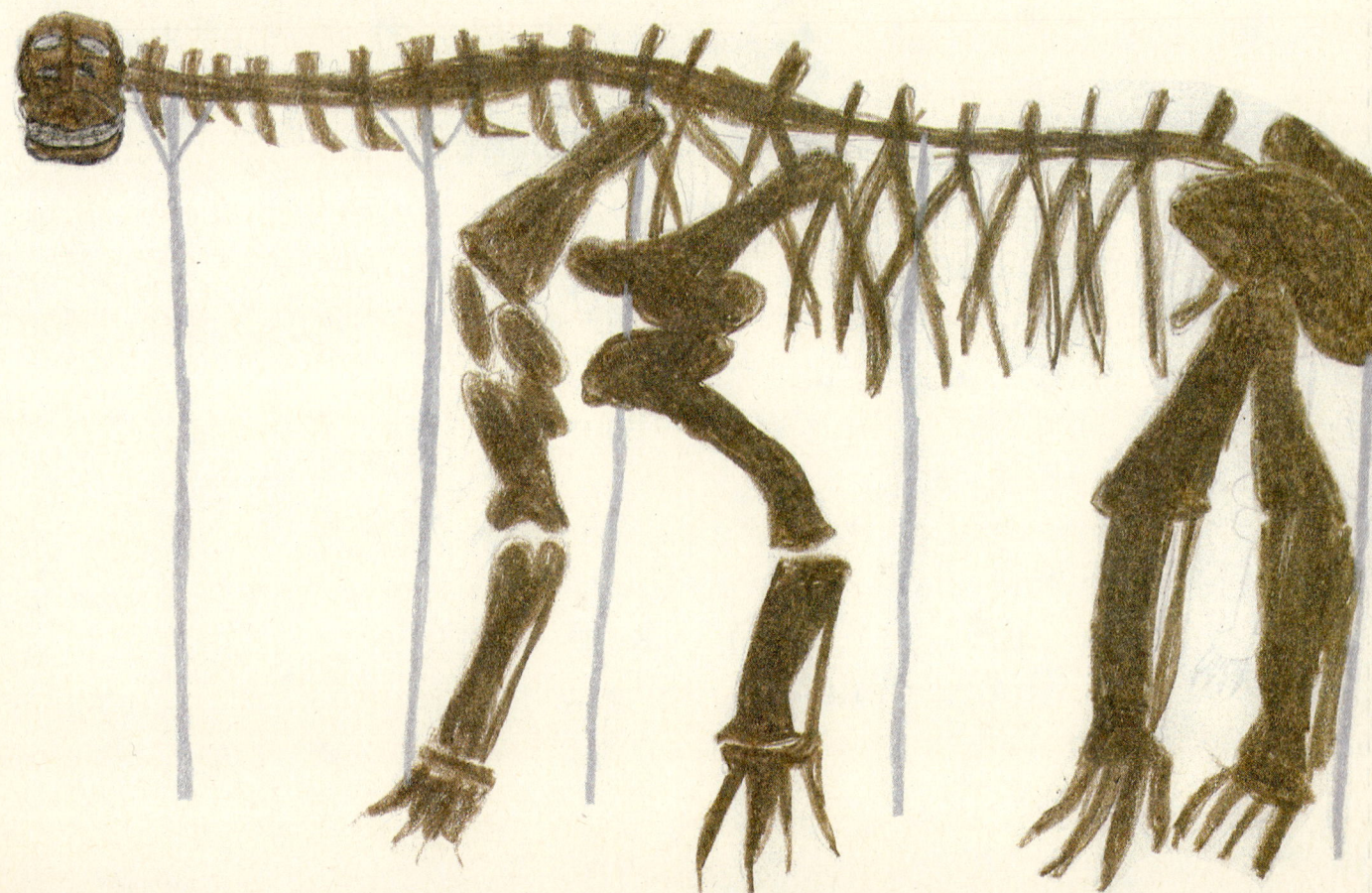

Stegosaurus had four spikes on its tail and plates on its back. In the pictures you see of Stegosaurus, he is usually fighting Allosaurus, but Allosaurus wasn't in the museum. There were other dinosaurs in the room that I wanted to draw pictures of, but Daddy would say, "Come on, it's late! Let's go to the next room!"

We'd go to the early American Indian room. First I'd see all kinds of masks. Then I'd see models of Indian villages. After that, I'd go see a gigantic canoe with all kinds of Indians in it.

After that, we'd go to the basement and go to the gift shop. I'd see all kinds of puzzles and books and toys and jewelry and models. My favorite room was really the gift shop, because I would always get something. That day I got a dinosaur puzzle.

Then we'd leave the museum and go out to Central Park to play frisbee. When we'd get tired of playing, we'd take a walk.

Then when it became almost night, my dad would say, "Jamie, let's go home. Mommy is waiting for us." Usually I'd want to stay there forever, but this time I said, "Okay, okay," because I was anxious to get home and show my drawings to my mom. We walked to Broadway and got on the bus and went home.

That was such a nice day! I wish I could go there again.

Respond

1. Think about the things James likes to do. Would you like to get to know him better? Why?

Discuss

2. What does James tell about himself in his story?
3. What do you think James likes best about the museum? How does he let you know this?

Name _____

Thinking As a Writer
Studying a Personal Story

Writer's Guide

♦ A personal story tells about something you have done.
♦ It can tell how you feel about something.
♦ A story tells what happened in order.

James wrote a personal story. That means he wrote a story about himself.

When you write about yourself, you can tell about something you have done. You can tell how you feel about something.

Read part of James's story.

> I'd say, "Come on, Dad!" **Then** we'd run in. At the gate we'd get a badge with a Stegosaurus on it. The **first** thing I'd see was a part of a giant tree.
> **Then** I'd see a giant spider. **After** that, we'd see a giant squid. **Then** I'd see fireflies.
> **Later**, we'd go downstairs.

Time-order words help show the order in which things happen.

Discuss

1. How do you know James wrote about himself?
2. What things does James do in this part of the story? In what order does he do them?

60   READING ↔ WRITING CONNECTION

Try Your Hand

A. Write the Story in Order Write the sentences in order so they tell a story. Write your own ending sentence.

I took out my paints.

I wrapped my picture.

I painted a picture.

First, _____

Next, _____

Then, _____

Last, _____

B. Tell About Pictures in Order Draw four things you do after school. Use <u>first</u>, <u>next</u>, <u>then</u>, and <u>last</u> to tell a friend about your pictures.

Name _____

Thinking As a Writer
Grouping Ideas by Topic

> **Writer's Guide**
> ◆ In a personal story, good writers tell about one topic.
> ◆ Good writers use only details that tell about the topic.

A good writer writes a personal story about one topic. The **topic** is the one idea the whole story is about.

James wrote a good story because he wrote about one topic. His topic is going to the museum.

James wrote many ideas that only tell about the museum. These are called **details**. James may have made a list like this before he wrote his story.

Topic		
going to the museum		
Details		
giant tree	Tyrannosaurus rex	Indian masks
blue whale	Brontosaurus	giant canoe

Discuss

1. Why should a personal story have only one topic?
2. Which detail would you add to James's story? Why?
   a. I'd ride a pony.   **b.** I'd see Indian clothes.

Try Your Hand

Tell About a Topic   Make a list of details that tell about this topic.

Topic: games I like to play

Developing the Writer's Craft
Using Synonyms

Synonyms are words that have almost the same meaning. Glad and thrilled are synonyms.

1. James was glad about seeing the dinosaurs.
2. James was thrilled about seeing the dinosaurs.

The word thrilled gives a clearer picture of how James feels.

Writer's Guide
- Good writers choose words to write exactly what they mean to say.

Words for Feelings

mad	furious
scared	terrified
glad	thrilled
sad	gloomy

Discuss

1. What other words could the writer have used to show how happy James was to see the dinosaurs?
2. If the dinosaur room had been closed, would sad or disappointed give a clearer idea of how James felt?

Try Your Hand

Use Exact Words Write a sentence to tell how you would feel if you saw a cute puppy.

READING ↔ WRITING CONNECTION

Name _____

1 Prewriting
Personal Story

You are going to write a story about yourself. Get ready to tell about something special that you did. Look at what Becky did to plan her story.

Becky followed the **Writer's Guide.** First, she thought about things she had done.

Writer's Guide

- ☑ Make a list of story ideas.
- ☑ Decide who will read your story.
- ☑ Choose an idea that you and your readers will like. This is your topic.
- ☑ Write details that tell about your topic.
- ☑ Put the details in order.

64 COMPOSITION: PREWRITING Personal Story

Name _____

Becky wrote her ideas in a list. These were her story ideas.

```
1. skiing with Mom
2. riding in Mr. Reed's balloon
3. learning how to swim
```

Becky was writing the story for her classmates. She chose the balloon ride because her class had been reading stories about ways to travel. Becky drew a line around that idea. This was her topic.

Next, Becky wrote details to tell about her ride. Then, she read her ideas. She took out a detail that did not tell about her topic. She wrote numbers beside the details to show the order in which they happened.

```
Topic
riding in Mr. Reed's balloon

Details
   ate breakfast
4  waved to friends
1  set up balloon
2  got in balloon basket
3  went up into the sky
```

Discuss

1. What did Becky do to follow the **Writer's Guide**?
2. Why did Becky cross out "ate breakfast"?

COMPOSITION: PREWRITING   Personal Story   **65**

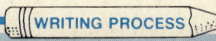

Name _____

Try Your Hand

Now plan your story.

A. Think of Story Ideas
Write a list of special things you have done. You may want to look through your journal for ideas.

B. Choose a Topic   Decide who will read your story. Draw a line around a topic that your readers will like.

C. Plan Details   Write many details to tell about your topic. You may wish to make a list in the way Becky did.

D. Check Details   Cross out any details that do not tell about your topic.

E. Put Details in Order
Number your details in the order in which they happened.

Eagle Ideas

1. Did something special happen on your birthday?
2. Have you taken a fun trip? What happened?
3. What did you do to surprise someone?

 Put your plan in your **Writer's Notebook**. You will use it when you write your story.

Name _____

Listening and Speaking
How to Tell About Ideas in Order

You can tell someone a story about yourself. To help your listener understand your story, tell it in order. Use time-order words such as <u>first</u>, <u>next</u>, <u>then</u>, and <u>last</u>.

Practice

A. Look at the pictures. Listen to the story. Listen for words that tell the order in which things happen.

B. Now draw four pictures that tell a story about something you did. Then tell the story. Use the words <u>first</u>, <u>next</u>, <u>then</u>, and <u>last</u>.

1	2
3	4

LISTENING/SPEAKING Personal Story

Name _____

2 Drafting
Personal Story

Look at what Becky did to write her story. First, she thought about her topic. She decided that she still wanted to write about the balloon ride. Then, Becky followed the **Writer's Guide** to write her first draft.

Writer's Guide

- ☑ Use your list for ideas.
- ☑ Write a sentence to tell what your topic is.
- ☑ Write details to tell about your topic.
- ☑ Write your details in order.

Topic
riding in Mr. Reed's balloon

Details
4 waved to friends
1 set up balloon
2 got in balloon basket
3 went up into the sky

One Saturday my sister Judy and I rode in Mr. Reed's balloon. First, we got the balloon ready. Next, we got into a basket tied to the balloon. Then, the balloon went up into the sky. I waved to my friends. Mary is my best friend. They were really surprised!

68 COMPOSITION: DRAFTING Personal Story

Name _____

Discuss

1. What is the topic of Becky's story?
2. Why did Becky write the details in the order she wrote them in?

Try Your Hand

Now write your personal story.

A. Think About Your Topic Do you still like your topic? If not, choose another topic and make a new story plan.

B. Read Your Story Plan Add any details that would make your story clearer. Take out details that do not tell about your topic.

C. Keep an Eagle Eye on Who, What, and Why Think about your readers. Remember that you are writing to tell about something you did.

D. Write Your First Draft Follow the **Writer's Guide** to write your first draft. Write quickly. You can correct any mistakes later.

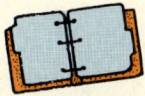 Put your first draft in your **Writer's Notebook**. You will check it in the next lesson.

COMPOSITION: DRAFTING   Personal Story

Name _____

3 Responding and Revising
Personal Story

Becky used the **Writer's Guide** to make her story clearer. She and Peter talked about her story.

> **Peter:** A balloon ride sounds fun! Why did you tell about Mary?
>
> **Becky:** I should take that part out. Mary was not there the day I rode in the balloon.

Writer's Guide

- ☑ Read your story to yourself or to a friend.
- ☑ Think about your story. Be sure you told the things your readers want to know.
- ☑ Be sure your details tell about one topic.
- ☑ Be sure your details are in order.
- ☑ Make changes.

Becky thought about her talk with Peter. She took out a sentence that did not tell about her topic. She used this mark ✂.

> One Saturday my sister Judy and I rode in Mr. Reed's balloon. First, we got the balloon ready. Next, we got into a basket tied to the balloon. Then, the balloon went up into the sky. I waved to my friends. ~~Mary is my best friend.~~ They were really surprised!

Take out

70 COMPOSITION: RESPONDING/REVISING Personal Story

Name _____

Discuss

1. What information did Becky take out? Why?
2. What other changes could Becky have made?

Try Your Hand

Check your story. Use the **Editor's Marks** to show your changes.

A. Think About Your Story   Read your story to yourself or to a friend. Did you tell everything your readers might want to know?

B. Make Changes

◆ Do your details tell about one topic? Take out sentences that do not tell about the topic. Use this mark ℒ .

◆ Do the detail sentences tell your story in order? Try to use time-order words.

Editor's Marks

∧ Add something.
ℒ Take out something.
⌃ Change something.
↶ Move something.

C. Check Your Story   Make changes until you feel your story is just right.

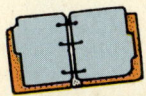 Put your story in your **Writer's Notebook.** In the next lesson, you will fix any mistakes.

Listening and Speaking
How to Work in a Response Group

A good way to make your writing better is to work with a partner. Each person should take a turn being the speaker and being the listener.

When You Are the Speaker
1. Read your writing to your partner.
2. Ask your partner questions about your writing.
3. Talk about your ideas for making your writing better.
4. Thank your partner for helping you.

When You Are the Listener
1. Listen carefully. Think about how the writing makes you feel.
2. Tell which parts you like best and why.
3. Ask questions about parts you do not understand.
4. Tell ideas you think should be added, changed, or taken out.

Name _____

4 Proofreading
Personal Story

Becky used the **Writer's Guide** to correct the mistakes in the next part of her story. Look at what she did.

> Mr. Reed helped us land the balloon in a big field. when I got out, i helped carry the lunches for a picnic. People ran over to see our big balloon

Writer's Guide

- ☑ Be sure that the word I is a capital letter.
- ☑ Be sure that each sentence begins with a capital letter.
- ☑ Be sure that each sentence ends with an end mark.
- ⇨ Use the **Writer's Handbook** for help.

Editor's Marks

- ≡ Use a capital letter.
- ⊙ Add a period.
- ∧ Add something.
- ℯ Take out something.
- ⁄ Change something.
- ◯ Check the spelling.

Discuss

1. Why did Becky use this mark ≡ ?
2. How did Becky show that the last sentence is a complete thought?

Try Your Hand

Now correct any mistakes in your story. Follow the **Writer's Guide.** Use the **Editor's Marks** to show your changes.

 Put your story in your **Writer's Notebook.** You will share it in the next lesson.

COMPOSITION: PROOFREADING   Personal Story   **73**

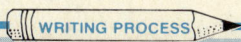

5 Publishing
Personal Story

Before Becky shared her story, she followed the **Writer's Guide.** Then she made her story into a book and shared it with her class. If you want to read Becky's finished story, you can find it on page 23 of the **Writer's Handbook.**

Writer's Guide
- ☑ Copy your story over neatly.
- ☑ Be sure nothing is left out.
- ☑ Be sure there are no mistakes.
- ☑ Share your story in an interesting way.

Becky made a tape.

Becky made a cover.

Becky shared her story with her classmates.

74 COMPOSITION: PUBLISHING Personal Story

Name _____

Discuss

1. How did Becky share her story? Why is this a good way to share a story about yourself?
2. Name other ways Becky could share her story.

Try Your Hand

Share Your Story   Follow the **Writer's Guide.** You may want to share your story in the way Becky did or try this idea.

- Glue your story onto a large sheet of paper. Draw a design around your story. Cover it with plastic wrap and use it for a placemat.

My Dog and Me
On Saturday I took my dog for a walk. We went to the park and played ball. Then we rolled in the leaves. I really had fun with my dog.

COMPOSITION: PUBLISHING   Personal Story   **75**

Writing in the Content Areas

Use what you learned to write a story about something your class did. Use one of these ideas or an idea of your own.

Science

Scatter crumbs or birdseed in an open spot near a window. Draw pictures of birds that come to feed. Then write a story telling what you did and learned. Make your story into a book. Write a title and your name on the cover. Read your book to a first-grade class.

Writer's Guide

When you write, use the stages of the Writing Process.
- Plan your writing.
- Write what you want to say to your readers.
- Talk with your classmates about your writing.
- Make your writing clear. Change words if you need to.
- Fix any mistakes.
- Share your writing.

Mathematics

Carry a pencil and paper with you tomorrow. Write what you are doing at each of the times shown. Write the time you do each thing.

Then write a story telling about your day. Be sure to tell the time you did each thing.

Name _____

CONNECTING
WRITING AND LANGUAGE

When you write a story about yourself, you tell about people, animals, places, and things you know about. Here is a story a girl named Lisa wrote. What does she tell about?

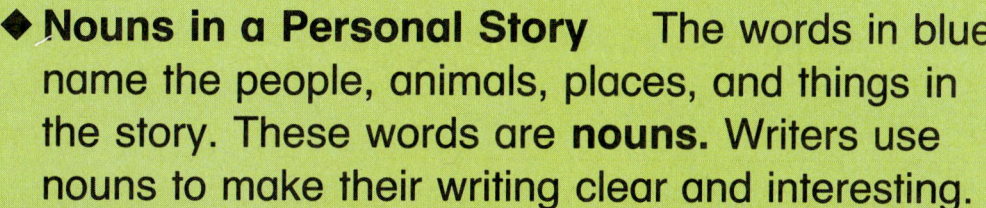

My secret friend is Chip. Chip lives in a tree in my backyard. I put raisins on the branches for him. Then Chip comes down the tree. He stuffs his cheeks with the food.

◆ **Nouns in a Personal Story**   The words in blue name the people, animals, places, and things in the story. These words are **nouns.** Writers use nouns to make their writing clear and interesting.

◆ **Language Focus: Nouns**   In the next lessons, you will learn about nouns and how to use them when you write.

CONNECTING WRITING AND LANGUAGE   77

Name _____

1 Naming Words for People and Animals

◆ **FOCUS** A word that names a person or an animal is called a **noun**.

mother

worker

gardener

sister

father

Many words are naming words.

1. My father works.   2. The dog plays.

Which words in the picture name people? Which words name animals?

Guided Practice

A. Find each noun that names a person or an animal.

1. My father builds a house of adobe bricks.
2. Our mother helps to make the bricks.
3. A worker pushes the bricks.
4. Our little dog rolls in the dust.

cat

dog

Write the nouns.

5. _____   6. _____

7. _____   8. _____

Name _____

THINK AND REMEMBER
◆ Use **nouns** to name people and animals.

Independent Practice

B. Writing Nouns Write a noun to finish the sentence. Use the words in the box.

Workers	Family	Animals
gardener	sister	cat
mover	father	dog
painter	aunt	horse

9. The ________ lifts boxes.

10. The _____ plants flowers.

11. The room belongs to my _____.

12. There is a bed inside for my _____.

13. My _____ stays outside.

Application—Writing

Sentences Draw a picture. Show a person doing his or her job. Write a sentence under the picture. Use a noun that names the person.

GRAMMAR Naming Words for People and Animals **79**

Name _____

2 Naming Words for Places and Things

◆ **FOCUS** A word that names a place or a thing is called a **noun**.

Words that name places or things are also nouns.

1. The bus stops.   2. We see the camp !

Name the places and things in the picture.

Guided Practice

A. Find the nouns that name places or things.

1. We rode a bus to the camp.
2. A flag flies from the flagpole.

Now write the nouns.

3. _____   4. _____

5. _____   6. _____

80   GRAMMAR   Naming Words for Places and Things

Name _____

THINK AND REMEMBER
◆ Use **nouns** to name places and things.

Independent Practice

B. Finding Nouns   Draw a line under each noun. Then write the nouns that name places or things.

The campers sit on logs around a campfire.

7. logs _____   _____

Swimmers play with a ball in the water.

8. _____   _____

Two boys find rocks in the pond.

9. _____   _____

The girls walk down the road to the river.

10. _____   _____

One girl throws bread to the ducks on the grass.

11. _____   _____

Application—Writing

Message   Imagine that you are at Camp Martin. Write four sentences. Tell about the people, animals, places, and things.

GRAMMAR   Naming Words for Places and Things   **81**

Name _____

3 Nouns That Name More Than One

◆ **FOCUS** Some nouns name more than one.

A noun can name one or more than one. Add the letter s to most nouns to name more than one.

Which nouns in the picture name more than one?

one tree

two trees

Guided Practice

A. Name the noun that tells about the picture. Write the noun.

1.  rock   rocks _____

2.  bone   bones _____

3.  birds   bird _____

4.  frogs   frog _____

Name _____

> **THINK AND REMEMBER**
> ◆ Add <u>s</u> to most nouns to name more than one.

Independent Practice

B. Proofreading Nouns Make the noun above the line mean more than one. Write the noun.

dinosaur

5. Dinosaur
   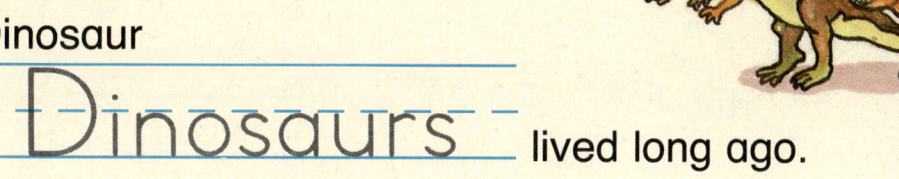 lived long ago.

dinosaurs

6. Scientists study dinosaur _____bone_____ .

7. Baby dinosaurs hatched from _____egg_____ .

8. They liked green _____plant_____ to eat.

9. Is it true that their _____neck_____ were long?

Application—Writing and Speaking

Poster Draw a dinosaur to show a younger student. Write sentences about it. Use nouns that name more than one.

Name _____

4 More Nouns That Name More Than One

◆ **FOCUS** Some nouns end with <u>es</u> to name more than one.

Some nouns end with <u>s</u>, <u>x</u>, <u>ch</u>, and <u>sh</u>. Add <u>es</u> to those nouns to tell about more than one.

    dress—dress**es**   peach—peach**es**

Find more nouns in the picture that name more than one.

Guided Practice

A. Choose the noun that tells about the picture. Write the noun.

1. bench   benches
    _____

2. fox   foxes
    _____

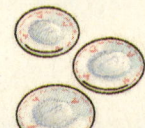
3. bus   buses
    _____

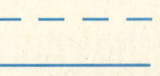
4. dish   dishes
    _____

Name _____

THINK AND REMEMBER
♦ Add <u>es</u> to nouns that end in <u>s</u>, <u>x</u>, <u>ch</u>, and <u>sh</u> to name more than one.

Independent Practice

B. Writing Nouns Choose a noun from the box to finish the sentence. Make the noun mean more than one. Write the noun.

lunch	bench
box	peach
dish	glass

5. The ____ at the fair taste good.   lunches

6. The food comes in paper ____.

7. Are there ____ of lemonade?

8. The shiny ____ are beautiful!

9. The ____ are nice and ripe.

10. We sit on the ____ to eat.

Application—Writing

List Imagine that your class is going on a picnic. Make a list of things to bring. Use nouns that end with <u>es</u> to name more than one.

GRAMMAR/SPELLING   More Nouns That Name More Than One   85

Name _____

5 Other Nouns That Name More Than One

◆ **FOCUS** Some nouns change spelling to name more than one.

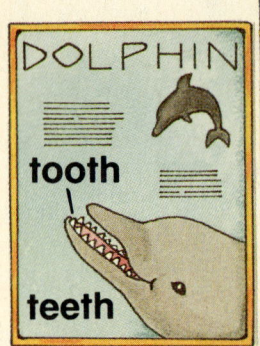

Remember that many nouns end with <u>s</u> or <u>es</u> to name more than one. Other nouns change spelling to name more than one.

one foot   two feet

Which nouns in the picture name one? Which name more than one?

Guided Practice

A. Choose the noun that tells about the picture. Write the noun.

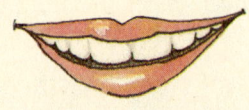   tooth / teeth

1. _____

   woman / women

2. _____

   child / children

3. _____

   man / men

4. _____

86   GRAMMAR/SPELLING   Other Nouns That Name More Than One

Name _____

> **THINK AND REMEMBER**
> ◆ Change the spelling of some nouns to name more than one.

Independent Practice

B. Proofreading Nouns   Make the noun in the ( ) mean more than one. Write the noun.

(woman)

5. The two ___women___ are divers.

(foot)

6. The divers kick their _____.

(man)

7. Are some _____ divers, too?

(tooth)

8. Do dolphins have _____?

(child)

9. The _____ are having fun.

Application—Writing

Sentences   Imagine you are one of the children in the picture. Write sentences to tell what you see. Use <u>children</u>, <u>feet</u>, <u>teeth</u>, and <u>women</u>.

GRAMMAR/SPELLING   Other Nouns That Name More Than One   **87**

Name _____

6 Nouns That Name Special People and Animals

◆ **FOCUS** Some **proper nouns** are the names of special people and animals.

A proper noun is a noun that names a special person, animal, place, or thing. Proper nouns begin with capital letters.

Jennifer **L**ee likes zoos.

Use proper nouns to tell about the picture.

Guided Practice

A. Find each proper noun.
 1. Jennifer Lee drew a lion.
 2. A picture shows Black Beauty.

Write the proper nouns.

3. _____

4. _____

88   GRAMMAR   Nouns That Name Special People and Animals

Name _____

THINK AND REMEMBER
◆ Use **proper nouns** to name special people and animals. Begin proper nouns with capital letters.

Independent Practice

B. Writing Proper Nouns   Write a proper noun from the picture to finish each sentence.

5. _____Marcus Jackson_____ tells about famous animals.

6. He writes about _____ the gorilla.

7. _____ is a big elephant.

8. Pilar Reyes likes the dog _____.

9. _____ tells about Elsa.

10. A huge animal is the whale _____.

Application—Writing and Speaking

Sentences   Draw an animal you would add to the picture. Write sentences about it. Tell its special name. Share your work with your class.

Name _____

7 Nouns That Name Special Places

◆ **FOCUS** Some **proper nouns** are the names of special places.

Noun	Proper Noun
city	Boston
lake	Bear Lake
park	Moss Park
river	Snake River

The names of special places are proper nouns. They begin with capital letters.

Tell about the picture. Use the names of special places.

Guided Practice

A. Find the nouns that name special places.
1. Tim lives in a city called Boston.
2. He lives in the state of Massachusetts.
3. His house is on Mill Road.

Write the nouns.

4. _____

5. _____

6. _____

GRAMMAR   Nouns That Name Special Places

Name _____

> **THINK AND REMEMBER**
> ◆ Use **proper nouns** to name special places. Begin proper nouns with capital letters.

Independent Practice

B. Proofreading Proper Nouns   Use the proper noun in the ( ) to finish each sentence. Write the noun correctly.

7. Tim's cousin Sara lives in (cleveland) Cleveland.

8. That big city is in (ohio) _____.

9. Sara goes to (timber school) _____.

10. Sara plays at (brookside park) _____.

11. She lives on (long street) _____.

Application—Writing

Postcard   Make a postcard for a relative. On one side write sentences about your town. Use nouns that name special places. On the other side draw a picture.

GRAMMAR   Nouns That Name Special Places   91

Name _____

8 Days, Months, and Holidays

◆ **FOCUS**   The names of days, months, and holidays are proper nouns.

Each day, month, and holiday has a special name. These names begin with capital letters. Only the important words in the name of a holiday begin with capital letters.

   1. Friday   **2.** May   **3.** Fourth of July

Guided Practice

A. Find each proper noun. Then write the proper noun.

1. School begins in September.

2. It starts after Labor Day.

3. On Tuesday we go to class.

92   GRAMMAR Days, Months, and Holidays

Name _____

> **THINK AND REMEMBER**
> ◆ Begin the names of days, months, and holidays with capital letters.

Independent Practice

B. Proofreading Proper Nouns   Read the sentences. Write the proper nouns correctly.

The month of february is special.

4. *February*

It comes after january.

5. _____

On friday it is valentine's day.

6. _____

Then comes presidents' day.

7. _____

The next month is march.

8. _____

Application—Writing

Sentences   Write three sentences about your favorite holiday. Tell when the holiday is.

9 Words That Take the Place of Nouns

◆ **FOCUS** A **pronoun** is a word that takes the place of a noun.

Mike is painting the moon.

He is doing a good job.

A pronoun can take the place of a noun. He, she, it, and they are pronouns.

Noun   1. Mike paints a picture.

Pronoun   2. He paints a picture.

He and she tell about people. It tells about animals and things. They tells about more than one.

Guided Practice

A. Choose the pronouns for the words in the ( ).

1. (The boy) paints a picture.   He, She
2. Is (the picture) beautiful?   it, they
3. (The stars) are pretty.   It, They

Now write the pronouns.

4. _____   5. _____   6. _____

94   GRAMMAR/USAGE   Words That Take the Place of Nouns

Name _____

THINK AND REMEMBER

◆ Use the **pronouns** he, she, it, and they to take the place of nouns.

Independent Practice

B. Writing Pronouns   Read each sentence. Write a pronoun for the word or words above the line.

Paintings
7. <u>They</u> are fun to make.

The paintings are nice.
They are nice.

Mr. Jones
8. _____ is my art teacher.

Ellen
9. Everyone likes the drawing that _____ makes.

my painting
10. I will take _____ home today.

Application—Writing

Sentences   Write sentences about the paintings to show a friend. Use he, she, it, and they.

GRAMMAR/USAGE   Words That Take the Place of Nouns   **95**

Name _____

10 The Pronouns I and Me

◆ **FOCUS**   The pronouns I and me should be used correctly.

The pronouns I and me take the place of some nouns. Use I in the naming part of a sentence. Use me in the telling part of a sentence.

Naming Part   I am behind a tree.

Telling Part   My friend calls me.

Guided Practice

A. Name the pronoun that tells about you.

1. I look for Alicia.
2. Alicia looks for me.
3. I have a hiding place.
4. She will never find me.

Write the pronouns.

5. _____   6. _____   7. _____   8. _____

96   GRAMMAR/USAGE   The Pronouns I and Me

Name _____

THINK AND REMEMBER
◆ Use <u>I</u> in the naming part of a sentence.
◆ Use <u>me</u> in the telling part of a sentence.

Independent Practice

B. Writing Nouns and Pronouns Write the correct word or words for each sentence.

(I and Jan, Jan and I)

9. <u>Jan and I</u> are friends.

(I, Me)

10. _____ have other friends.

(Max and I, I and Max)

11. Are _____ friends?

(I, me)

12. May _____ play at your house?

(I, me)

13. I hope you can ride bikes with _____.

Jan and I are friends.

Application—Writing

Sentences Write four sentences for your class about playing with a friend. Use <u>I</u> and <u>me</u>.

GRAMMAR/USAGE The Pronouns <u>I</u> and <u>Me</u> **97**

Building Vocabulary
Compound Words

A **compound word** is made up of two words. The two words together make a new word.

star + fish = starfish

Reading Practice

Read the poem. Find the compound words.

If you want to find a compound word . . .
Wade at the seashore. Wave at a starfish.
Talk to the lifeguard. Look for a goldfish.
If these things you are willing to do,
You will find a compound word or two.

Writing Practice

Write sentences about a visit to the sea. Use the compound words in the poem.

Project

List compound words that you find in books and magazines. Make a card for each word.

- Draw or cut out a picture to show each part of the word.
- Glue the pictures on the front of a card.
- Write the compound word on the back.
- Have a partner look at the pictures and name the word.

Name _____

Listening and Speaking
Poetry

What could be inside a pocket? Listen to the nouns in this poem.

Sing a Song of Pockets
by Beatrice Schenk de Regniers

Sing a song of pockets
A pocket full of stones
A pocket full of feathers
Or maybe chicken bones
A pocket full of bottle tops
A pocket full of money
Or if it's something sweet you want
A pocket full of honey . . .
ugh!

Name _____

Language Enrichment
Nouns

Use what you know about nouns to do these activities.

Noun Tree

Work with your class. Make a noun tree.
- On a big sheet of paper, draw a tree with branches.
- List nouns. Draw and cut out their shapes.
- Hang each shape on the tree.
- Write the nouns on the trunk.

PEACHES! PEACHES!

Use the rhyme below to play jump rope.
- Call out a word from the box each time someone starts to jump.
- The jumper adds <u>s</u> or <u>es</u> to make the word mean more than one.
- Then the jumper uses the word in place of the words in blue.

I went to the store.
This is what I bought.
Peaches! Peaches!
Now I have a lot of
P-E-A-C-H-E-S and
   O-U-T spells OUT!

glass	brush
box	ribbon
doll	door

100   LANGUAGE ENRICHMENT   Nouns

CONNECTING
LANGUAGE AND WRITING

In this unit you learned about nouns.

◆ **Using Nouns in Your Writing** Knowing about nouns will help you write and say exactly what you mean. Use nouns to do these activities.

Boots and Bookends

- List things that come in pairs, such as shoes and gloves.
- Choose one pair.
- Write a story about the pair of things.
- Make a book in the shape of the word.

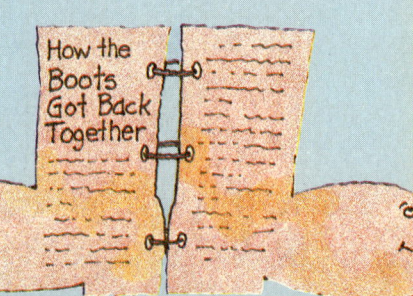

Stacking Stories

You learned about compound words. Write a stacking story like this one. Use the **Word Bank.**

Word Bank

mailbox
dollhouse
classroom
backpack

On the <u>playground</u> there is a <u>sandbox</u>.
In the sandbox there is a <u>pail</u>.
In the pail there is a <u>shovel</u>.
In the shovel there sits a <u>flea</u>.
But the flea hops away!

Name _____

2 Unit Checkup

Personal Story   pages 60–61
Read Sarah's personal story. Follow the directions.

> Captain Lee took me on a boat ride. The boat had a glass bottom. First, I helped him steer the boat. Next, Captain Lee showed me how to look through the glass. I saw turtles and plants. It was fun!

1. Draw a line around the words that help you know that Sarah wrote a story about herself.
2. Draw a line under the words in the story that show the order in which things happened.

Grouping Ideas by Topic   page 62
Draw a line under the details that tell about each topic.

3. Topic: playing baseball
   - hit a home run
   - caught a fly ball
   - jumped over the net

4. Topic: going shopping
   - rode on the plane
   - tried on shoes
   - bought a shirt

Using Synonyms   page 63
Write a word to take the place of the underlined word.

| cheerful   sleepy |

5. Sharon is happy.

6. Connie feels tired.

102   UNIT CHECKUP   Unit 2

Name _____

The Writing Process pages 64–75
Draw a line under the answer to each question.

7. What should you do first to plan a personal story?

   a. Write a first draft.   **b.** Make a list of story ideas.

8. Pretend you are checking your personal story. You find a sentence that does not tell about your topic. What should you do with the sentence?

   a. Take it out.   **b.** Keep it in.

Naming Words for People and Animals pages 78–79
Draw a line under each noun that names a person or an animal.

9. My mother is a special doctor.

10. This woman helps a sick pet.

11. The man thanks her for making his dog better.

Naming Words for Places and Things pages 80–81
Draw a line under each noun. Write each noun that names a place or thing.

12. My family leaves the city to go to the beach.

13. My sister looks for shells by the water.

Unit 2   UNIT CHECKUP   103

Name _____

Nouns That Name More Than One pages 82–83
Draw a line around each noun that names more than one.

14. The boys saw maps of the moon at the science fair.

15. Are there plants and flowers on the moon?

More Nouns That Name More Than One pages 84–85
Draw a line under the noun that names more than one.

16. Two classes were on a hike.

17. Suddenly they saw some bushes move.

18. Three little foxes ran out!

Other Nouns That Name More Than One pages 86–87
Draw a line under the correct noun.

19. Two (man, men) at the zoo tell us about lions.

20. We see some of the lion's sharp (tooth, teeth).

21. Look at its four huge (foot, feet)!

Nouns That Name Special People and Animals
pages 88–89
Write a proper noun from the picture to finish each sentence.

Bambi Lassie

Pam

22. _____ likes her book.

23. She drew a deer called _____.

24. The dog's name is _____.

104 UNIT CHECKUP Unit 2

Name _____

Nouns That Name Special Places   pages 90–91
Draw a line under the proper noun that is written correctly.

25. Lee lives in (Pineville, pineville).

26. She rides her bike to (Todd School, todd school).

Days, Months, and Holidays   pages 92–93
Draw a line around each letter that should be a capital letter.

27. flag day is in june.   **28.** It is on monday.

29. The next month is july.   **30.** sunday is independence day.

Words That Take the Place of Nouns   pages 94–95
Draw a line around the pronoun that can take the place of the underlined word or words.

31. Ellen wrote a wonderful story.   He, She

32. The story is about a friendly snake.   They, It

33. Matt and Sue enjoyed reading Ellen's story.   They, It

The Pronouns I and Me   pages 96–97
Draw a line under the correct word or words in the ( ).

34. Pam lives near (I, me).   **35.** (I, Me) go to her house.

36. (Pam and I, I and Pam) play.   **37.** Then (I, me) go home.

Compound Words   page 98
Join the underlined words. Write each compound word.

38. I sleep in a bed + room.

39. I kick the foot + ball.

UNIT CHECKUP   Unit 2   **105**

Name _____

1–2 Cumulative Review

What Is a Sentence? pages 28–29
Draw a line under each group of words that tells a complete thought.

1. The story is funny.
2. about a clown
3. makes us laugh
4. The clown does tricks.

Naming and Telling Parts of Sentences pages 30–33
Write a naming part or a telling part to finish each sentence.

5. _____ has a pet frog named Ribbit.

6. The frog _____ .

7. _____ hops around the yard.

8. Ribbit _____ .

Word Order in a Sentence pages 34–35
Draw a line under each group of words that is in the correct order.

9. writes a newspaper Our class.
10. Jill tells about the museum.
11. draws pictures Jack for the stories.
12. We write jokes for the newspaper.

Name _____

Kinds of Sentences   pages 36–43
Read each sentence. Draw a line around the word that tells what kind of sentence it is.

13. I have a new game.   statement   question   exclamation
14. What are the rules?   statement   question   exclamation
15. This game is fun!   statement   question   exclamation

Nouns   pages 78–81
Draw a line under each noun. Write the nouns that name people or animals.

16. The teacher took her students to the circus.

   _____   _____

17. One girl laughed at monkeys wearing hats.

   _____   _____

18. My brother saw a pony with a long tail.

   _____   _____

Nouns That Name More Than One   pages 82–85
Draw a line around the nouns that name more than one.

19. In our science classes we study insects.
20. We keep many bugs in large jars.
21. We give them twigs from bushes to eat.

CUMULATIVE REVIEW Units 1–2

Name _____

Other Nouns That Name More Than One   pages 86–87
Write the correct noun for each sentence.

22. Two (child, children) wore costumes.

23. Their masks had many (teeth, tooth).

24. They wore big shoes on their (foot, feet).

25. Several (man, men) laughed at the silly costumes.

26. All the (women, woman) had fun too.

Proper Nouns   pages 88–91
Write the correct noun for each sentence.

chinatown, Chinatown

27. We rode the bus to _____.

Jill Wong, jill wong

28. Mom took us to visit _____.

Kimo, kimo

29. We saw a statue of _____ the dragon.

108   CUMULATIVE REVIEW   Units 1–2

Name _____

Days, Months, and Holidays pages 92–93
Draw a line around the sentence that is written correctly.

30. Thanksgiving is Thursday.   thanksgiving is thursday.

31. Is labor day in may?   Is Labor Day in May?

Pronouns pages 94–95
Write a pronoun from the box to take the place of the underlined words.

| he   It   she   They |

32. Mom and Tim looked for whales.

33. Soon Tim saw a whale.

34. The whale dived under the water.

35. Then Mom saw a big whale dive.

The Pronouns I and Me pages 96–97
Write I or me to finish each sentence.

36. Will Sam eat lunch with _____?

37. Sharon and _____ eat apples.

38. _____ share my grapes with Sam.

CUMULATIVE REVIEW Units 1–2   **109**

UNIT 3

Sharing Your News

◆ **COMPOSITION FOCUS:** Friendly Letter
◆ **LANGUAGE FOCUS:** Verbs

When you don't see your friends every day, how do you tell them what you have been doing? You can share ideas by calling your friends on the telephone. You can also write letters to them.

Shannon and David are good friends. When Shannon moved away, she and David shared their ideas by writing friendly letters.

In this unit, you will learn how to write a friendly letter to someone you know.

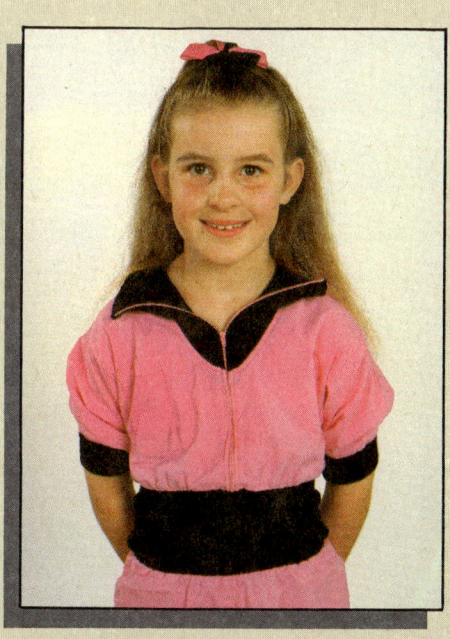 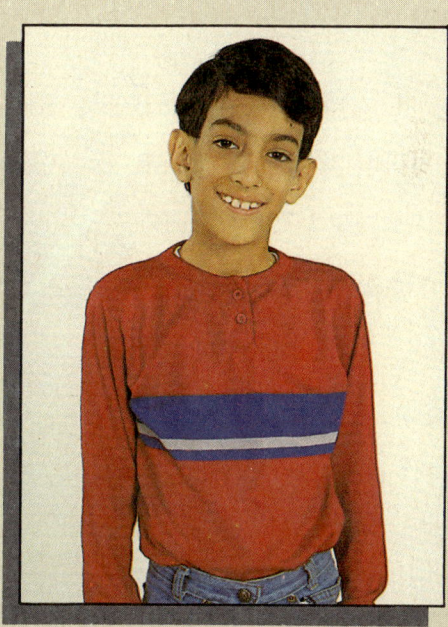

Shannon and David wrote letters to tell each other about their lives.

UNIT 3

Reading with a Writer's Eye
Friendly Letter

Read the friendly letters that Shannon and David wrote to each other. Think about why each letter was written.

July 15, 1990

Dear Shannon,
   I am having a birthday party. We are going swimming. The party will start at 1:00 P.M. We will have the party on Sunday, July 24. The party will be at Elm Park. Can you come to my party?

   Your pal,
   David

July 29, 1990

Dear Shannon,
   Thank you for giving me the nice presents. I like the paper, the eraser, the pencil, and the watch. I will use them in school. Did you get a pet for your birthday?

   Your pal,
   David

Name _____

August 3, 1990

Dear David,

    Yesterday I got a new cat! Her name is Snowball. She is all white. She likes to play with red yarn. She is a year old. Her favorite color is red. My cat climbs into my bed at night so she can sleep with me. David, does your dog do tricks?

                Your friend,
                Shannon

Shannon Tyler
422 Maple Street
Daytona Beach, Florida 320

    David Allan
    310 Laurel Road
    Orlando, Florida 32803

Respond

1. Would you like to write a letter to Shannon or David? What would you tell about?

Discuss

2. Why does David write his first letter to Shannon? Why does he write the second letter?

3. Look at the letter Shannon wrote. Why does she tell David about her cat?

READING ↔ WRITING CONNECTION

Name _____

Thinking As a Writer
Studying a Friendly Letter

Writer's Guide
◆ A friendly letter has five parts.

You can write a **friendly letter** to tell a friend about yourself. You can ask a friend questions. A friendly letter has five parts.

Look at David's letter to Shannon.

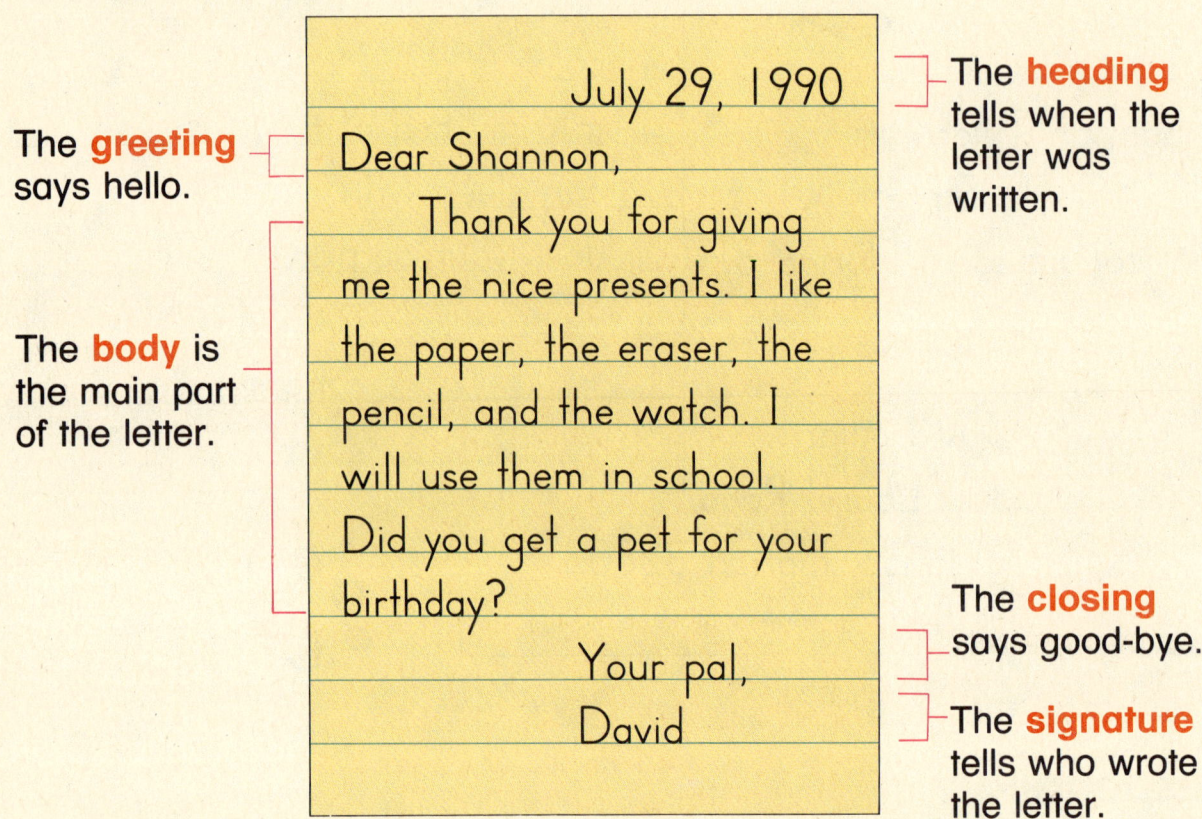

The **greeting** says hello.

The **body** is the main part of the letter.

The **heading** tells when the letter was written.

The **closing** says good-bye.

The **signature** tells who wrote the letter.

Notice how a **comma** (,) is used in the heading, greeting, and closing. Notice which parts begin with capital letters.

Discuss

1. Why does David write this letter?
2. What does each part of David's letter do?

114   READING ↔ WRITING CONNECTION

Name _____

Try Your Hand

A. Write the Parts of a Letter   Read the letter. Write each letter part on the line next to its name.

> May 6, 19--
>
> Dear Erin,
>   Thanks for the beautiful plant! I put it in my room.
>   Your friend,
>   Carol

1. Heading

2. Greeting

3. Body

4. Closing

5. Signature

B. Find Parts of a Letter   Read Shannon's letter to David. What are the parts of her letter? Why do you think Shannon wrote this letter?

READING ↔ WRITING CONNECTION   **115**

Thinking As a Writer
Picturing Events

You can picture things that have happened by closing your eyes. You can see the things again in your mind.

Before writing, Shannon closed her eyes and pictured what she wanted to write about. Then she drew a picture.

> **Writer's Guide**
> ◆ Good writers picture events in their minds before they write about them.

Discuss

1. What did Shannon do before writing?
2. How did picturing Snowball help Shannon write her letter?

Try Your Hand

Picture an Animal   Close your eyes. Picture what your favorite animal does. Draw a picture to show what you saw in your mind.

Developing the Writer's Craft
Writing for Your Reader

Before writing a friendly letter, a good writer decides who will read the letter. The writer chooses ideas that are interesting to the reader. A good writer also decides whether to share news, invite someone, or thank someone.

Read this friendly letter.

Writer's Guide
- Good writers decide <u>who</u> will read their writing.
- Good writers decide <u>why</u> they are writing.

July 15, 19--

Dear Mary,
    I am on an airplane. My family is coming back from Washington, D.C. We saw the White House. I took a lot of pictures. I will show them to you at school.

                      Your friend,
                      Bill

Discuss

1. Why does Bill write this letter?
2. What does Bill write that Mary might like to read?

Try Your Hand

Tell About Reasons   Tell a partner a reason for writing to each of these people.

    1. a fire fighter   2. a librarian

READING ↔ WRITING CONNECTION

Name _____

1 Prewriting
Friendly Letter

> **Writer's Guide**
>
> ☑ Decide who will get your letter and why you are writing it.
> ☑ Draw pictures of your ideas.
> ☑ Choose an idea your reader will like. This is your topic.
> ☑ Picture in your mind what happened.
> ☑ Write details about your topic.

Look at what Randy did to plan a friendly letter.

Randy followed the **Writer's Guide.** He decided to write to his friend Carl. He drew pictures of what he wanted to share with Carl. Randy decided to tell about washing the car because something funny had happened that day. Randy drew a line around that picture.

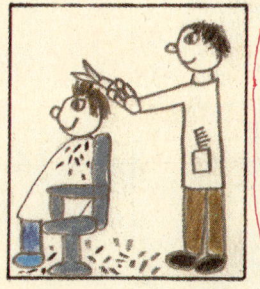  

Randy pictured that day in his mind. He wrote details to help Carl "see" what had happened. He wrote the details in a drawing.

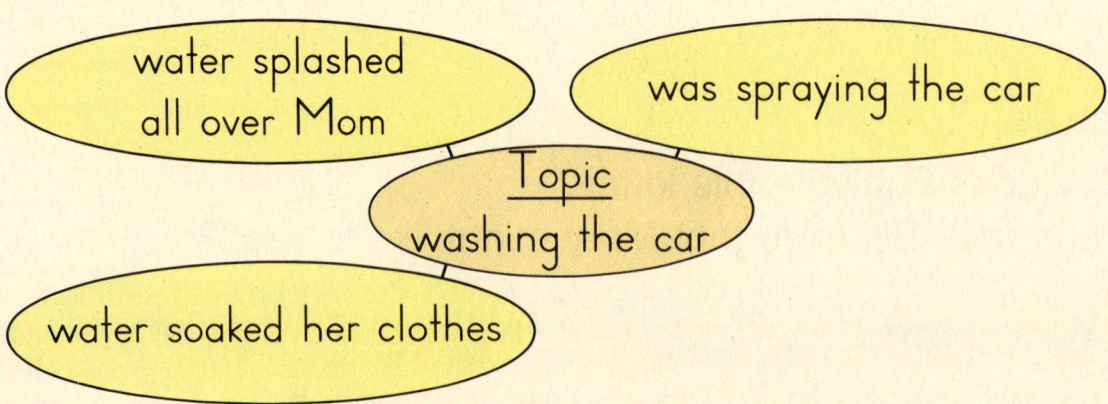

118 COMPOSITION: PREWRITING Friendly Letter

Name _____

Discuss

1. How does Randy follow the **Writer's Guide**?
2. What helps Randy think of ideas for his letter?

Try Your Hand

Now plan your friendly letter.

A. Think About Why and Who
Decide <u>why</u> you are writing.
Decide <u>who</u> will read your letter.

B. Think of Writing Ideas
Draw pictures of interesting things that have happened.

Eagle Ideas

1. Has anything funny happened to you lately?
2. What is new at school?
3. What would you like to thank someone for?

C. Choose a Topic Choose an idea your friend will like. This is your topic.

D. Plan Your Details Close your eyes and picture your topic. Write details. You may wish to make a drawing as Randy did.

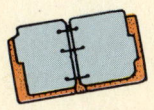 Put your plan in your **Writer's Notebook.** You will use it when you write your letter.

COMPOSITION: PREWRITING Friendly Letter **119**

Name _____

2 Drafting
Friendly Letter

Before writing the first draft of his letter, Randy looked at his drawing. He noticed that he had left out an important detail. He added a detail about not seeing Mom.

Writer's Guide

☑ Write a heading.
☑ Write a greeting.
☑ Write the body. Use your drawing for ideas.
☑ Write a closing. Sign your name.

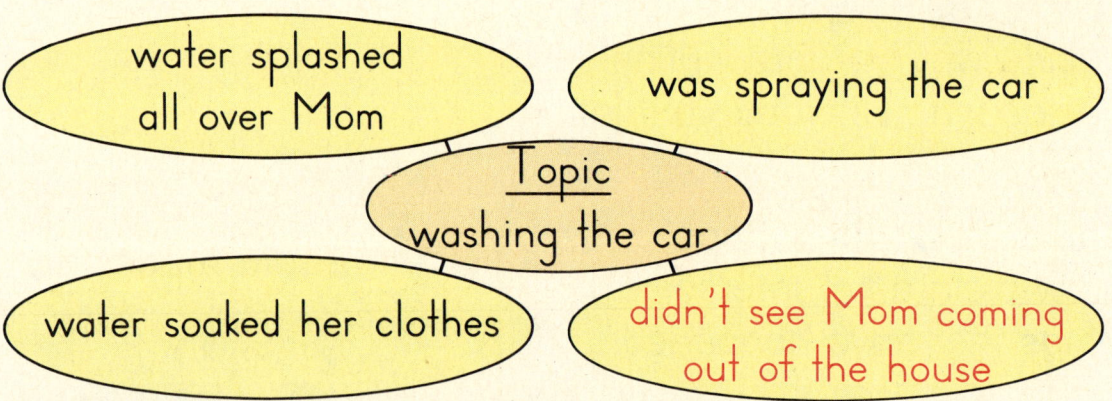

Randy used the details in his drawing to write his letter. He followed the **Writer's Guide.**

> July 12, 1990
>
> Dear Carl,
>   A funny thing happened when I washed our car. I was spraying the car with the hose. I didn't see Mom coming out of the house. The water splashed all over Mom. The water soaked her clothes.
>
>   Your buddy,
>   Randy

120 COMPOSITION: DRAFTING Friendly Letter

Discuss

1. Why is it important that Randy added that he did not see his mom coming out of the house?
2. What else could Randy add to his letter?

Try Your Hand

Now write your friendly letter.

A. Think About Your Topic   Do you still want to write about your topic? If not, choose a new topic and make another plan.

B. Read Your Plan   Add any details that would make your letter clearer. Change words to say exactly what you mean.

C. Keep an Eagle Eye on Who, What, and Why   Remember that you are writing to tell about something that happened to you.

D. Write Your First Draft   Write the heading, greeting, body, closing, and signature of your letter.
   Write quickly. You can correct any mistakes later.

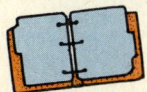
Put your first draft in your **Writer's Notebook**. You will check it in the next lesson.

Name _____

3 Responding and Revising
Friendly Letter

Randy used the **Writer's Guide** to help him check his letter. Then Randy showed his letter to Lisa. They asked each other questions. Later Randy thought about his talk with Lisa.

Writer's Guide

- ☑ Read your letter to yourself or to a friend.
- ☑ Think about your letter. Be sure you told what your reader would like to know.
- ☑ Be sure your words tell exactly what happened.
- ☑ Be sure your letter has five parts.
- ☑ Make changes.

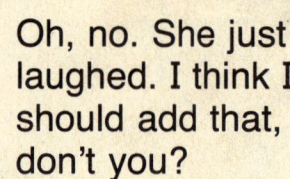

I think Carl will like your letter, Randy. Your story is funny. Did your mom get mad?

Oh, no. She just laughed. I think I should add that, don't you?

122 COMPOSITION: RESPONDING/REVISING Friendly Letter

Name _____

Look at Randy's letter. He used this mark ∧ to add a sentence and a question. He also joined two sentences that have the same naming part. He used this mark ⌒.

> July 12, 1990
>
> Dear Carl,
>   A funny thing happened when I washed our car. I was spraying the car with the hose. I didn't see Mom coming out of the house. The water splashed all over Mom⌒ The water —— Change
> and
> soaked her clothes. She laughed. Has anything funny happened to you, Carl? —— Add
>
>   Your buddy,
>   Randy

Discuss

1. Why do you think Randy joined two sentences?

2. What is the first sentence Randy added to his letter? Why did he add it?

3. Why do you think Randy added a question to his letter?

COMPOSITION: RESPONDING/REVISING Friendly Letter

Name _____

Try Your Hand

Now check your letter. Use the **Editor's Marks** to show your changes.

A. Think About Your Letter   Read your letter to yourself or to a classmate. Will your letter be clear to your reader?

B. Check the Five Parts   Be sure your letter has these parts.
- a heading
- a greeting
- a body
- a closing
- a signature

C. Make Changes
- Are your details clear? To change something, use this mark ⊼. To add something, use this mark ∧.
- Use the **Word Book** to help you find exact words to make your letter clear.

Editor's Marks

∧ Add something.
⌒e Take out something.
⊼ Change something.
↷ Move something.

D. Join Sentences   Look for sentences that can be joined.

E. Check Your Letter   Read your letter again. Make changes until your letter is clear.

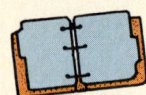 Put your letter in your **Writer's Notebook.** In the next lesson, you will fix any mistakes.

Name _____

Revising Workshop
Joining Sentences

Writers often join two sentences into one. The new sentence says the same thing in fewer words. Read these sentences.

1. Ted opened the book.   **2.** Ted looked at the pictures.

Each sentence has the same naming part, but a different telling part. You can put these two sentences together. How is the new sentence better?

3. Ted opened the book and looked at the pictures.

Practice

Read each pair of sentences. Use the word <u>and</u> to join the two sentences into one. Write the new sentence.

Gina dances. Gina sings.

1. _____

Don read the letter. Don smiled.

2. _____

Paul paints. Paul reads.

3. _____

COMPOSITION: REVISING WORKSHOP   Friendly Letter   **125**

Name _____

4 Proofreading
Friendly Letter

Carl wrote a letter back to Randy. He used the **Writer's Guide** for help.

> July 27, 1990
>
> dear Randy,
>   Thanks for your letter! Something funny happened on Saturday. My family and I were leaving for a picnic. Dad saw something dripping from the car. He thought it wuz oil. (was) It was honey from our picnic lunch!
>
>   your friend,
>   Carl

Writer's Guide

☑ Check for commas in the heading, greeting, and closing.

☑ Check for capital letters in the heading, greeting, and closing.

☑ Check your spelling.

⇨ Use the **Writer's Handbook** for help.

Editor's Marks

≡   Use a capital letter.
⊙   Add a period.
∧   Add something.
⤴   Take out something.
⋀   Change something.
◯   Check the spelling.

Discuss

1. Where does Carl add **commas (,)**? Why?
2. Why does Carl use this mark ≡?
3. Which word is not spelled correctly?

Try Your Hand

    Now correct any mistakes in your letter. Follow the **Writer's Guide.** Use the **Editor's Marks** to show your changes.

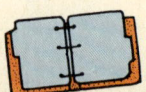 Put your letter in your **Writer's Notebook.** You will share it in the next lesson.

Name _____

5 Publishing
Friendly Letter

Before sharing his letter, Randy followed the **Writer's Guide**. Then he sent his letter to Carl. If you want to read Randy's finished letter, you can find it on page 28 of the **Writer's Handbook**.

Writer's Guide

- ☑ Copy your letter over neatly.
- ☑ Be sure nothing is left out.
- ☑ Be sure there are no mistakes.
- ☑ Share your letter.

Randy addressed an envelope.

Randy put his letter in the envelope. He added a stamp.

Randy mailed his letter to Carl.

Name _____

Discuss

1. How does Randy share his letter?
2. Why is this a good way to share a letter?
3. Name other ways Randy could share his letter.

Try Your Hand

Share Your Letter   Follow the **Writer's Guide** to get your letter ready for sharing. You may want to share your letter in the way Randy did or try one of these ideas.

- Change your letter into a puzzle. First glue your letter onto a piece of paper. Then cut the letter into six big pieces. Make each piece a different shape. Mail the puzzle to your friend.
- Copy your letter onto a long sheet of paper. Then roll it up. Tie it with yarn or string. Give your letter to your friend.

128   COMPOSITION: PUBLISHING   Friendly Letter

Name _____

Listening and Speaking
How to Talk on the Telephone

A telephone can help you share information. What are Kathy and Mark saying on the telephone?

Kathy: Hello. May I speak to Barbara, please?
Mark: Barbara isn't home. May I take a message?
Kathy: This is Kathy. Please tell Barbara the swim team is meeting on Saturday at ten o'clock at Brook Park.
Mark: I will write that down. Good-bye!

Now read the message that Mark wrote.

> Dear Barbara,
>   Kathy called. Your swim team is meeting on Saturday at ten o'clock at Brook Park.
>   Mark

When Someone Calls
- Speak clearly and politely.
- Listen carefully.
- If the call is for someone who is not at home, write a message.

When You Write a Message
- Write the caller's name.
- Write what the caller said.
- Make sure the message is complete and correct.

LISTENING/SPEAKING Friendly Letter

Name _____

Writing in the Content Areas

Use what you learned about a friendly letter to write to people you know. Use one of these ideas.

Writer's Guide

When you write, use the stages of the Writing Process.

- Plan your writing.
- Write what you want to say to your readers.
- Talk with your classmates about your writing.
- Make your writing clear. Change words if you need to.
- Fix any mistakes.
- Share your writing.

Physical Education

Write a letter to your family. Tell about a funny game or sport that your class has played. Draw a picture to go with the letter.

Social Studies

Read about Abraham Lincoln, Pocahontas, or another person from long ago. Then imagine that you are that person. Write a letter telling about your life. Put your Letters from Long Ago into a class mailbox. Read each other's letters.

Name _____

CONNECTING
WRITING AND LANGUAGE

When you write a friendly letter, you write about things that happened to you. You can use words that tell about actions.

Here is a letter Lee wrote to Jeff. What actions does Lee tell about?

> July 31, 1990
>
> Dear Jeff,
>   My dog Lucky and I *swim* almost every day. I *jump* in the water first. Then Lucky *dives* off the dock. I *splash* and *kick*. Lucky *paddles* and *barks*. Then we *race* to the float.
>   Your friend,
>   Lee

◆ **Verbs in a Friendly Letter**   The words shown in blue tell about actions. These words are called **verbs.** Writers use verbs to tell what people, animals, and things do.

◆ **Language Focus: Verbs**   In the next lessons, you will learn how to use different kinds of verbs in your writing.

CONNECTING WRITING AND LANGUAGE   **131**

Name _____

1 Action Verbs

◆ **FOCUS** An **action verb** is a word that tells what someone or something does.

The children play.

The telling part of a sentence can tell what someone or something does. The word that names the action is an action verb.

1. The children laugh .   2. Mike hops for fun.

Tell what the children in the picture do.

Guided Practice

A. Find the action verb in each sentence.
1. Lee waves his arms.
2. Mike kicks his leg.
3. The children sing.

Write the action verbs.

4. _____   5. _____   6. _____

132 GRAMMAR Action Verbs

Name _____

THINK AND REMEMBER
◆ Use an **action verb** to tell what someone or something does.

Independent Practice

B. Completing Sentences   Write an action verb to finish each sentence. Use words from the box.

grabs	races
paints	shines
tags	picks

7. Roger _____ red rowboats.   races

8. Susan _____ silver skates.

9. Patty _____ purple pictures.

10. Greta _____ green grapes.

11. Tom _____ Tina two times.

12. Peter Piper _____ peppers.

Application—Writing and Speaking

Poem   Write a poem using action verbs. Tell your classmates how you dance. Use the **Word Bank.** Use page 25 of the **Writer's Handbook** to help you write a poem.

Word Bank
skip—flip
jump—bump
shake—break
twirl—swirl

GRAMMAR Action Verbs   133

Name _____

2 Verbs That Tell About Now

◆ **FOCUS**   A verb can tell about an action that happens now.

Add <u>s</u> to an action verb that tells what one person, animal, or thing does. Do not add <u>s</u> to an action verb that tells about more than one.

1. The door opens .
2. The apples fall .

Use action verbs to tell about the picture.

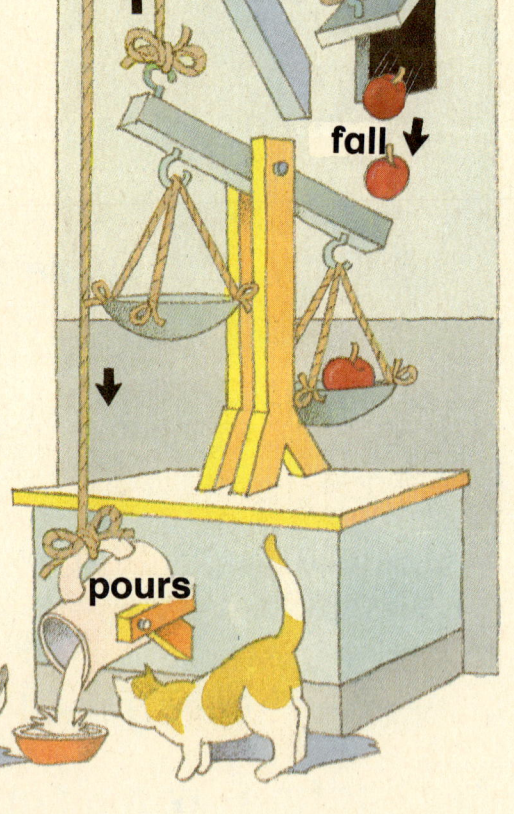

Guided Practice

A. Choose the correct verb. Tell why.

1. The scale (pull, pulls) the string.
2. The pitcher (spill, spills) the milk.
3. The bowl (fill, fills) with milk.
4. The cats (drink, drinks) the milk.

Now write the verbs.

5. _____   6. _____

7. _____   8. _____

134   GRAMMAR/USAGE   Verbs That Tell About Now

Name _____

THINK AND REMEMBER

◆ Add s to an action verb that tells what one person, animal, or thing does now.

Independent Practice

B. Writing Verbs   Look at the picture. Then use a word from the box to finish each sentence. Add s to the verb if you need to.

| find | jump | skate | wind | beat |

9. The children ___find___ the toys.

10. The girl _____ up each toy.

11. The cow _____ .

12. A monkey _____ a drum.

13. Two mice _____ up.

Application—Writing and Speaking

Sentences   Draw a picture of a wind-up toy. Write sentences about your toy. Use action verbs. Act out your sentences.

GRAMMAR/USAGE   Verbs That Tell About Now

Name _____

3 Verbs That Tell About the Past

◆ **FOCUS**   A verb can tell about an action that happened in the past.

Ruff jumped in a puddle this morning.

Now Ruff jumps out of the tub!

Many verbs end with <u>ed</u> to tell about the past.

    Now   1. Today Mike walks to school.

  The Past 2. Yesterday Mike walked to the store.

Use verbs that end with <u>ed</u> to tell what happened in the pictures.

Guided Practice

A. Choose the verbs that tell about the past.

1. Mike and Ruff (walk, walked) home this morning.

2. It (rains, rained) on the way home.

3. Mike (pulled, pulls) up his hood.

Now write the verbs that tell about the past.

4. _____ 5. _____ 6. _____

136   GRAMMAR/USAGE   Verbs That Tell About the Past

Name _____

THINK AND REMEMBER
◆ Add <u>ed</u> to many verbs to tell about the past.

Independent Practice

B. Revising Sentences Finish each sentence with a verb from the box. Make the verb tell about the past.

play	laugh
jump	kick
soak	clean

7. Ruff ____ in a puddle.   played

8. Mike ____ the dog.

9. Ruff ____ the water everywhere.

10. The water ____ Mike.

11. Ruff ____ out of the tub.

12. Dad and Mike ____.

Application—Writing

Story Write a story. Imagine that you are Ruff. Write about something silly you did. Use verbs that tell about the past. If you need help writing a story, use page 24 of the **Writer's Handbook.**

GRAMMAR/USAGE Verbs That Tell About the Past 137

Name _____

4 The Verbs Is and Are

◆ **FOCUS** The verbs <u>is</u> and <u>are</u> tell what something is like.

The school is fun.   **The clowns are silly.**

The verbs <u>is</u> and <u>are</u> do not tell about action. These verbs tell what something is like. These verbs tell about now. Use <u>is</u> with nouns that name one. Use <u>are</u> with nouns that name more than one.

1. One clown is funny.   2. Some dishes are broken.

Use <u>is</u> and <u>are</u> to tell about the picture.

Guided Practice

A. Choose <u>is</u> or <u>are</u> to finish each sentence. Then write the verb.

1. The clowns (is, are) funny.   _____

2. That car (is, are) little!   _____

3. The balls (is, are) red.   _____

138 GRAMMAR/USAGE <u>Is</u> and <u>Are</u>

Name _____

THINK AND REMEMBER

◆ Use <u>is</u> or <u>are</u> to tell what something is like.

◆ Use <u>is</u> to tell about one. Use <u>are</u> to tell about more than one.

Independent Practice

B. Finishing Sentences   Finish each sentence. Use <u>is</u> or <u>are</u>. Use the picture for ideas.

4. The girl   is a clown.

5. Her shoes _____.

6. Her ears _____.

7. A cat _____.

8. The hat _____.

9. A flower _____.

10. The clown _____.

Application—Writing and Speaking

Poster   Draw a picture of the clowns doing a trick. Write sentences on your picture. Use <u>is</u> and <u>are</u>.

GRAMMAR/USAGE   <u>Is</u> and <u>Are</u>   **139**

Name _____

5 The Verbs Was and Were

◆ **FOCUS**   The verbs <u>was</u> and <u>were</u> tell what something was like.

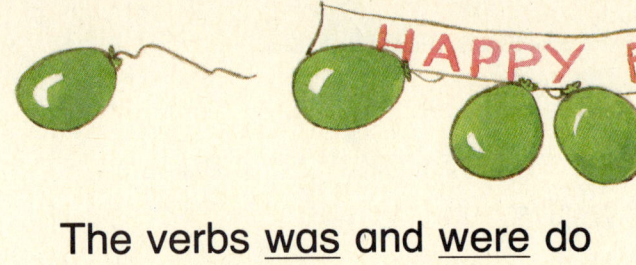

The verbs <u>was</u> and <u>were</u> do not tell about action. These verbs tell what something was like. These verbs tell about the past. Use <u>was</u> with nouns that name one. Use <u>were</u> with nouns that name more than one.

1. The girl was a clown.
2. The children were funny!

Use <u>was</u> and <u>were</u> to tell about the picture.

The children <u>were</u> excited.
The party <u>was</u> fun.

Guided Practice

A. Choose the correct verb. Tell why it is correct.

1. We children (was, were) guests at a party.
2. Dan (was, were) a cook.
3. His hat and coat (was, were) white.

Now write the verbs.

4. _____   5. _____   6. _____

140   GRAMMAR/USAGE   <u>Was</u> and <u>Were</u>

Name _____

THINK AND REMEMBER
◆ Use <u>was</u> or <u>were</u> to tell what something was like.
◆ Use <u>was</u> to tell about one. Use <u>were</u> to tell about more than one.

Independent Practice

B. Writing Verbs Read each sentence. Write <u>was</u> or <u>were</u> to finish the sentence.

7. The bug **was** big.

8. The bee _____ all wet.

9. The ants _____ very busy.

10. The fleas _____ small.

11. The fox _____ brown.

12. The bats _____ fast asleep.

Application—Writing, Listening, and Speaking

Riddle Imagine that you went to a costume party. Write sentences for your family about your costume. Do not tell what it was. Use <u>was</u> and <u>were</u>. Can your family guess your costume?

GRAMMAR/USAGE <u>Was</u> and <u>Were</u> 141

Building Vocabulary
Words That Have More Than One Meaning

Some words have more than one meaning. In sentence **1**, bat names a baseball bat. In sentence **2**, bat names an animal.

1. Bill swings the bat.   2. The bat lives in a cave.

Reading Practice

Read each pair of sentences. Tell the meanings of the underlined words.

1. The weather is cold.
   I sneeze when I have a cold.

2. We play on the swings.
   I am Cinderella in a play.

Writing Practice

Write two sentences each for fly, pen, and letter. Tell a different meaning of the word in each sentence. Share your sentences with a classmate.

Project

Make a picture dictionary with your class. Use words with more than one meaning.
- Write each word on a sheet of paper.
- Write sentences and draw pictures to show the different meanings of the word.
- Put the pages together to make a book.

Listening and Speaking

Poetry

What has a tongue but cannot talk? Listen to this poem. Think about the action verbs.

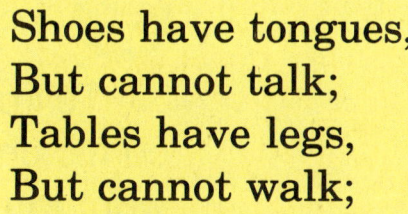

Shoes Have Tongues
by Ilo Orleans

Shoes have tongues,
But cannot talk;
Tables have legs,
But cannot walk;

Needles have eyes,
But cannot see;
Chairs have arms,
But they can't hug me!

Name _____

Language Enrichment
Verbs

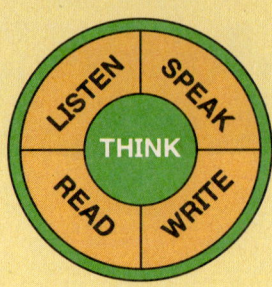

Use what you know about verbs to do these activities.

 **Action-Packed**

- Look at something you see every day, such as a leaf, a rock, a bag, or a book.
- Write the name of the thing.
- Make a list of action verbs that go with it. For example, a leaf can grow, hang, spin, fall, rustle, or float.
- Choose one verb from your list to act out for your classmates. Have them guess the verb.

Melf is a tiny elf.

His friends are tiny too!

 **Funny Faces**

Tell about a favorite comic character. You may want to use books or newspapers to find a character.

- Draw large comic-strip frames on paper.
- Write a story about your character in the frames. Use is, are, was, and were.
- Draw pictures in the frames to go with the sentences.
- Share your comic strip.

Name _____

CONNECTING
LANGUAGE AND WRITING

You have learned about verbs in this unit.

◆ **Using Verbs in Your Writing**   Knowing how to use verbs will help you make your writing clear and interesting. Use verbs to do these activities.

Midnight Magic

Imagine that your favorite toys came to life one night! Write a story about your toys. Use some verbs from the box to tell what they did. Add <u>ed</u> to the verbs to show the past. Read your story to a classmate.

bump	clean	climb
whisper	open	jump
walk	look	laugh

Double Talk

You learned about words with more than one meaning. Now look at each picture. Read the riddle. Name the word with two meanings. Tell the meanings.

1. Why did the machine go to the movies? It was a fan.

2. Why did the bird pay for its beak? It was a bill.

Name _____

3 Unit Checkup

Friendly Letter   pages 114–115

Read Tom's letter. Draw a line under the answer to each question.

> November 14, 1990
>
> Dear Ben,
>   My class made puppets. I made a puppet with big shoes and baggy pants. I painted a silly face on it. We laughed at my puppet. What are you doing at school?
>
>   Your pal,
>   Tom

1. Why did Tom write this letter?

    a. to share news about himself with his friend

    b. to thank his friend for a gift

2. Which of these letter parts is the greeting?

    a. November 14, 1990   b. Dear Ben,

Picturing Events   page 116

Think about Tom's letter. Draw a line under the answers to the questions.

3. Which details help you "see" Tom's puppet?

    a. big shoes, baggy pants, silly face   b. school, puppets

4. What may have helped Tom write clear details?

    a. He pictured things in his mind before he wrote.

    b. He asked his classmates what happened.

Name _____

Writing for Your Reader   page 117

Draw a line under the answer to each question.

5. What is the first thing you should do to plan a letter?

   a. Sign your name.   **b.** Decide why you are writing it.

6. It is a good idea to decide who will read your letter before you write it. Why?

   a. You can choose ideas that will interest your reader.

   b. You can write quickly.

The Writing Process   pages 118–128

Draw a line under the answer to each question.

7. Pretend that you are planning your letter. What should you do to help you write your ideas clearly?

   a. Picture in your mind what happened.

   b. Address an envelope.

8. What should you do when you write a first draft?

   a. Ask someone how to spell words.

   b. Write quickly to get all your ideas down on paper.

Action Verbs   pages 132–133

Write an action verb to finish each sentence. Use the words in the box.

| lands   throws |

9. Dad ____ his hat into the air.

10. The hat ____ on his head!

UNIT CHECKUP   Unit 3   **147**

Name _____

Verbs That Tell About Now pages 134–135
Write a word from the box to finish each sentence. Add <u>s</u> to the verb if you need to.

| throw play |
| ride run |

11. Ed _____ a game.   12. We _____ bikes.

13. I _____ a ball.   14. He _____ to catch it.

Verbs That Tell About the Past pages 136–137
Draw a line around the verb that tells about the past.

15. Cory just ____ the fence green.   paint   painted

16. His cat ____ into the fence!   bumped   bump

17. Cory ____ his cat.   washed   wash

18. He ____ the cat's fur.   brush   brushed

The Verbs Is and Are pages 138–139
Finish each sentence. Write <u>is</u> or <u>are</u> in the sentence. Tell what the elephant looks like.

19. The elephant _____.

20. Its trunk _____.

21. Its ears _____.

148 UNIT CHECKUP Unit 3

Name _____

The Verbs Was and Were pages 140–141
Read each sentence. Write was or were to finish the sentence.

22. At the silly zoo the lions _____ tiny.

23. A monkey _____ as big as an elephant.

24. Some bears _____ purple.

25. The giraffes _____ green and red.

26. A pink snake _____ fuzzy.

Words That Have More Than One Meaning page 142
Look at the underlined word in each sentence. Think about its meaning. Then use the word in a new sentence. Show a different meaning for the word.

The <u>bark</u> on the tree trunk is brown.

27. _____

Dad gave Mom a pretty <u>ring</u> for her finger.

28. _____

UNIT CHECKUP Unit 3 **149**

UNIT 4

Telling What Things Are Like

◆ **COMPOSITION FOCUS:** Paragraph That Describes
◆ **LANGUAGE FOCUS:** Describing Words

When you tell your friends what something is like, you are describing it. A **description** is a word picture. The words in a good description help your friends picture in their minds what you are talking or writing about.

The book Under the Lemon Tree by Edith Thacher Hurd gives a good word picture of a donkey and of where the donkey lives. The author's descriptions help you picture in your mind how things look, taste, smell, feel, and sound.

In this unit you will learn to write a good description.

Edith Thacher Hurd wrote Under the Lemon Tree for people to enjoy and to describe a little donkey and the place where it lives.

Reading with a Writer's Eye
Description

Read this story to find out how the author describes a little donkey and the place where the donkey lives.

Under the Lemon Tree
by Edith Thacher Hurd

Once there was an old lemon tree where the lemons hung big and fat and as yellow as butter.

Under the lemon tree lived a little gray donkey. In the winter, the thick leaves of the lemon tree kept the cold wind from blowing on the little donkey. In the summertime, the leaves kept the hot sun from shining on her, and in the springtime, the bees went HUM-HUM-HUM in the sweet, white blossoms of the lemon tree.

The lemon tree stood in the farmyard of a little farm, so the donkey was close to the big white rooster that the farmer loved more than anything else in all the world. The little donkey was also close to the ten white chickens and close to the yellow ducks on the pond.

Name _____

Not too far from the little farm, just over the hill and into the woods, lived a sly mother fox and her five little, sly little foxes, who were always hungry for something good to eat.

One dark night, the mother fox came out of the woods and over the hill and into the farmyard. She was looking for something for herself and her five little foxes to eat.

The little donkey, under the lemon tree, had big ears, and she heard the mother fox, and she saw her two bright eyes shining in the darkness.

Name _____

The little donkey opened her mouth. EE-AW-EE-AAW, bawled the donkey. The donkey woke up the rooster. COCK-A-DOODLE-DO, crowed the rooster.

The rooster woke up the chickens. CLUCK-CLUCK-CLUCK, clucked the chickens. The rooster and the chickens woke up the ducks. QUACK-QUACK-QUACK, quacked the ducks.

They all made such a noise that they frightened the fox away, and they woke up the farmer, and they woke up the farmer's wife.

The farmer and his wife ran to the window, but they did not see the fox, and they did not know that she had been in their farmyard that night.

"Oh," said the sleepy farmer to his wife the next morning. "Why does our donkey make such a terrible noise?"

"Well," said his gentle wife, "that is the only kind of a noise she knows how to make."

"Then it would be better if she made no noise at all," grumbled the farmer. "Tonight I will take her far away so that neither you nor I nor anyone else will hear her."

And that's just what the farmer did. When it grew dark and the fireflies were bright, the farmer took his little donkey far away and tied her to an old fig tree.

Name _____

The little donkey had never slept anywhere but under the lemon tree in the farmyard. Now she was far from the big white rooster, far from the chickens, and far from the ducks in the pond. She could not sleep all alone under the fig tree.

Late that night the mother fox crept out again, out of the woods, over the hill, and into the farmyard.

There was no little donkey to hear her and nobody there to see her bright eyes shining as she crept closer and closer to the big white rooster.

Name _____

Then all of a sudden the rooster began to squawk, the chickens to cluck, and even the ducks went QUACK-QUACK-QUACK.

When the farmer and his wife heard all the noise, they jumped out of bed and ran down the stairs, for they knew it couldn't be the little donkey who had woken them up this time.

Away ran the fox.

Away ran the farmer, and the farmer's wife ran as fast as she could behind them.

The mother fox was in such a hurry that she did not see where she was going. She did not see the donkey under the fig tree.

READING ↔ WRITING CONNECTION

Name _____

But the little donkey had not closed her eyes all night, so she saw the fox running, and she heard the rooster squawking.
    EE-AAW-EE-AAW-EE-AAW.
    EE-AAW-EE-AAW-EEEEE!
bawled the donkey. She had never bawled like this before in all her life.

When the fox heard this terrible noise she opened her mouth and dropped the rooster on the ground.

The rooster jumped up and began to crow.
    COCK-A-DOODLE-DO.
    COCK-A-DOODLE-DO.
The farmer and his wife came running and shouting, "Stop thief! Stop thief! Stop that fox!"

And that was the last that anyone ever saw of the fox, for she never came back to the farmyard again.

"How lucky we are!" cried the farmer, as soon as he could catch his breath. "How lucky we are to have the noisiest donkey in all the world!"

"Yes indeed," said his gentle wife, "or else you would have lost your beautiful big white rooster."

The farmer picked up the rooster, and his wife put her arm around the neck of the little donkey, and they all walked back to the farmyard together.

Then the sun came up, the rooster crowed, the chickens clucked, the ducks quacked, and the bees went HUM-HUM-HUM in the sweet, white blossoms of the lemon tree.

The farmer's wife tied the donkey under the lemon tree and, from that time on, the little donkey never lived anywhere else.

Respond

1. Do you like the donkey? What does the writer tell you that makes you feel this way about the donkey?

Discuss

2. How does the writer describe where the donkey lives?
3. Use your own words to describe the fox.

Thinking As a Writer
Studying a Paragraph That Describes

A **paragraph** is a group of sentences that tells about one main idea. The first word of a paragraph is written a little to the right. It is **indented**.

The paragraph below is a paragraph that describes. It tells what something is like. Words that tell how things <u>look</u>, <u>taste</u>, <u>smell</u>, <u>feel</u>, and <u>sound</u> are used to give a good word picture.

Writer's Guide

- A paragraph that describes tells what someone or something is like.
- The topic sentence names the topic.
- The other sentences give details about the topic.

> A beautiful lemon tree grows in the farmyard. The lemons are big and yellow and sour. Its thick, green leaves are shiny. In the spring, birds chirp in the sweet, white blossoms of the lemon tree.

The **topic sentence** names the topic.

The **detail sentences** tell about the topic.

Discuss

1. What is the topic of the paragraph?
2. Which words give you the best picture of the lemon tree?
3. What other details could you add to this paragraph?

160 READING ↔ WRITING CONNECTION

Name _____

Try Your Hand

A. Find the Topic Sentences   Read each paragraph. Write the topic sentence.

   The farmhouse is pretty. It is clean and white. It has a little round window.

1. _____

   The mother fox does many things. She takes care of five baby foxes. She hunts for food at night.

2. _____

B. Find and Write Details   Read the paragraph about the farmhouse again. Write another detail sentence that you could add to the paragraph.

3. _____

C. Write Words That Describe   Draw a picture of a room in your house. Then write words under the picture to tell what the room is like.

READING ↔ WRITING CONNECTION   161

Name _____

Thinking As a Writer
Paying Attention to Details

Good writers use many details to give a good word picture. They use their five senses to find out how things look, taste, smell, feel, and sound.

The author of <u>Under the Lemon Tree</u> may have made a chart like this before she described the lemon tree.

Writer's Guide

- Good writers use their five senses to study what they will describe.
- They use words to describe what they notice.

Looks	Tastes	Smells	Feels	Sounds
yellow big white	sour	sweet fresh	smooth bumpy	hum loud

Discuss

1. Look at the picture on the first page of the story. Name words to describe things.
2. Which words could you add to the chart?

Try Your Hand

Collect Details What is your classroom like? Think about how things look, taste, smell, feel, and sound. Then list words to describe the place. You may want to use a chart.

Name _____

Developing the Writer's Craft
Using Colorful Words

Colorful words help readers tell what something is like.

> Not too far from the little farm, just over the hill and into the woods, lived a <u>sly</u> mother fox and her five little, <u>sly</u> little foxes, who were always hungry for something good to eat.

Writer's Guide

◆ Good writers choose colorful words to tell what something is like.

The writer could have said that the foxes are smart. The word <u>sly</u> is more colorful, or interesting. It helps you picture just how smart the foxes are.

Discuss

1. What colorful word could you use instead of <u>good</u> to describe the foxes's food?
2. Picture the five little foxes in your mind. What colorful words could describe them?

Try Your Hand

Use Colorful Words Write sentences to describe the woods. Use colorful words.

_____
_____
_____

READING ↔ WRITING CONNECTION

Name _____

1 Prewriting
Paragraph That Describes

Steven followed the **Writer's Guide** to write a paragraph that describes. First, he talked about writing ideas with some friends. He made a list of ideas.

> 1. building my dream treehouse
> 2. watching a rocket blast off
> 3. being in a jungle

Writer's Guide

- ☑ Talk with others about writing ideas. Make a list of ideas.
- ☑ Decide who will read your paragraph.
- ☑ Choose an idea that you and your readers will like. This is your topic.
- ☑ Draw or find a picture.
- ☑ Write words that describe your topic.

Steven wanted his friends to read his paragraph. He decided to write about a rocket because he and his friends had seen a rocket blast off. Steven wrote that idea on a piece of paper.

Next, Steven found a picture of the rocket he had seen. He noticed all the details in the picture. He closed his eyes and pictured what had happened on the day the rocket took off. He wrote words in a chart to describe the rocket.

164 COMPOSITION: PREWRITING Paragraph That Describes

Name _____

<u>watching a rocket blast off</u>

Looks	Tastes	Smells	Feels	Sounds
smooth tall big engines white smoke giant		strong smoky	ground shakes bumpy hot	roar hiss whoosh rumble

Steven read his chart. He added more details.

Discuss

1. How does Steven follow the **Writer's Guide**?
2. Why does Steven add details to his chart?
3. Does Steven need to use any words to describe taste? Why or why not?

COMPOSITION: PREWRITING   Paragraph That Describes   **165**

Name _____

Try Your Hand

Now plan your paragraph.

A. Think of Writing Ideas   Think of interesting people, animals, places, or things to describe. They can be be real or make-believe.

B. Choose a Topic   Decide who will read your paragraph. Choose an idea your readers will like. This is your topic.

C. Use a Picture   Draw or find a picture to show your topic.

D. Plan Your Details   Close your eyes and picture your topic. Then use the picture and what you "see" in your mind to write words to describe your topic. You may wish to make a chart.

E. Check Your Details   Read your details and look at your picture. Do you want to add or change any words?

Eagle Ideas

1. Imagine a wonderful place to take a vacation.
2. What is your favorite animal like?
3. What does your dream room look like?

Put your plan in your **Writer's Notebook.** You will use it when you write your paragraph.

166   COMPOSITION: PREWRITING   Paragraph That Describes

Name _____

2 Drafting
Paragraph That Describes

Writer's Guide

- ☑ Use your picture and chart for ideas.
- ☑ Write a topic sentence to name your topic.
- ☑ Write detail sentences to explain the topic.
- ☑ Use words that give a good word picture.

Look at what Steven did to write his paragraph.

Before writing, Steven thought about his topic. He decided that he still wanted to describe the rocket. Then he followed the **Writer's Guide** to write his first draft.

> A rocket is ready to blast off into space. The tall rocket looks like a giant jet. There are many big engines. Suddenly they roar! The ground shakes. White smoke and flames come out of the engines. The rocket goes up slowly. It leaves a strong smell behind in the air.

Discuss

1. What is Steven's topic sentence?
2. Which words helped you picture the rocket?

COMPOSITION: DRAFTING   Paragraph That Describes

Name _____

Try Your Hand

Now write your paragraph that describes.

A. Think About Your Topic   Do you still want to write about your topic? If not, choose another topic and make a new plan.

B. Look at Your Plan   Look at your picture and your chart. Add any details that would make your paragraph more interesting.

C. Keep an Eagle Eye on Who, What, and Why   Think about who will read your paragraph. Remember that you are describing something that you want your readers to picture in their minds.

D. Write Your First Draft   Write a topic sentence to name your topic. Write detail sentences that describe your topic.

Write your ideas quickly. You will have time later to fix any mistakes.

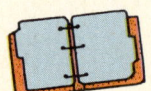 Put your first draft in your **Writer's Notebook.** You will check it in the next lesson.

Name _____

3 Responding and Revising
Paragraph That Describes

Steven used the **Writer's Guide** to help him write a better paragraph. He and Pam talked about the paragraph.

> **Pam:** What do the flames look like?
> **Steven:** They're yellow and orange. I'll add that.

Steven added words to make his paragraph clearer. He used this mark ∧. He changed one word. The new word had just the right meaning. He used this mark ∧.

Writer's Guide
- ☑ Read your paragraph to yourself or to a friend.
- ☑ Be sure you name what you are describing.
- ☑ Be sure your sentences tell about your topic.
- ☑ Can your readers picture what you wrote?
- ☑ Make changes.

A rocket is ready to blast off into space. The tall rocket looks like a giant jet. There are many big engines. Suddenly they roar! The ground shakes. White smoke and ∧^(yellow and orange) flames come out of the engines. The rocket goes up slowly. It leaves a ^(smoky) strong smell behind in the air.

— Add

— Change

COMPOSITION: RESPONDING/REVISING   Paragraph That Describes   **169**

Name _____

Discuss

1. What information does Steven add? How do these words make the paragraph better?
2. Which word does Steven change? Why?

Try Your Hand

Now check your paragraph. Use the **Editor's Marks** to show your changes.

A. Think About Your Writing Read your paragraph to yourself or to a friend. Does your paragraph give a good word picture?

B. Make Changes

- Does one sentence name your topic? You may need to add a sentence.
- Do your detail sentences describe your topic? You may want to add words that describe. Use this mark ∧. Use page 171 for help.
- Does your writing say what you want it to? Use this mark ∧ to change words.

Editor's Marks

∧ Add something.
⌿ Take out something.
∧ Change something.
↷ Move something.

C. Check Your Paragraph Read your paragraph again. Make changes until you feel it gives the best word picture.

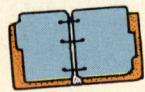 Put your paragraph in your **Writer's Notebook**. In the next lesson, you will fix any mistakes.

Name _____

Revising Workshop
Adding Describing Words to Sentences

Writers often make a sentence clearer.
1. The man crosses the field.
2. The <u>tall</u> man crosses the <u>green</u> field.

How is the second sentence better?

Here is how to add words to make a clear sentence.
- Find the nouns in the sentence.
- Think about what else you can tell about the nouns.
- Choose words to describe the nouns.
- Add the new words.

Practice

Find the nouns. Think of words that describe the nouns to add to each sentence. Write the new sentences.

The boy has a jacket.

1. _____

The car stops.

2. _____

The dog runs.

3. _____

COMPOSITION: REVISING WORKSHOP   Paragraph That Describes   171

4 Proofreading
Paragraph That Describes

Steven used the **Writer's Guide** to correct the mistakes in his next paragraph. Look at what he did.

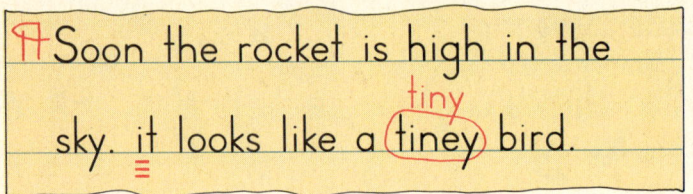

Writer's Guide

☑ Be sure to indent your paragraph.

☑ Be sure each sentence begins with a capital letter.

☑ Check your spelling.

⇨ Use the **Writer's Handbook** for help.

Discuss

1. Why does Steven use this mark ⁋ ?
2. Why does Steven use this mark ≡ ?
3. Which word does Steven draw a line around? Why?

Try Your Hand

Now correct any mistakes in your writing. Follow the **Writer's Guide.** Use the **Editor's Marks** to show your changes.

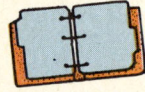 Put your paragraph in your **Writer's Notebook.** You will share it in the next lesson.

Editor's Marks

≡ Use a capital letter.

⊙ Add a period.

∧ Add something.

℮ Take out something.

⋀ Change something.

◯ Check the spelling.

⁋ Indent the paragraph.

Name _____

5 Publishing
Paragraph That Describes

Here is how Steven shared his work. First, he followed the **Writer's Guide.** Then, he made a model to go with his description. He shared it with his friends. If you want to read Steven's finished description, you can find it on page 21 of the **Writer's Handbook.**

Writer's Guide
- ☑ Copy your paragraph over neatly.
- ☑ Be sure nothing is left out.
- ☑ Be sure there are no mistakes.
- ☑ Share your work in an interesting way.

Steven wrote his paragraphs neatly.

Steven made a model of the rocket.

Steven shared his work with his friends.

COMPOSITION: PUBLISHING Paragraph That Describes **173**

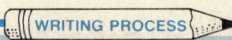

Name _____

Discuss

1. How does Steven share his writing?
2. Why is this a good way to share a paragraph that describes?
3. How would you share a paragraph that describes?

Try Your Hand

Share Your Description Follow the **Writer's Guide.** You may want to share your work in the way Steven did. You may wish to try this idea.

♦ Make a large painting to show what you wrote about. First, copy your description on a large piece of paper. Then, paint a picture on the rest of the paper.

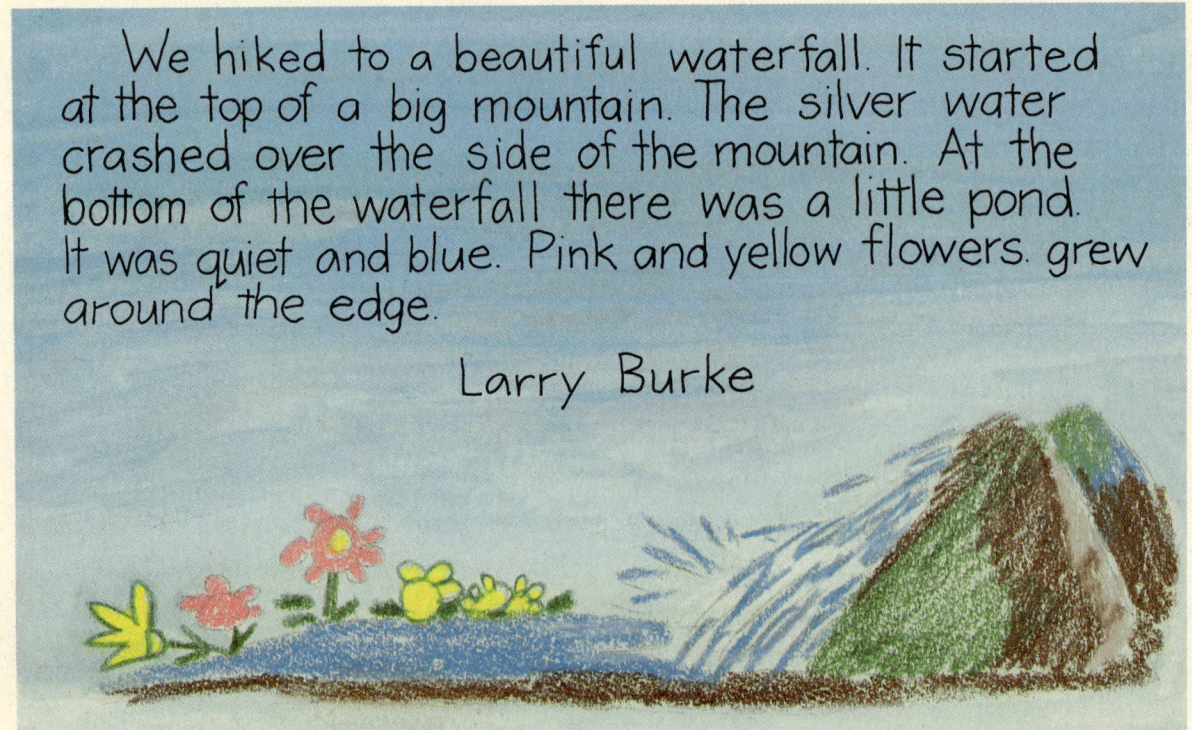

Listening and Speaking
How to Give an Oral Description

When you speak, you can tell what someone or something is like.

Before You Describe Something
- Think of interesting people, animals, places, or things to talk about.
- Decide who is going to hear you speak.
- Choose a topic your listeners will like.

As You Describe Something
- Speak slowly and clearly.
- Use words that tell how things look, taste, smell, feel, and sound to help your listeners picture what you are describing.

Practice

With a partner, take turns describing something you see every day. It might be a bowl of crunchy cereal, a woolly sweater, or a big red book. Compare the words that you use.

Name _____

Writing in the Content Areas

Use what you learned about writing a paragraph that describes. Use one of these ideas.

Writer's Guide

When you write, use the stages of the Writing Process.
- Plan your writing.
- Write what you want to say to your readers.
- Talk with your classmates about your writing.
- Make your writing clear. Change words if you need to.
- Fix any mistakes.
- Share your writing.

Art

Use color words to tell about a make-believe person, animal, place, or thing. Write a paragraph to describe your topic. Then draw a picture to go with your description. Glue your picture and writing on a piece of paper. Make a Color Corner in your classroom.

Social Studies

Do you speak another language? Have you ever lived in another country? Does your family eat special foods from other lands?

Ask someone in your family these questions. Then write a paragraph that describes a special kind of food, clothing, place, or holiday. Share your work.

Lederhosen are shorts that are worn in Germany.

Name _____

CONNECTING
WRITING AND LANGUAGE

When you write a paragraph that describes, you tell what someone or something is like.

Here is a paragraph that describes a house. Which words tell about the house?

> The **tiny** house is **beautiful**. It has a **red** roof, a **white** door, and **round** windows. Near the house is a **big** garden filled with **many** flowers.

◆ **Describing Words in a Paragraph** Read the paragraph again. The words shown in blue are **describing words.** Writers use describing words to tell what people, animals, places, and things are like.

◆ **Language Focus: Describing Words** In the next lessons, you will learn about describing words and how to use them to tell more about nouns.

CONNECTING WRITING AND LANGUAGE 177

Name _____

1 Describing Words

◆ **FOCUS**   A **describing word** tells about a noun.

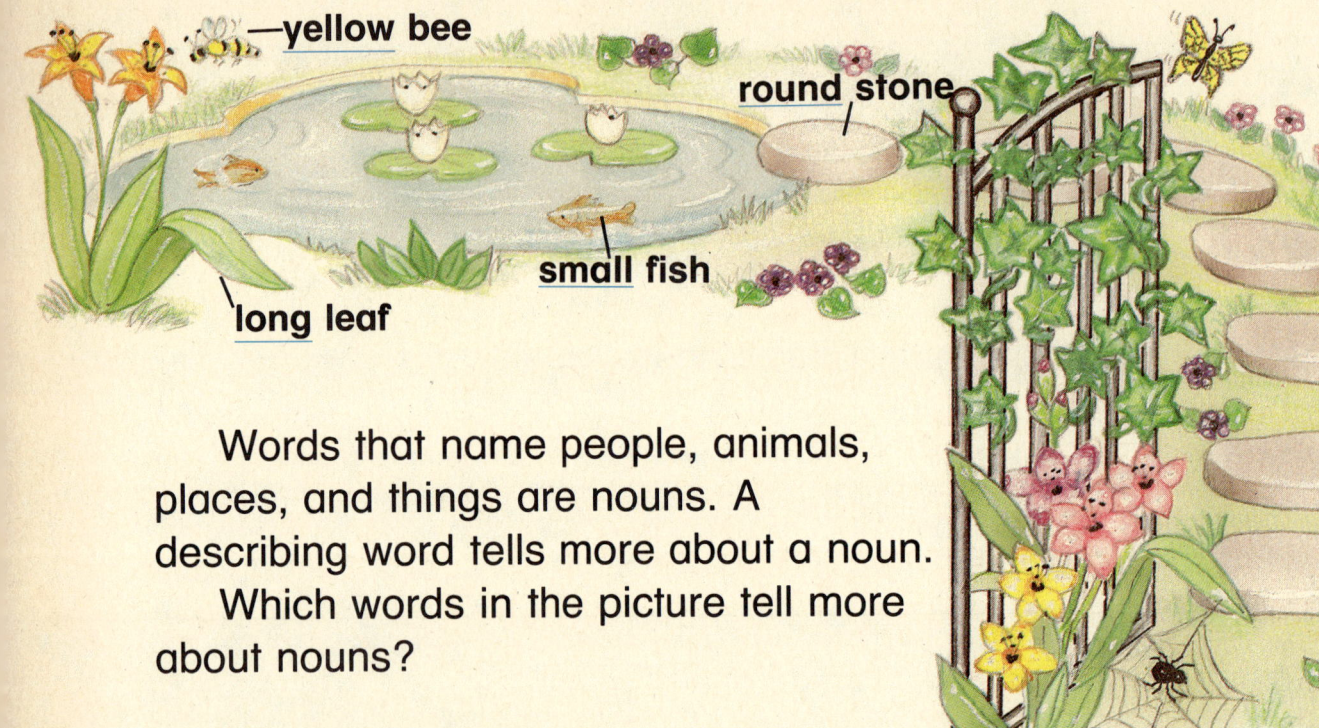

Words that name people, animals, places, and things are nouns. A describing word tells more about a noun. Which words in the picture tell more about nouns?

Guided Practice

A. Which word tells about the underlined noun?

1. The <u>garden</u> is beautiful.
2. Do you see the yellow <u>butterfly</u>?
3. The <u>flowers</u> are huge!
4. There is a black <u>spider</u>.

Now write the describing words.

5. _____

6. _____

7. _____

8. _____

178   GRAMMAR   Describing Words

Name _____

THINK AND REMEMBER
◆ Use **describing words** to tell more about nouns.

Independent Practice

B. Writing Describing Words
Choose a describing word to finish each sentence. Write the word.

Word Bank
cold   round
green two
heavy warm
little white

9. A pond is round .

10. There are _____ flowers around it.

11. Are _____ fish in the pond?

12. Does the water feel _____?

13. Here is a _____ stone.

14. The leaves are _____.

Application—Writing

Invitation   Make a card to invite your teacher to visit a garden. Write sentences that tell what he or she will see. Use describing words. Use page 29 of the **Writer's Handbook** to help you write an invitation.

GRAMMAR Describing Words 179

Name _____

2 Describing Words for Shape and Color

FOCUS
- Some describing words tell about shape.
- Some describing words tell about color.

Describing words tell more about nouns. They can describe the shape and color of a person, animal, place, or thing.

1. square rug   2. white cat

Use describing words to tell about the picture.

Guided Practice

A. Find the noun in each sentence. Then find the describing word that tells about it. Write the describing word.

1. The pillow is purple. _____

2. Do you see a red table? _____

3. I like the square blocks. _____

180 GRAMMAR Describing Words for Shape and Color

Name _____

THINK AND REMEMBER
♦ Use **describing words** to tell about the shape and color of a person, animal, place, or thing.

Independent Practice

B. Using Describing Words Finish each sentence. Use a describing word that tells about the shape or color of the toy.

4. The robot's face is <u>square</u>.

5. The bear has a _____ face.

6. The fur on the bear is _____.

7. A _____ horn is near a drum.

8. Is the drum _____?

9. Do you see the _____ frog?

Application—Writing and Speaking

List What would you put in a playhouse? Make a list. Use describing words for shape and color to tell about the things.

Name _____

3 Describing Words for Size and Number

FOCUS
- Some describing words tell about size.
- Some describing words tell how many.

The describing words tiny and tall tell about size.

The describing words one and two tell exactly how many. Other describing words for how many are many, few, and some.

Use describing words for size and how many to tell about the picture.

Guided Practice

A. Which word tells about the underlined noun? Write the describing word.

1. There are two monsters.

2. The monsters have a big basket.

3. Many ants are on the blanket.

Name _____

THINK AND REMEMBER

◆ Use **describing words** to tell about size and <u>how many</u>.

Independent Practice

B. Writing Describing Words   Write a describing word to finish each sentence. Use the **Word Bank**.

Word Bank
big   many
five   six
Four   small
little two

4. ____ monsters go to a park.

5. They stay for ____ hours.

6. The ____ monsters swim in the lake.

7. Then they eat a ____ lunch.

8. The monsters brought ____ sandwiches.

9. After lunch the ____ monsters play.

Four
_____
_____
_____
_____
_____

Application—Writing

Postcard   Make a postcard for a friend. Use describing words to describe your favorite place.

front   back

GRAMMAR Describing Words for Size and Number   183

Name _____

4 Describing Words for Taste, Smell, Feel, and Sound

◆ **FOCUS** Some describing words tell how something tastes, smells, feels, or sounds.

Describing words can tell how things taste, smell, feel, and sound.

The apple tastes sweet.

Tell how things in the picture might taste, smell, feel, and sound.

Guided Practice

A. Which word describes each underlined noun?

1. The <u>water</u> tastes salty.
2. The <u>air</u> smells fresh.
3. I like the smooth <u>sand</u>.
4. I hear the noisy <u>waves</u>.

Now write the describing words.

5. _____   6. _____

7. _____   8. _____

184   GRAMMAR   Describing Words for Taste, Smell, Feel, and Sound

Name _____

THINK AND REMEMBER
◆ Use **describing words** to tell how things taste, smell, feel, and sound.

Independent Practice

B. Writing Describing Words   Write a describing word to finish each sentence. Use the **Word Bank**.

Word Bank
cool   smoky
loud   soft
salty spicy
slippery warm

9. I hear the ___soft___ sound of the wind.

10. The fish feels _____.

11. We listen to the _____ waves.

12. We swim in the _____ water.

13. Our campfire smells _____.

14. Does the food taste _____?

Application—Writing and Speaking

Travel Folder   Imagine a wonderful place and draw a picture. Write sentences that describe the place.

front   inside

GRAMMAR   Describing Words for Taste, Smell, Feel, and Sound   185

Name _____

5 Describing Words for Feelings

◆ **FOCUS** Some describing words tell about feelings.

Remember that describing words can tell how things look, taste, smell, feel, and sound. Describing words can also tell about feelings.

Use describing words to tell how the people in the picture feel.

Guided Practice

A. Which word describes how the person feels?

1. Is the girl surprised?
2. That woman is angry.
3. A frightened man runs away.
4. The proud boy smiles.

Now write the describing words.

5. _____
6. _____
7. _____
8. _____

Name _____

THINK AND REMEMBER
♦ Use **describing words** to tell about feelings.

Independent Practice

B. Writing Describing Words
Add describing words to finish the sentences. Use the **Word Bank.**

Word Bank
afraid	pleased
angry	proud
frightened	sad
happy	unhappy

9. Sometimes I yell when I am _angry_.

10. When I do a good job, I am _____.

11. When Karen is _____, she cries.

12. He feels _____ when he sees scary movies.

13. A _____, _____ boy smiles.

Application—Writing and Speaking

Song How would you feel if you were in the flying car? Write a song about your feelings to share with your class. Use these rhyming words.
    proud—cloud   mad—glad   shy—fly

GRAMMAR Describing Words for Feelings

Name _____

6 Describing Words with er and est

FOCUS
- ◆ A describing word that ends with er compares two things.
- ◆ A describing word that ends with est compares more than two things.

Bop
loud bark

Lad
louder bark

Max
loudest bark

Describing words can tell how things are different from each other. Add er to most describing words to compare two things. Add est to most describing words to compare more than two.

Use describing words with er and est to tell about the pictures.

Guided Practice

A. Choose the correct word for each sentence. Write the word.

1. Lad is (louder, loudest) than Bop. _____

2. Bop is the (darker, darkest) dog of all. _____

3. Max is (stronger, strongest) than Lad. _____

188 GRAMMAR/USAGE Describing Words with er and est

Name _____

> ### THINK AND REMEMBER
> ◆ Add er to most describing words to compare two nouns.
> ◆ Add est to most describing words to compare more than two.

Independent Practice

B. Using Describing Words   Add er or est to the word in the ( ) to finish each sentence.

4. Nina has the __(smart)__ smartest _____ dog of all.

5. Her dog is __(loud)__ _____ than thunder.

6. Her dog's tail is __(long)__ _____ than a snake.

7. Nina's dog is the __(strong)__ _____ dog I know.

Application—Writing and Speaking

Dog Report   Write sentences to tell how Max, Lad, and Bop are different. Use describing words with er and est.

GRAMMAR/USAGE   Describing Words with er and est   **189**

Building Vocabulary
Antonyms

Antonyms are words whose meanings are very different from each other. Antonyms are also called **opposites**. Wet is the opposite of dry. Wet and dry are antonyms.

cold   hot

full   empty

Reading Practice

Read the poem. Name the antonyms.

> **Dreams**
>
> Dreams are good. Some are bad.
> Dreams are happy. Some are sad.
> Dreams are short. Some are long.
> I dream I'm a bear, big and strong.

Writing Practice

Look at the poem again. Write a poem of your own with opposite words. You may want to use words from the **Word Bank**.

Word Bank
first—last
heavy—light
hot—cold
short—tall

Project

Find six antonym pairs. Make this game.
- Draw lines on cards to make different puzzles.
- Write an antonym pair on each card. Write one word in each part.
- Cut the cards. Put the pieces in an envelope.
- Trade envelopes with a partner. Put the antonym pairs together.

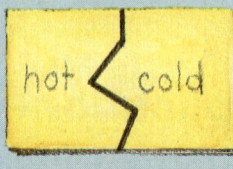

Name _____

Listening and Speaking

Poetry

Listen for the words in this poem that describe colors.

Just for a Change
by William Cole

I wish that things didn't all have to be
The colors you always *expect* to see:

Just imagine a sky of green,
A sky that's never, ever seen;
And from it shines on everyone
A great big cheerful purple sun!

Over the grass of bright, bright red
Orange flowers and black are spread;
One other thing not seen before—
A silver house, a golden door . . . .

I know it sounds silly, crazy, and strange,
But *I'd* like to see it just for a change.

Name _____

Language Enrichment
Describing Words

Use what you know about describing words to do these activities.

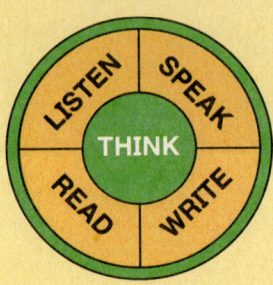

Shape and Tell

Cut triangles, squares, and circles out of colored paper. Make different sizes and colors. Then glue the shapes on paper to make a picture. Show your picture to the class. Use describing words for <u>shape</u>, <u>size</u>, <u>color</u>, and <u>how many</u> to tell about your picture.

Guess What?

Play this guessing game.
- Write describing words to tell about something.
- Use your words to write a riddle on a card.
- On the other side of the card, write the answer.
- Trade cards with a partner. Take turns reading each other's riddles out loud. Answer the riddle you read.

I am red.
I am round.
I grow on a tree.
What am I?

front

I am an apple.

back

Name _____

CONNECTING
LANGUAGE AND WRITING

In this unit you learned that describing words tell more about nouns.

◆ **Using Describing Words in Your Writing**

Use describing words to help people imagine what you are writing about. Think about describing words as you do these activities.

Forest Fantasy

Pretend that you are tiny, and that you live in a town in a forest. Write a letter to a partner about your town. Use describing words. Then trade letters with your partner. Draw pictures of each other's towns.

Odd Opposites

Lem: The soup is too thin.
Mel: The soup is too thick.

Lem: The bread is too soft.
Mel: It is hard as a brick!

Think about what you learned about antonyms. Then work with a classmate. Write a play like the one about Lem and Mel. Use some antonyms from the **Word Bank.**

Word Bank
good—bad
happy—sad
wrong—right
new—old

CONNECTING LANGUAGE AND WRITING 193

Name _____

4 Unit Checkup

Paragraph That Describes   pages 160–161

Read Dan's paragraph. Draw a line under the answer to each question.

> Mr. Gibb has a special toy parrot in his store. The parrot has blue and red wings. Its long, orange beak moves when it sings!

1. What is the topic of Dan's paragraph?

    a. a special toy parrot   b. Mr. Gibb's store

2. Which detail would you add to Dan's paragraph?

    a. I like the red train.   b. The parrot's body is yellow.

Paying Attention to Details   page 162

Look at the pictures. Think about how things look, taste, smell, feel, and sound. Write a word to describe each picture.

3.  _____

4.  _____

Using Colorful Words   page 163

Draw a line under the answer to each question.

5. Which word describes the taste of a lemon better?

    a. good   b. sour

6. Which of these sentences describes a rabbit better?

    a. A rabbit has fur.   b. A rabbit has soft, fluffy fur.

194   UNIT CHECKUP   Unit 4

Name _____

The Writing Process   pages 164–174

Draw a line under the answer to each question.

7. When you write the first draft of a paragraph, what should you do first?

   a. Write detail sentences to describe your topic.

   b. Write a topic sentence to name your topic.

8. Imagine you find a word in your paragraph that does not give the best word picture. What should you do?

   a. Change it to a more colorful word.   b. Take it out.

Describing Words   pages 178–179

Finish each sentence. Use a describing word from the box.

| prickly   bright   cool   tiny |

9. I saw a _____ cactus in my dream.

10. The night air felt _____.

11. There were _____ stars in the sky.

12. I saw some _____ animals.

UNIT CHECKUP Unit 4   **195**

Name _____

Describing Words for Shape and Color pages 180–181
Finish each sentence. Use a describing word that tells about the shape or color of the penguin.

13. My penguin has _____ eyes.

14. Its wings and head are _____.

Describing Words for Size and Number pages 182–183
Draw a line under each describing word that tells about size. Draw a line around each describing word that tells how many.

15. One day there was a big flood.

16. A crocodile saved three little animals from the flood.

17. The large crocodile had many friends.

Describing Words for Taste, Smell, Feel, and Sound
pages 184–185
Write a describing word to finish each sentence. Use the words in the box.

| sweet | fluffy |
| fresh | loud |

18. If I were a squirrel, I would make _____ sounds.

19. I would sleep in a _____ bed in a tree.

20. I would smell the _____ air in the morning.

21. I would eat food that tastes _____.

Name _____

Describing Words for Feelings pages 186–187
Read each sentence. Draw a line around the
word that describes how Lisa feels.

22. Lisa could not find her cat, Zip.   worried   cheerful
23. She heard a noise under a bed.   angry   surprised
24. She smiled when she saw Zip there.   happy   sad

Describing Words with er and est pages 188–189
Add er or est to the word in the ( ) to finish each sentence.

(tall)
25. Vern is the _____ dragon on earth.

(smart)
26. Puff is a _____ dragon than Vern.

Antonyms page 190
Choose the word from the box that means
the opposite of the word above the
line. Write it in the sentence.

| huge   soft |

little
27. Bear lives in a _____ cave.

hard
28. Each day Bear hops out of his _____ bed.

UNIT CHECKUP Unit 4 **197**

1–4 Cumulative Review

Naming and Telling Parts of a Sentence   pages 30–33
Write a naming part or a telling part to finish each sentence.

1. _____ writes a story.

2. The story _____.

3. _____ is the hero.

4. The hero _____.

Kinds of Sentences   pages 36–43
Write each sentence correctly. Make **5** a statement, make **6** a question, and make **7** an exclamation.

we went to the beach

5. _____

did you have fun

6. _____

watch out for the waves

7. _____

Name _____

Nouns   pages 78–81
Draw a line under each noun. Draw a line around each noun that names a thing or a place.

8. A girl watches the rocket blast off.

9. This spaceship is going to the moon.

10. Two men and a woman ride in the rocket.

Nouns That Name More Than One   pages 82–85
Draw a line around the nouns that name more than one.

11. Two classes at Elm School put on plays.

12. One play is about two foxes and their friends.

13. The other play is called Three Wishes.

Other Nouns That Name More Than One   pages 86–87
Draw a line under the correct noun for each sentence.

14. Many (children, child) played in the snow.

15. Their (tooth, teeth) chattered in the cold.

16. The children wore warm boots on their (foot, feet).

Proper Nouns   pages 88–91
Draw a line around the correct proper noun for each sentence.

17. People wrote about ____.   paul bunyan   Paul Bunyan

18. He and his ox ____ were   Babe   babe
    famous.

19. They dug a lake in ____.   Michigan   michigan

CUMULATIVE REVIEW   Units 1–4   **199**

Days, Months, and Holidays pages 92–93
Find each proper noun that is written incorrectly.
Write it correctly.

20. Memorial Day is in may.

21. Monday is flag day.

22. Our flowers bloom in april.

23. Veterans Day will be on friday.

Pronouns pages 94–97
Draw a line under the pronoun that can take the place of the underlined words.

24. My uncle catches a fish.   He   She   It   They
25. The fish is huge!   He   She   It   They

Draw a line under the pronoun that finishes the sentence.

26. Mom and ___ go to the beach.   I   me
27. Mom takes pictures of ___.   I   me

Action Verbs pages 132–133
Draw a line under the action verb in each sentence.

28. Tom tells tall tales.   **29.** Silly snakes sing songs.
30. A fast frog flies.   **31.** Lizards leap over lions.

Name _____

Verbs That Tell About Now pages 134–135
Write the correct verb for each sentence.

(draw, draws)

32. Dan _____ a picture of a robin.

(paint, paints)

33. He _____ it brown and orange.

(hang, hangs)

34. Mom and Dad _____ the picture on the wall.

(look, looks)

35. His friends _____ at the painting.

Verbs That Tell About the Past pages 136–137
Write a verb from the box to finish each
sentence. Make the verb tell about the past.

| work | pick |
| clean | plant |

36. Yesterday we _____ around the house.

37. I _____ up the leaves.

38. Dad _____ the garage.

39. Then Mom _____ some flowers.

CUMULATIVE REVIEW Units 1–4 **201**

Name _____

The Verbs Is, Are, Was, and Were   pages 138–141
Write the correct verb for each sentence.

40. Now Rob and Sarah (is, are) ready to walk the dogs.

41. Today it (is, are) a beautiful day.

42. Yesterday this dog (was, were) very playful.

43. Last year the dogs (was, were) little puppies.

Describing Words   pages 178–183
Draw a line around the describing words. Draw a line under the nouns they tell about.

44. The green frogs lived by a pond.

45. They made a round boat from leaves.

46. They made long, brown paddles from twigs.

47. They sailed across the pond in their tiny boat.

Describing Words for Taste, Smell, Feel, and Sound
pages 184–185
Draw a line to the describing word that finishes each sentence.

48. If I were a lemon, I would taste   squeaky.

49. If I were a knife, I would feel   sharp.

50. If I were a pizza, I would smell   sour.

51. If I were a mouse, I would sound   spicy.

Name _____

Describing Words for Feelings pages 186–187
Write a describing word from the box to finish each sentence.

| proud   bored   happy   worried |

52. I feel _____ when I have nothing to do.

53. The _____, _____ boy showed us his prize.

54. I feel _____ when my puppy is sick.

Describing Words with er and est pages 188–189
Add er or est to the word in the ( ) to finish each sentence.

(old)
55. Buck is the _____ of all the robots.

(short)
56. Elmer is _____ than Buck.

(long)
57. His feet are _____ than Buck's feet.

(tall)
58. Buck is the _____ robot of all.

CUMULATIVE REVIEW Units 1–4 **203**

UNIT 5

Telling Stories

◆ **COMPOSITION FOCUS:** Story
◆ **LANGUAGE FOCUS:** Verbs

How do you and your friends have fun? Do you play games? Do you go to the movies or the park?

Another way to have fun is to make up stories for each other to enjoy. In a story you can write about whatever you want. You decide who the people in the story will be. You think of what will happen to them.

Michael Foreman wrote a book called Cat and Canary. He drew pictures to go with his story. This story tells about people, animals, and events that the author made up in his mind.

In this unit you will learn how to write a story.

Michael Foreman made up Cat and Canary for people to enjoy.

UNIT 5 **205**

Reading with a Writer's Eye
Story

Usually cats and birds do not play together, but in a story anything can happen. Read to find out about the exciting adventure Michael Foreman made up in Cat and Canary.

from Cat and Canary
by Michael Foreman

It was dawn in the city. Cat watched the winter sky change from night to day. Canary was still asleep in her cage.

Every day Cat watched his master get ready for work. Every day the man said, "You are lucky. You just lie around the house all day, lazy cat." Then he put on his hat and coat and went to work.

Every day, though, as soon as the man had left, Cat let Canary out of her cage. Canary always flew around the room a few times. Then they had breakfast together and went up to the roof.

Cat watched Canary dive and whirl around in the sky. He wished he could fly with his friend above the streets and bridges to the land beyond the river.

Cat often watched other cats on other roofs chasing birds. He never chased birds. After all, his best friend was a canary. All the birds flocked to his roof. Most days his roof was a blizzard of birds.

Name ______________________________

One windy day Cat found a kite tangled on a television antenna. When he untied it, he became caught in the string. Suddenly the wind came up, and Cat was whisked into the air and over the streets. The cats on the other roofs were amazed to see Cat flying.

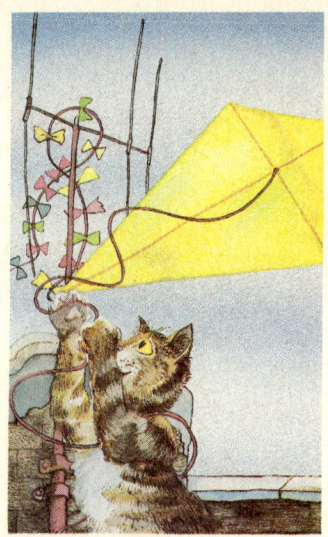

Winds rushing between the high buildings blew him higher until he was flying among the tallest skyscrapers. Canary tried desperately to keep up with him.

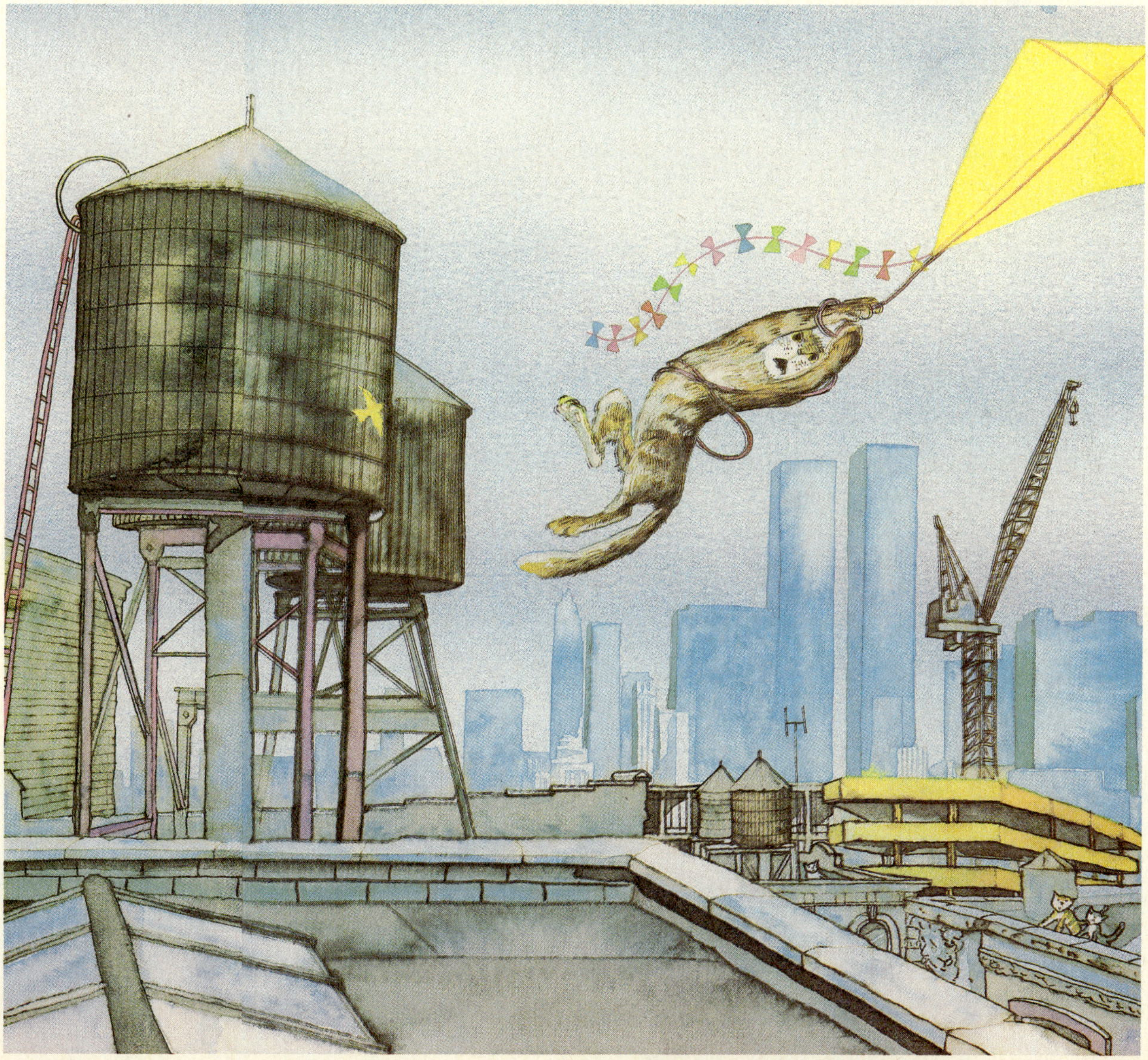

Cat was thrilled to be suddenly soaring free as a bird. The sun turned the great buildings to gold and silver, and threw Cat's giant shadow across surprised people far below.

Soon, though, the sun was covered by storm clouds and Cat no longer felt free as a bird. The huge buildings now looked dangerous and threatening. There was no way Cat could control the kite. He was being blown farther and farther from home. Below he could see the icy river. Snow began to fall.

Name _____

Just as Cat was about to give up, Canary appeared with a large flock of birds. They took the kite strings and turned toward home.

Down they went, through the snow toward the bright flashing lights of the city.

They landed on their roof just as their master turned the corner. The man did not see them. His head was bent against the wind, and snow blew into his face and down his neck. "Oh, to be a cat," he thought, "to stay home where it's cozy and do nothing."

Cat waved to the birds and tied the kite back onto the television antenna. "Tomorrow," he thought, "if we all fly together, we can go to the land beyond the river and still be back by nightfall."

Then Cat and Canary raced downstairs. When their master opened the door, Canary was swinging in the cage and Cat was curled up on the mat with his eyes closed.

"What a lazy cat!" said the man. "I bet you haven't moved all day."

Respond

1. Which part of the story do you think the author makes the most exciting? Why?

Discuss

2. What is Cat's problem? How does Canary help?
3. How does the author let you know that Cat and Canary are different from real animals?

READING ↔ WRITING CONNECTION

Name _____

Thinking As a Writer
Studying a Story

    A story can tell about real or make-believe events. A story has characters. The **characters** are the people or animals the story is about. Here are some story characters.

> Cat
> Canary
> Winnie-the-Pooh
> Snow White

    A story has a setting. The **setting** is when and where the story takes place. Here are some story settings.

> in a castle long ago
> in your backyard
> in a city on the moon

    A **story map** shows the parts of a story. It shows the **beginning,** the **middle,** and the **ending.**

    Think about what happened to Cat and Canary in the story you just read. Study the story map on the next page.

Writer's Guide

- A story has a beginning, a middle, and an ending.
- A story is often about solving a problem.
- A story has a title.

Name _____

Title: Cat and Canary

— The **title** gives a hint about the story.

Beginning

Who? Cat, Canary, master
When and where? winter in the city
What is the problem? Cat gets caught in a kite string and is blown away.

— The **beginning** tells who the characters are, what the setting is, and what the problem is.

Middle

1. Cat has fun flying with the kite.
2. A storm comes up.
3. Cat is blown far away.
4. Cat cannot get home.

— The **middle** tells what happens. It tells what the characters do.

Ending

1. Canary and other birds take the kite string and pull Cat home.
2. Cat and Canary are safely back by the time their master comes home.

— The **ending** tells what happens when the problem is solved.

Discuss

1. Read the first page of Cat and Canary again. Who are the characters? What is the setting?
2. Which story part tells how Cat gets into trouble?
3. Is Cat's problem solved by the end of the story? Explain your answer.

READING ↔ WRITING CONNECTION

Name _____

Try Your Hand

Find Story Parts Listen as your teacher reads a story. Fill in this map to go with the story.

Beginning

Who? Mr. Raccoon
_____

When and where? _____
_____

What is the problem? _____
_____
_____

Middle

1. The river floods Mr. Raccoon's house.
_____

2. _____

Ending

1. The storm stops.
_____

2. _____
_____

3. _____

216 READING ↔ WRITING CONNECTION

Thinking As a Writer
Thinking About What Might Happen

> **Writer's Guide**
>
> ◆ Good writers create an interesting problem in the beginning of a story.
>
> ◆ Then they plan what will happen to solve the problem.

To finish a story, a writer plans what will happen to solve a character's problem. The author of <u>Cat and Canary</u> may have made a chart like this before he chose a way to solve Cat's problem.

Problem	Ways to Solve It
Cat is carried away on a kite.	1. Cat lets go of the kite. 2. Canary and other birds pull Cat home. 3. Cat lands safely.

Discuss
1. How would you have solved Cat's problem?
2. Suppose Cat fell into the river. How could Canary and his friends get Cat home?

Try Your Hand
Solve a Problem   Read about Cat's new problem below. With a partner, make a chart to show ways to solve the problem. Share your ideas.

   <u>Cat takes a walk and gets lost in the city.</u>

READING ↔ WRITING CONNECTION

Name _____

Developing the Writer's Craft
Using Enough Details

Writer's Guide

◆ Good writers use enough details to help readers picture what happens in a story.

Good writers use many details to help readers know what is happening in a story. Read these sentences that tell what happened when Cat was in danger.

> There was no way Cat could control the kite. Snow began to fall.

> There was no way Cat could control the kite. He was being blown farther and farther from home. Below he could see the icy river. Snow began to fall.

The second group of sentences is clearer. It has many details to <u>show</u> how much danger Cat was really in.

Discuss

1. In the second group of sentences, which words did the writer use to help you picture what is happening?
2. Do you think the writer used enough details to show the danger? Why or why not?
3. What details would you add to the second group of sentences?

Name _____

Try Your Hand

Add Details   Add sentences to this paragraph. Give enough details to show how sad Cat is.

> Cat looks at the empty cage. He wishes Canary would come back from the bird doctor.

READING ↔ WRITING CONNECTION

Name _____

1 Prewriting
Story

Kim followed the **Writer's Guide** to plan her story. First, she thought of story ideas. She really liked reading <u>Cat and Canary</u>. She decided to write a new story to share with younger students. Her story would be about two animals who are friends.

Next, Kim drew a picture to show her characters and the setting. She wrote a sentence to tell about her picture.

Writer's Guide
☑ Think of story ideas. Choose the best idea.
☑ Draw a picture to plan your characters and your setting.
☑ Decide what the problem will be.
☑ Plan what the characters will do.
☑ Decide how the problem will be solved.

220 COMPOSITION: PREWRITING Story

Name _____

Then, Kim thought about what could happen to cause a problem for Mouse or Fox. She made a list of ideas. She drew a line around the most exciting story idea.

1. Fox can't find Mouse.
2. Mouse doesn't want to play with Fox.
3. A rock has rolled into Mouse's doorway, and she can't get out.

Kim thought about how to solve the problem. She decided to have Fox help Mouse. She made a **story map** to plan what was going to happen. Then, she read her map carefully. She added an important detail.

Beginning
1. Mouse and Fox
2. evening in a forest
3. A rock has rolled into Mouse's doorway, and she can't get out.

Middle
1. Fox sees the rock and knows Mouse is trapped.
2. Fox thinks of a way to help.

Ending
1. Fox helps Mouse get out.
2. Mouse plays with Fox.

COMPOSITION: PREWRITING Story

Name _____

Discuss

1. How does Kim follow the **Writer's Guide**?
2. What is the problem in Kim's story? How will it be solved?

Try Your Hand

Now plan your story.

A. Think of Story Ideas Think of stories you have read, things you have done, and people you know. Use your journal or **Writer's Notebook**. Make a list of ideas.

Eagle Ideas

1. What was the most exciting story you ever read?
2. Imagine a character who is like someone you know.
3. What problems have you had? How did you solve them?

B. Choose a Story Idea Who will read your story? Choose an idea that you and your readers will like.

C. Plan Your Story
- Draw a picture to show your characters and your setting.
- Decide what the problem will be.
- Decide what will happen to the characters.
- Decide how the problem will be solved.

You may wish to make a story map in the way Kim did.

D. Check Your Plan Read your plan. Do you want to add any details?

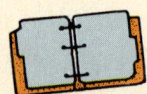 Put your plan in your **Writer's Notebook**. You will use it when you write your story.

Name _____

2 Drafting
Story

Look at what Kim did to write her story. Before writing, she thought about her story idea. She decided that it would still make the best story.

Then Kim followed the **Writer's Guide.** She used her picture and her map to write the first draft.

Writer's Guide

- ☑ Write the beginning of your story. Tell the characters, the setting, and the problem.
- ☑ Write the middle. Tell what happens to the characters.
- ☑ Write the ending. Tell how the problem is solved.
- ☑ Write a title for your story.

Fox to the Rescue

Mouse and Fox lived in a beautiful forest. One evening, Fox came to visit his friend Mouse. Mouse had just woken up from her nap. She couldn't get out of her house, though. A big rock had rolled into her doorway.

When Fox saw the big rock, he knew Mouse was trapped! Then Fox thought of a way to help.

Fox gathered all his strength and helped Mouse get out. Mouse was so happy! She hurried outside to play with Fox.

COMPOSITION: DRAFTING   Story

Name _____

Discuss

1. In which story part does Kim name the characters and the setting?

2. What other details could be added to Kim's story?

Try Your Hand

Now write your story.

A. Think About Your Story Problem Do you still think your idea would make the best story? If not, choose another idea and make a new plan.

B. Keep an Eagle Eye on Who, What, and Why Think about your readers. Remember that you are making up a story for them to enjoy.

C. Write Your First Draft Write the beginning, the middle, and the ending of your story. Write a title for your story.

Write quickly. You can fix any mistakes later.

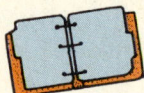 Put your first draft in your **Writer's Notebook**. You will check it in the next lesson.

Name _____

3 Responding and Revising
Story

Kim used the **Writer's Guide** to help her write a better story. First, she read her story to herself. Then, she read it to Matt. They asked each other questions.

Writer's Guide
- ☑ Read your story to yourself or to a friend.
- ☑ Be sure the beginning tells about the characters, the setting, and the problem.
- ☑ Be sure the middle tells what happens to the characters.
- ☑ Be sure the ending tells how the problem is solved.
- ☑ Be sure you use enough details.
- ☑ Make changes.

Your story is good, but I don't understand how Fox helps Mouse. Can you make that part clearer?

Yes. I can tell what Fox did to help. Do you think I should also tell more about Mouse's problem?

COMPOSITION: RESPONDING/REVISING Story **225**

Name _____

Kim thought more about her talk with Matt. She used this mark ∧ to add an important sentence. She used this mark ⌒ to change a sentence to make it clearer.

> ### Fox to the Rescue
>
> Mouse and Fox lived in a beautiful forest. One evening, Fox came to visit his friend Mouse. Mouse had just woken up from her nap. She couldn't get out of her house, though. A big rock had rolled into her doorway.∧ *She pushed and puffed, but she couldn't move it.* — **Add**
>
> When Fox saw the big rock, he knew Mouse was trapped! Then Fox thought of a way to help.
>
> Fox gathered all his strength and *pushed the rock away.* ~~helped Mouse get out.~~ Mouse was — **Change**
> so happy! She hurried outside to play with Fox.

226 COMPOSITION: RESPONDING/REVISING Story

WRITING PROCESS

Name _____

Discuss

1. Which sentence does Kim add? How does it help you know more about Mouse's problem?
2. Which sentence does Kim change? How does this change make her story clearer?

Try Your Hand

Now check your story. Use the **Editor's Marks** to show your changes.

A. Think About Your Story   Read your story to yourself or to a friend. Did you tell everything your readers need to know?

B. Make Changes

- Do you need to add details to the beginning, the middle, or the ending? Use this mark ∧.
- Do you need to change words to make your story clearer? Use this mark ⌒.

Editor's Marks

∧ Add something.
℮ Take out something.
⌒ Change something.
↶ Move something.

C. Check Your Story   Make changes until your story is clear.

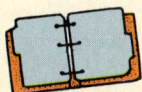 Put your story in your **Writer's Notebook.** In the next lesson, you will fix any mistakes.

COMPOSITION: RESPONDING/REVISING   Story   227

Name _____

4 Proofreading
Story

Kim used the **Writer's Guide** to correct the mistakes in another story that she wrote about Mouse and Fox. Look at what she did.

> one morning Fox and Mouse
> ≡
> decided to go swimming⊙ They
>   picnic
> made a (picnick) lunch and walked
> to the lake.

Writer's Guide

☑ Be sure each sentence begins with a capital letter.
☑ Be sure each sentence ends with an end mark.
☑ Check your spelling.
⇨ Use the **Writer's Handbook** for help.

Discuss

1. Why does Kim use this mark ≡ ?
2. Why does Kim use this mark ⊙ ?
3. Why does Kim draw a line around a word?

Editor's Marks

≡ Use a capital letter.
⊙ Add a period.
∧ Add something.
⊢ Take out something.
⋏ Change something.
◯ Check the spelling.
¶ Indent the paragraph.

Try Your Hand

Now correct any mistakes in your story. Follow the **Writer's Guide**. Use the **Editor's Marks** to show your changes.

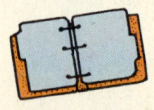
Put your story in your **Writer's Notebook.** You will share it in the next lesson.

Name _____

5 Publishing
Story

Before Kim shared her story, she followed the **Writer's Guide.** Then she made puppets to help her share her story with younger students. If you want to read Kim's finished story, you can find it on page 24 of the **Writer's Handbook.**

> **Writer's Guide**
> ☑ Copy your story over neatly.
> ☑ Be sure nothing is left out.
> ☑ Be sure there are no mistakes.
> ☑ Share your story in an interesting way.

Kim made a neat copy of her story.

Kim made puppets to help her tell her story.

Kim told her story to younger students.

COMPOSITION: PUBLISHING Story **229**

Name _____

Discuss

1. How does Kim share her story?
2. Why is this a good way to share a story?
3. Name other ways Kim could share her story.

Try Your Hand

Share Your Story   Follow the **Writer's Guide.**
You may want to share your story in the way Kim did or try one of these ideas.

- Fold a big piece of construction paper into three equal parts. Write the beginning, the middle, and the ending of your story on the parts of the large paper. Draw pictures. Stand your story on a table.

- Draw the shape of your main character on a big piece of construction paper. Cut out the shape. Glue a neat copy of your story on it. Put your story on a bulletin board.

Name _____

Listening and Speaking
How to Give Reasons

Giving reasons is a good way to make someone do or believe something. Kim is giving reasons to Mike. Read what she says.

I think you should read my story, Mike. You are a good reader. You'll have fun reading it. It's exciting! I will be happy.

When you give reasons to make someone do or believe something, remember these things.

◆ Tell what you want the other person to do or believe.
◆ Tell why the other person should do or believe what you want.
◆ Tell how it will help you or others.

LISTENING/SPEAKING Story

Writing in the Content Areas

Use what you learned to write a story. Choose one of these ideas or an idea of your own.

Literature

Work with a group. Think of a story that everyone likes. Use the characters and setting in that story to write a new story. Think of a new problem for your story. Decide how the problem will be solved. Give a play for your class.

Writer's Guide

When you write, use the stages of the Writing Process.
- ◆ Plan your writing.
- ◆ Write what you want to say to your readers.
- ◆ Talk with your classmates about your writing.
- ◆ Make your writing clear. Change words if you need to.
- ◆ Fix any mistakes.
- ◆ Share your writing.

Art

Find a picture that shows some people or animals doing something. Make up a story about the picture. Name the characters, the setting, and the problem. Tell how things work out.

After you finish, copy your story onto a big piece of paper. Draw a picture on the paper to go with your story.

Name _____

CONNECTING
WRITING AND LANGUAGE

The things that happen in a story often take place in the **past,** or some time ago.

Here is a story written by Rosa. Find out what happened on Squirrel's birthday.

> Last week Squirrel **gave** a birthday party. Robin, Chipmunk, and Ladybug **came** to Squirrel's house. They **hid** Squirrel's gifts behind their backs.
>
> Squirrel **was** sad. He thought his friends **did** not bring gifts.
>
> Then they **gave** him big, bright gifts. Squirrel **was** so surprised!

◆ **Verbs in a Story** The words shown in blue are verbs. They do not end with <u>ed</u> to tell about the past. These verbs change spellings to show the past. Writers must understand these verbs to help them write clearly and correctly about the past.

◆ **Language Focus: Verbs** In the next lessons, you will learn how to use verbs in your writing.

Name _____

1 Verbs That Tell About Now or the Past

◆ **FOCUS** **Verbs** can tell about actions that happen now or actions that happened in the past.

Verbs can tell about now. Add <u>s</u> to a verb that tells about one person, animal, or thing.

Verbs can tell about the past. Add <u>ed</u> to many verbs to tell about the past.

Now   1. Dad hikes in the woods.

2. We hike with him.

The Past   3. Last night the family cooked fish.

Use verbs to tell about the picture.

Guided Practice

A. Read each sentence. Choose the correct verb. Then write the verb.

1. They (walk, walks) into the woods. _____

2. The girl (sing, sings) a song. _____

3. Yesterday we (rest, rested) by a lake. _____

4. Last week I (packed, packs) for a trip. _____

Name _____

THINK AND REMEMBER

- Add <u>s</u> to a verb to tell what one person does now.
- Add <u>ed</u> to many verbs to tell about the past.

Independent Practice

B. Using Verbs   Use a verb from the **Word Bank** to finish each sentence. Add <u>s</u> to the verb to tell what one person does now. Add <u>ed</u> to the verb to tell about the past.

Word Bank
call	pick
climb	rent
enjoy	sail
gather	visit
join	walk

5. My family ____visits____ the lake each year.

6. Last year we _____ a boat.

7. Now we _____ up a mountain.

8. Yesterday I _____ wildflowers.

9. Now Father _____ us for dinner.

Application—Reading, Writing, and Speaking

Story   Write a story about a camping trip to read to a partner. Tell what happened yesterday. Then tell what happens now.

GRAMMAR/USAGE   Verbs That Tell About Now or the Past

Name _____

2 The Verbs Is, Are, Was, and Were

FOCUS
♦ The verbs is and are tell about now.
♦ The verbs was and were tell about the past.

Is, are, was, and were tell what something is like or was like. Is and was tell about one. Are and were tell about more than one.

Now
1. The house is spooky!
2. Two boys are outside.

The Past
3. Mom was inside.
4. The boys were scared.

Guided Practice

A. Choose the verb that goes in the sentence. Write the verb.

1. The house ____ old.   is   are

2. The rooms ____ dark.   is   are

3. Our visit ____ fun.   was   were

4. The boys ____ sad to leave. was   were

236 GRAMMAR/USAGE Is, Are, Was, and Were

Name _____

THINK AND REMEMBER
- Use <u>is</u> and <u>are</u> to tell about now.
- Use <u>was</u> and <u>were</u> to tell about the past.

Independent Practice

B. Writing Verbs   Read each sentence. Write <u>was</u> or <u>were</u> to finish the sentence.

5. John ____was____ in the house.

6. Shadows _____ on the wall.

7. A monster _____ hungry.

8. Its claws _____ sharp.

9. Its eyes _____ big and bright.

10. It _____ only a cat!

Application—Writing

Poem   Write a spooky poem for your class about the haunted house. Use <u>is</u>, <u>are</u>, <u>was</u>, and <u>were</u>. Use page 25 of the **Writer's Handbook** to help you write a poem.

GRAMMAR/USAGE   <u>Is</u>, <u>Are</u>, <u>Was</u>, and <u>Were</u>   **237**

Name _____

3 The Verbs Has, Have, and Had

FOCUS
- The verbs has and have tell about now.
- The verb had tells about the past.

Use has to tell about one. Use have to tell about more than one. Use had to tell about one or more than one.

Now
1. The driver has a car.
2. Drivers have helmets.

The Past
3. Yesterday we had a flat tire.
4. The tire had a hole.

Use has, have, and had to tell about the pictures.

Guided Practice

A. Read each sentence. Choose the correct verb. Write the verb.

1. Pilots (has, have) exciting jobs.

2. Yesterday an airplane (had, have) a broken door.

3. A jet (has, have) strong engines.

4. Long ago airplanes (have, had) wings made from cloth.

238 GRAMMAR/USAGE   Has, Have, and Had

Name _____

> **THINK AND REMEMBER**
> ◆ Use has and have to tell about now.
> ◆ Use had to tell about the past.

Independent Practice

B. Writing Verbs   Finish each sentence. Use has or have to tell about now. Use had to tell about the past.

5. A fire fighter ___has___ special clothes.

6. Fire fighters _____ boots.

7. Their trucks _____ big hoses.

8. Each fire engine _____ a tall ladder.

9. Yesterday the fire fighters _____ a busy day.

10. After work they _____ a good rest.

Application—Writing and Speaking

Job Form   What exciting job would you like? Fill out a job form. Use has, have, and had. Tell why you would be good at the job.

Name _____
Job _____
Reasons _____
_____
_____

GRAMMAR/USAGE   Has, Have, and Had   239

Name _____

4 Helping Verbs

◆ **FOCUS** A **helping verb** works with the verb to show action.

Has, have, and had can be helping verbs. They can work with other verbs to show action in the past.

1. The man has worked.   2. Dogs had pulled a sled.

Has tells about one. Have tells about more than one. Had tells about one or more than one.

Guided Practice

A. Find the helping verb in each sentence. Which verb does it help?

1. Jim had climbed a hill.
2. He has cooked dinner.
3. The log has burned.
4. The dogs have rested.

Write each helping verb and the verb it helps.

5. _____   6. _____

7. _____   8. _____

240 GRAMMAR/USAGE Helping Verbs

Name _____

> **THINK AND REMEMBER**
>
> ◆ Use has, have, and had with other verbs to show action that happened in the past.

Independent Practice

B. Writing Helping Verbs   Write has, have, or had to finish each sentence.

9. Jim _____ gathered the firewood.

10. We _____ helped him with the wood.

11. Our cat _____ curled up by the fire.

12. The dogs _____ stopped playing.

13. Terri _____ opened a good book.

14. Jim _____ fixed popcorn after dinner.

15. We _____ worked hard all day.

had

Application—Writing

Sentences   Write sentences for a classmate about the cabin in the picture. Use has, have, and had with other verbs to tell about the past.

GRAMMAR/USAGE   Helping Verbs   **241**

Name _____

5 The Verbs Come and Run

FOCUS
◆ The verbs come and run tell about now.
◆ The verbs came and ran tell about the past.

The horses run.

The verbs come and run tell about now. The spelling of these verbs changes to came and ran to tell about the past.

Now   1. A horse runs .

The Past   2. Yesterday a horse ran to the river.

Use come, came, run, and ran to tell about the picture.

Guided Practice

A. Read each sentence. Choose the correct verb. Then write the verb.

1. Now a horse (came, comes) to drink water. _____

2. Then two raccoons (run, ran) from the horse. _____

3. Last night the horse (runs, ran) to the hills. _____

242   GRAMMAR/USAGE/SPELLING   Come and Run

Name _____

> **THINK AND REMEMBER**
> ◆ Use <u>come</u> and <u>run</u> to tell about now.
> ◆ Use <u>came</u> and <u>ran</u> to tell about the past.

Independent Practice

B. Revising Sentences Write each sentence. Change the verb to tell about the past.

Two dogs come to a cave.

4. Two dogs came to a cave.

One dog runs inside.

5. _____

A bear comes out.

6. _____

Both dogs run from the bear.

7. _____

The bear runs into the water.

8. _____

Application—Writing, Listening, and Speaking

Game Make two teams. Write <u>come</u>, <u>run</u>, <u>came</u>, and <u>ran</u> in sentences. Share your work with the other team. Vote on the best sentence.

GRAMMAR/USAGE/SPELLING <u>Come</u> and <u>Run</u>

Name _____

6 The Verbs Go and Do

FOCUS
- The verbs go and do tell about now.
- The verbs went and did tell about the past.

The verbs go and do tell about now. The spelling of these verbs changes to went and did to tell about the past.

To make go and do tell about one, change them to goes and does.

Now   **1.** Pam goes on a ride.

The Past   **2.** Everyone went home.

Use go, do, went, and did to tell about the picture.

We go to the park.

Guided Practice

A. Choose the correct verb. Tell how you know it is correct.

1. Last week we (go, went) to the park.
2. Lori (go, goes) to the ticket booth.
3. We (do, does) the same thing.

Write the verbs.

4. _____   5. _____   6. _____

Name _____

> **THINK AND REMEMBER**
> ◆ Use <u>go</u> and <u>do</u> to tell about now.
> ◆ Use <u>went</u> and <u>did</u> to tell about the past.

Independent Practice

B. Revising Sentences   Read each sentence. Change the verb to tell about the past.

7. What ~~does~~ _did_ Bob see at Land of Adventure?

8. He ~~goes~~ _____ there with his best friend.

9. They ~~do~~ _____ many things.

10. The boys ~~go~~ _____ in a huge spaceship!

Application—Writing

Story   Write a story about a day at Land of Adventure to show your family. Use <u>went</u> and <u>did</u> to tell about the morning. Use <u>go</u> and <u>do</u> to tell what happens now.

GRAMMAR/USAGE/SPELLING   <u>Go</u> and <u>Do</u>   245

Name _____

7 The Verbs See and Give

FOCUS
◆ The verbs <u>see</u> and <u>give</u> tell about now.
◆ The verbs <u>saw</u> and <u>gave</u> tell about the past.

We <u>see</u> a movie.

The verbs <u>see</u> and <u>give</u> tell about now. The spelling of these verbs changes to <u>saw</u> and <u>gave</u> to tell about the past.

Now   1. He gives us tickets.

The Past   2. I gave a ticket away.

Use <u>see</u>, <u>saw</u>, <u>give</u>, and <u>gave</u> to tell about the picture.

Guided Practice

A. Choose the correct verb. Tell how you know it is correct.

1. Grandpa always (saw, sees) good seats.

2. Last night he (give, gave) the best seat to me.

Write the verbs.

3. _____ 4. _____

246   GRAMMAR/USAGE/SPELLING   <u>See</u> and <u>Give</u>

Name _____

> **THINK AND REMEMBER**
> ◆ Use <u>see</u> and <u>give</u> to tell about now.
> ◆ Use <u>saw</u> and <u>gave</u> to tell about the past.

Independent Practice

B. Revising Sentences Read each sentence. Change the verb to tell about the past.

see

5. I <u>saw</u> a Max Starr movie.

give

6. Two boys _____ Max a map.

gives

7. The map _____ clues about a treasure.

sees

8. Max _____ the treasure at last.

gives

9. He _____ the boys some jewels.

Application—Writing and Speaking

Movie Script Pretend that you will be in a movie. Write four sentences that you will say in the movie. Use <u>see</u>, <u>give</u>, <u>saw</u>, and <u>gave</u>. Say your sentences for a classmate.

GRAMMAR/USAGE/SPELLING <u>See</u> and <u>Give</u>

Name _____

8 Contractions

◆ **FOCUS**   A **contraction** is a short way to write two words.

Sometimes two words are put together to make one short word. The new word is a contraction. When a contraction is made, one or more letters are left out. An **apostrophe** (') takes the place of the missing letter or letters.

are + not = aren't

What two words make up the contraction in the picture?

Guided Practice

A. Name the contraction for the underlined words. Then write the contraction.

1. The boat <u>is</u> <u>not</u> big.

2. The winds <u>do</u> <u>not</u> stop.

3. The sun <u>did</u> <u>not</u> shine.

248   GRAMMAR/SPELLING   Contractions

Name _____

THINK AND REMEMBER

♦ Use a **contraction** to write two words in a shorter way.

♦ Use an **apostrophe** (') to take the place of the missing letter or letters.

Independent Practice

B. Writing Contractions Finish each sentence. Use a contraction for the two words.

　　　　　　　is not
4. The ocean ___isn't___ small.

　　　　　　　is not
5. The storm _____ over yet.

　　　　　　　are not
6. Many sailors _____ afraid.

　　　　　　　was not
7. The trip _____ easy.

　　　　　　　is not
8. The wind _____ calm.

Application—Writing

Journal Entry Write an adventure story in your journal. It can be real or make-believe. Use contractions.

GRAMMAR/SPELLING Contractions **249**

Building Vocabulary
Prefixes

A **prefix** is a group of letters added to the beginning of a word. A prefix changes the meaning of a word. <u>Un</u> and <u>re</u> are prefixes.

Prefix	Meaning	Example
un	not, the opposite of	unsafe
re	again	refill

Reading Practice

Name the word in each sentence with the prefix <u>un</u> or <u>re</u>. Tell the meaning of the word.

1. I untie my shoelaces.
2. He will reheat the cold soup.

Writing Practice

Add <u>un</u> or <u>re</u> to the words in the box. Use the new words to finish the sentences.

fair
paint

1. Please _____ the old doghouse.

2. Is the rule _____?

Project

Make "A Treasury of Words."
- Draw two chests on a sheet of paper.
- Write <u>un</u> or <u>re</u> on each chest. List words with the prefix in the chest.

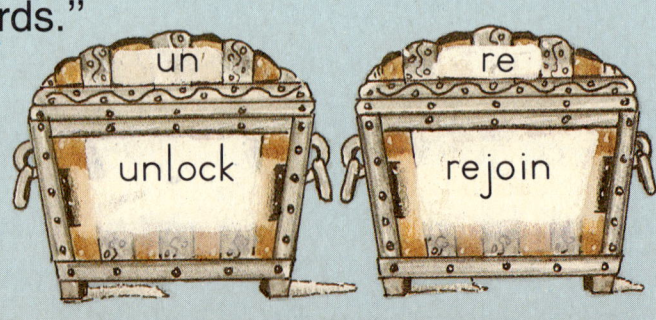

Listening and Speaking

Poetry

What is whistling and whirling? Listen to the verbs in this poem.

The Wind
by Ilo Orleans

I heard the wind blow.
I saw the wind blow.
   It whistled,
   It whirred,
   It whirled.

The branches crackled.
The green leaves shook,
   And twisted,
   And trembled,
   And curled.

The wind blew loud.
The wind blew long.
   It rumbled,
   It thundered,
   It roared.

The great trees swayed.
The sky grew black,
   And it rained,
   And it stormed,
   And it poured.

Language Enrichment
Verbs

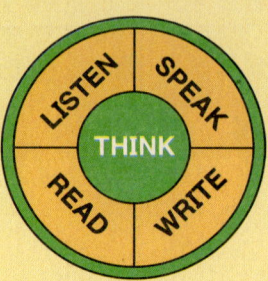

Use what you know about verbs to do these activities.

Contraction Action!

Write a poem about the weather, like the poem in the box. Use contractions such as <u>don't</u>, <u>didn't</u>, <u>aren't</u>, or <u>weren't</u>. These rhyming words may help you write.

blow—glow   here—near
wet—set   white—bright

Then share your poem.

The Weather That Wasn't

There isn't any weather today,
It didn't rain or snow,
The sky wasn't blue or gray,
The wind didn't blow.

Crash! Bang! Boom!

Word Bank

bang	have
bump	hiss
come	jump
crash	roll
do	run
gallop	see
go	thump

Work with a partner. Choose six verbs from the **Word Bank.** Use each verb in a sentence about something that was funny or exciting. Add <u>ed</u> to some verbs to tell about the past. Change the spelling of other verbs.

Then practice acting out your sentences as your partner reads them. Put on a show for your class!

Name _____

CONNECTING
LANGUAGE AND WRITING

In this unit you learned about verbs.

◆ **Using Verbs in Your Writing** Knowing how to use verbs will help you write clearly and correctly.

Once Upon a Time

Write a story to read to your class about an exciting person of long ago. Use verbs from the **Word Bank.** Change the verbs to show the past. Use words with the prefixes un and re.

Word Bank

come	give
crawl	knock
dash	peek
do	pretend
float	see
frighten	wish

Merry Music

Change the verbs in the song to tell about now. Then write verses about adventures Mary and the lamb have. Use contractions. Sing your song with your classmates!

Mary Had a Little Lamb

Mary had a little lamb,
Little lamb, little lamb.
Mary had a little lamb,
Its fleece was white as snow.

Name _____

5 Unit Checkup

Story pages 214–216

Match each picture or group of words to the name of a story part.

1.  •   • Title

2.  •   • Beginning

3. Starfish Saves the Day •   • Middle

4.  •   • Ending

Thinking About What Might Happen page 217

Think of another way to solve Bear's problem. Add your idea to the chart.

Problem
Bear is out fishing and his boat starts to sink.
Ways to Solve
Bear plugs up the holes with thick honey.
5. _____

Name _____

Using Enough Details   pages 218–219

6. Draw a line around the group of sentences that best tells what happened during the storm.

   a. The strong wind pushed the boat toward land. Big waves hit its sides.

   b. The strong wind pushed the boat toward land. The wind blew the cold rain into our faces. The boat filled up with water. Big waves hit its sides.

7. Look back at **6b**. Draw a line under the words that best helped you picture what happened.

The Writing Process   pages 220–230

Draw a line under the answer to each question.

8. Suppose you choose a story idea. What do you do next?

   a. Write a first draft.   **b.** Plan your story.

9. Suppose your classmate does not understand how your story ends. What should you do?

   a. Add more information.   **b.** Take out words.

Verbs That Tell About Now or the Past   pages 234–235

Draw a line around the correct verb for each sentence.

10. My father ____ a big truck.   drive   drives
11. He ____ vegetables to the stores.   takes   take
12. Last Saturday I ____ into the truck.   climb   climbed

UNIT CHECKUP   Unit 5   **255**

Name _____

The Verbs Is, Are, Was, and Were   pages 236–237
Draw a line under the correct verb for each sentence.

13. (Were, Are) you ready to go on a hike now?

14. Last year we (are, were) on a long hike.

15. That hike (was, is) fun.

16. I hope it (is, was) fun this year!

The Verbs Has, Have, and Had   pages 238–239
Draw a line around the correct verb for each sentence.

17. Mr. Howe _____ a little cabin at the lake.   has   have

18. His friends _____ fun when they visit him.   has   have

19. Last week two friends _____ fun fishing.   has   had

Helping Verbs   pages 240–241
Write has, have, or had to finish each sentence.

20. The children _____ visited the space museum.

21. Kim _____ stepped into an old spaceship!

22. Long ago the spaceship _____ traveled in space.

The Verbs Come and Run   pages 242–243
Draw a line under the correct verb in the ( ).

23. Yesterday, people (came, come) for a big race.

24. They always (run, runs) about twenty-six miles.

Name _____

The Verbs Go and Do   pages 244–245
Draw a line under the correct verb in the ( ).

25. Ann (did, does) many things outside last year.

26. Now she (goes, go) up a snowy hill.

27. Yesterday she (went, goes) skiing with her friend.

The Verbs See and Give   pages 246–247
Draw a line around the correct verb in the ( ).

28. Long ago my grandfather (sees, saw) a painting.

29. Last year he (gives, gave) it to my mom.

30. Now we (see, saw) the beautiful painting.

Contractions   pages 248–249
Write a contraction to take the place of the underlined words.

31. Cat <u>is not</u> looking at Mouse.

32. Cat <u>did not</u> see Mouse grab the cheese!

Prefixes   page 250
Add <u>un</u> or <u>re</u> to the words in the box. Use the new words to finish the sentences.

| wrap |
| wash |

33. I _____ my present.

34. Please _____ the dirty dish.

UNIT 6

Telling How to Do Something

◆ **COMPOSITION FOCUS:** How-to Paragraph
◆ **LANGUAGE FOCUS:** Mechanics Wrap-up

What do you know how to make or do? Have you ever tried to explain what you know to other people?

A good way to explain this kind of information is to write a how-to paragraph. A how-to paragraph tells the steps someone should follow to make or do something.

In the story "Carmen's Surprise" by Lorenca Rosal, a girl named Carmen makes something special. The author put a how-to paragraph in the story to tell what Carmen makes and how she makes it.

In this unit you will learn how to write a how-to paragraph.

Lorenca Rosal wrote "Carmen's Surprise" for people to enjoy. She also explained how to make something special.

UNIT 6

Reading with a Writer's Eye
Story

Read this story to find out how the writer, Lorenca Rosal, tells how Carmen surprises Grandfather.

Carmen's Surprise
by Lorenca Rosal

Drip, Drip, Drip! Splash, Splash, Splash! Ever since Grandfather had gone to the hospital, it had poured and poured. Carmen stared out the window at the rain. She missed Grandfather a lot, and the rain made her feel even sadder.

Carmen looked at Grandfather's car sitting out in the gray, misty weather. Grandfather used to take her places. Sometimes they drove to a movie. Other days they went to the library. Sometimes they drove to the beach and had a picnic.

There was one special trip, though, that Carmen liked best of all. She loved to go to town on Columbus Day. There was music, a barbeque, and a big parade. Everyone celebrated Christopher Columbus's discovery of America.

Name _____

Grandfather and Carmen had gone to the parade this year. Carmen began to daydream about what had happened that day.

Carmen and Grandfather watched the parade go by and picked out their favorite float. It looked like one of Christopher Columbus's ships. A flag with the words <u>Santa María</u> on it fluttered from the mast. Red, blue, and yellow <u>piñatas</u> hung from the sides of the float.

A <u>piñata</u> is a brightly decorated container filled with treats. Children break open the container with sticks.

READING ↔ WRITING CONNECTION 261

Name _____

    After the parade all the children were invited to break the piñatas. Carmen whacked one with a stick. It burst open! Candies and toys flew everywhere. Carmen and the other children hurried to pick them up.

    "That was the best Columbus Day ever!" Carmen told Grandfather as they drove home. "I wish we had our own piñata."

    "Well, that's easy," Grandfather answered. "We'll make one."

    Then Grandfather told Carmen all about making piñatas.

Now, though, Grandfather was in the hospital. It looked as if they would never get to make their piñata.

Just then Carmen's cat, Columbus, hopped onto the chair next to her and surprised her. Carmen looked at Columbus and suddenly got a great idea. She could make a piñata for Grandfather! She ran to the kitchen to tell her mother.

"That's a wonderful idea," Mother said. "We can take the piñata to him tomorrow when we visit."

READING ↔ WRITING CONNECTION

That afternoon Carmen made a beautiful piñata for Grandfather. First, she got a large paper bag, colored paper, ribbon, crayons, scissors, and tape. She found small boxes of raisins and nuts, and some magazines. Next, Carmen decorated the bag to look like a cat. Then, Carmen put the snacks and magazines into the bag. She taped the top shut. Last, she looped the ribbon through holes in the top of the bag.

The next day, Carmen and her mother drove to the hospital. A nurse led them to Grandfather's room. It was clean and sunny and bright.

"Grandfather!" Carmen cried. "Guess what? I have a special surprise for you."

She held up the piñata.

Grandfather smiled. "You did it, Carmen! You made our piñata. I couldn't have done better myself."

Carmen beamed.

"I have a surprise for you, too," Grandfather said. "Tomorrow I'm coming home!"

Respond

1. How does Carmen surprise Grandfather? What could you make to give to someone special?

Discuss

2. How does the writer tell how to begin making a piñata? Why is this important?

Name _____

Thinking As a Writer
Studying a How-to Paragraph

A **how-to paragraph** gives directions. The sentences in the paragraph are in the correct order to tell how to make or do something. If the paragraph is about making something, the first step should tell the things you need.

This paragraph from the story tells how to make a piñata.

Writer's Guide

- A how-to paragraph tells how to make or do something.
- The topic sentence names the topic of the paragraph.
- The detail sentences explain the steps in order.
- The paragraph is indented.

That afternoon Carmen made a beautiful piñata for Grandfather. First, she got a large paper bag, colored paper, ribbon, crayons, scissors, and tape. She found small boxes of raisins and nuts, and some magazines. Next, Carmen decorated the bag to look like a cat. Then, Carmen put the snacks and magazines into the bag. She taped the top shut. Last, she looped the ribbon through holes in the top of the bag.

— Topic Sentence

— Detail Sentences

— Time-order words tell the order of the steps.

Discuss

1. What is the paragraph about?
2. Which words tell the order of the steps? Why are these words important?
3. Why is the first step important?

266 READING ↔ WRITING CONNECTION

Name _____

Try Your Hand

A. Find Parts of a How-to Paragraph Read this how-to paragraph. Draw a line under the sentence that tells what you need for a treasure hunt. Draw a line around the words that tell the order of the steps.

> Set up a treasure hunt for a friend. First, get a bag of bread crumbs and a prize. Next, make a trail outside with the bread crumbs. Then, put the prize at the end of the trail. Last, tell your friend to follow the trail and find the prize!

B. List Things You Need Write a list of all the things that someone would need to make a sandwich. Then write a sentence to tell this information.

Name _____

Thinking As a Writer
Connecting Ideas in Sequence

Writer's Guide

◆ In a how-to paragraph, good writers tell the steps in the correct order.

In a how-to paragraph, good writers tell <u>all</u> the steps in order that are needed to make or do something.

Lorenca Rosal may have made a drawing like this before writing about how to make a piñata.

1. Get a large bag, colored paper, ribbon, crayons, scissors, tape, and some treats.

↓

2. Decorate the bag.

↓

3. Put the treats inside the bag and close it.

↓

4. Put ribbon through the holes in the top.

Discuss

1. Why is it important to write the steps in a how-to paragraph in order?
2. Where would this step go in the drawing? Why?
   <u>Wrap the treats in pretty paper.</u>

Try Your Hand

Write Steps in Order   Think of the steps to make a sandwich. Make a drawing like the one above. Tell what to do <u>first</u>, <u>next</u>, <u>then</u>, and <u>last</u>.

268   READING ↔ WRITING CONNECTION

Name _____

Developing the Writer's Craft
Getting the Reader's Interest

> **Writer's Guide**
> ◆ Good writers use good beginning sentences to interest their readers.

The beginning sentence is important because it gets the reader interested in what the writer has to say. Read this beginning sentence.

> *Imagine making your own robot that really works.*

Does this sentence make you want to read more? Tell why or why not.

Discuss

1. Would this sentence make a better beginning for a paragraph about making your own robot? Why or why not?
   <u>Here is how to make a robot</u>.
2. Which beginning sentence would make you more interested in reading a paragraph about a robot costume? Why?
   a. Do these things to make a robot costume.
   b. Turn yourself into an amazing robot!

Try Your Hand

Write a Beginning Sentence   With a classmate, write a good beginning sentence to go with each paragraph idea.

1. making a paper spider   2. growing a window garden

READING ↔ WRITING CONNECTION   269

Name _____

1 Prewriting
How-to Paragraph

Paula followed the **Writer's Guide** to plan her paragraph. First, she made a list of things she knew how to make or do. Then, Paula drew a line around <u>making a bird feeder</u>. She thought other students might like to feed the birds.

> 1. doing a cartwheel
> 2. making a bird feeder
> 3. making a puppet

Next, Paula made a drawing to show the steps for making a bird feeder. She wrote them in order.

> 1. Get a pine cone, string, peanut butter, a spoon, and birdseed.
>
> 2. Tie string around the pine cone.
>
> 3. Put peanut butter on the pine cone and roll it in birdseed.
>
> 4. Hang the pine cone in a tree.

Writer's Guide

☑ Make a list of ideas.

☑ Decide who will read your paragraph.

☑ Choose an idea your readers will like. This is your topic.

☑ Write steps in the correct order to tell about your topic.

270 COMPOSITION: PREWRITING How-to Paragraph

Name _____

Discuss

1. How does Paula follow the **Writer's Guide**?
2. What is the last step in making a bird feeder?

Try Your Hand

Now plan your paragraph.

A. Think of Things to Make or Do
Think about things you know how to make or do. Write them in a list.

Eagle Ideas

1. What special tricks can you do?
2. Do you know how to make something to wear or to eat?
3. Think of a wonderful toy. How would you make that toy?

B. Choose a Topic Decide who will read your paragraph. Choose an idea your readers will like. This is your topic.

C. Plan the Steps Write the steps in the correct order to tell about your topic. You may wish to make a drawing, as Paula did.

D. Check the Steps Be sure you told all the steps in the correct order. Move or add steps if you need to.

 Put your plan in your **Writer's Notebook.** You will use it when you write your paragraph.

COMPOSITION: PREWRITING How-to Paragraph **271**

Name _____

2 Drafting
How-to Paragraph

> **Writer's Guide**
> - ☑ Use your drawing for ideas.
> - ☑ Write a sentence to name your topic.
> - ☑ Write steps in the correct order to tell about your topic.
> - ☑ Use time-order words to show the order of the steps.

Look at what Paula did to write her paragraph. First, she thought about her topic. She decided that she still wanted to tell how to make a bird feeder. Then, Paula followed the **Writer's Guide** to write her first draft.

> How would you like to make a bird feeder? First, get a pine cone, string, peanut butter, a spoon, and birdseed. Next, tie the string around one end of the pine cone. Then, roll the pine cone in bird seed. Put peanut butter on the pine cone. Last, hang your bird feeder in a tree. You will enjoy your bird feeder. The birds will enjoy your bird feeder.

272 COMPOSITION: DRAFTING How-to Paragraph

Name _____

Discuss

1. What is Paula's paragraph about?
2. Which time-order words does Paula use to tell the order of the steps?

Try Your Hand

Now write your how-to paragraph.

A. Think About Your Topic   Do you still like your topic? If not, choose another topic and make a new plan.

B. Read Your Paragraph Plan   Add any steps that would make your paragraph clearer. Move steps to show the correct order.

C. Keep an Eagle Eye on Who, What, and Why   Think about your readers. Remember that you are writing to tell them how to make or do something.

D. Write Your First Draft   First, write an interesting sentence to name your topic. Then, write the steps in the correct order.
Write quickly. Do not worry about mistakes.

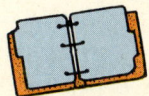 Put your first draft in your **Writer's Notebook**. You will check it in the next lesson.

COMPOSITION: DRAFTING   How-to Paragraph

Name _____

3 Responding and Revising
How-to Paragraph

Paula used the **Writer's Guide** to help her make her paragraph clearer. She read her paragraph to Miki. They talked about the paragraph.

Miki: I'd like to make this bird feeder! I think you should put the part about the peanut butter before the part about the seeds.

Paula: You're right! Is there anything else I can make clearer?

Writer's Guide

- ☑ Read your paragraph to yourself or to a friend.
- ☑ Think about your paragraph. Be sure your first sentence will interest your readers.
- ☑ Be sure you wrote all the steps that are needed.
- ☑ Be sure the steps are clear and in order.
- ☑ Make changes.

Name _____

Paula thought about her talk with Miki. She used this mark ↻ to move a sentence to a better place. She also put together two sentences that had the same telling parts. She used this mark ⋏.

> How would you like to make a bird feeder? First, get a pine cone, string, peanut butter, a spoon, and birdseed. Next, tie the string around one end of the pine cone. Then, roll the pine cone in birdseed. ⟨Put peanut butter on the pine cone.⟩ Last, hang your bird feeder in a tree. You will enjoy your bird feeder. The birds will enjoy your bird feeder.

— Move
— Change

Discuss

1. What does Paula move? How does this change make her paragraph better?
2. Why does Paula put two sentences together?

COMPOSITION: RESPONDING/REVISING   How-to Paragraph   **275**

Name _____

Try Your Hand

Now check your paragraph. Use the **Editor's Marks** to show your changes.

> **Editor's Marks**
>
> ∧ Add something.
> ℓ Take out something.
> ⋀ Change something.
> ◯ Move something.

A. Think About Your Paragraph
Read your paragraph to yourself or to a partner. Did you tell everything your readers need to know?

B. Make Changes
- Are the steps in order? Use this mark 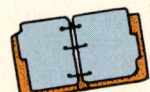 to move something.
- Are the steps clear? Use time-order words.
- Do some of your sentences have the same telling parts? You may want to join them. Use this mark ⋀ . Use page 277 for help.

C. Check Your Paragraph Read your paragraph again. Make changes until it is just right.

Put your paragraph in your **Writer's Notebook**. In the next lesson, you will fix any mistakes.

Name _____

Revising Workshop
Joining Sentences

Writers often join two sentences into one. The new sentence says the same thing in fewer words. Read these sentences.

1. Debby made a kite.
2. John made a kite.

Each sentence has the same telling part, but a different naming part. You can join these two sentences into one. How is the new sentence better?

3. Debby and John made kites.

Practice

Read each pair of sentences. Use the word <u>and</u> to join the two sentences into one. Write the new sentence.

Robins eat seeds. Sparrows eat seeds.

1. _____

The boys skate. The girls skate.

2. _____

Bears catch fish. Birds catch fish.

3. _____

Name _____

4 Proofreading
How-to Paragraph

Paula decided to write more about the bird feeder. She used the **Writer's Guide** to correct the mistakes in her next paragraph. Look at what she did.

> ¶ You can use different kinds of seeds to make this bird feeder. ⱻind out what the birds that ~~liv~~ *live* near you ~~lik~~ *like* to eat⊙

Writer's Guide

☑ Be sure you indented your paragraph.

☑ Be sure each sentence begins with a capital letter.

☑ Be sure each sentence ends with an end mark.

⇨ Use the **Writer's Handbook** for help.

Discuss

1. Why does Paula use this mark ¶ ?
2. Why does Paula use this mark ≡ ?
3. Why does Paula draw lines around two words?
4. How does Paula show that the second sentence is a complete thought?

Editor's Marks

≡ Use a capital letter.
⊙ Add a period.
∧ Add something.
ℯ Take out something.
⌒ Change something.
◯ Check the spelling.
¶ Indent the paragraph.

Try Your Hand

Now correct any mistakes in your paragraph. Follow the **Writer's Guide**. Use the **Editor's Marks** to show your changes.

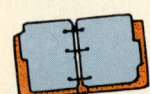 Put your paragraph in your **Writer's Notebook**. You will share it in the next lesson.

Name _____

5 Publishing
How-to Paragraph

Before Paula shared her work, she followed the **Writer's Guide.** Then she made a poster to help her share her writing with the students in another class. You can find Paula's finished paragraph on page 18 of the **Writer's Handbook.**

Writer's Guide
- ☑ Copy your paragraph over neatly.
- ☑ Be sure nothing is left out.
- ☑ Be sure there are no mistakes.
- ☑ Share your paragraph in an interesting way.

Paula made a poster. She showed the other students how to make the bird feeder.

Discuss

1. Why is this a good way for Paula to share a how-to paragraph?
2. How else could Paula share her work?

Try Your Hand

Share Your How-to Paragraph Follow the **Writer's Guide.** Share your paragraph in the way Paula did, or try this idea.

♦ Write each step on a separate piece of paper. Draw a picture to go with each step. Show the pictures and read the pages to your class.

COMPOSITION: PUBLISHING How-to Paragraph **279**

Listening and Speaking
How to Give Directions

Look at the pictures and read the steps. What is Richard telling Mary how to do?

When You Give Directions
- Think about the steps.
- Think about the order of the steps.
- Tell the steps in order.
- Use time-order words such as <u>first</u>, <u>next</u>, <u>then</u>, <u>last</u>.

Practice

Think of something you know how to make or do. Think of the steps in order. Then tell the steps to a partner. Ask your partner to follow the directions.

Listening and Speaking
How to Follow Directions

Look at the pictures. What is Mary thinking as she follows the directions?

When You Follow Directions
◆ Listen carefully to all the steps.
◆ Listen for time-order words such as <u>first</u>, <u>next</u>, <u>then</u>, <u>last</u>.
◆ Ask questions if you do not understand.
◆ Follow the steps.

Practice

Take out a sheet of paper. Then, follow the directions your teacher reads to you.

Name _____

Writing in the Content Areas

Use what you have learned to write a how-to paragraph. Use one of these ideas or an idea of your own.

Writer's Guide

When you write, use the stages of the Writing Process.
- Plan your writing.
- Write what you want to say to your readers.
- Talk with your classmates about your writing.
- Make your writing clear. Change words if you need to.
- Fix any mistakes.
- Share your writing.

Health

Think of a snack that is good for you and that tastes good too. Write a paragraph to tell how to make the snack. Then draw a picture of your snack. Share your work with your class.

Mathematics

Tell a classmate how to do a math problem. Tell about the kind of math problem you are learning this week. Tell each step your classmate should do to get the right answer. Write an example of the problem at the top of a piece of paper. Share your work.

282 COMPOSITION: WRITING IN THE CONTENT AREAS How-to Paragraph

CONNECTING
WRITING AND LANGUAGE

When you write a paragraph, you use capital letters and end marks to help your readers understand your writing.

Here is a paragraph that Sandy wrote. Can you tell where the sentences begin and end?

> You can make a valentine to give to a friend! First, get red paper, white paper, scissors, and glue. Next, cut a heart out of the red paper. Cut the white paper into a fancy shape. Then, glue the heart onto the white paper. Last, write a message on the heart!

◆ **Capital Letters and End Marks in a Paragraph** The capital letters and the end marks are shown in blue. Capital letters are used to show the beginning of sentences. End marks are used to show the end of sentences.

◆ **Language Focus: Mechanics** In the next lessons, you will learn how to use capital letters, end marks, and commas when you write.

Name _____

1 Sentences

◆ **FOCUS**   A sentence begins with a capital letter and ends with an end mark.

Remember that a sentence tells a complete thought. Every sentence begins with a capital letter.

A **statement** tells something. It ends with a **period** (.).

> A spaceship landed.

A **question** asks something. It ends with a **question mark** (?).

> Who are you?

An **exclamation** shows strong feeling. It ends with an **exclamation point** (!).

> He is so strange!

Use sentences to tell and ask about the picture.

Guided Practice

A. Tell the end mark that each sentence needs. Then write the end mark.

  1. A strange creature came to our city ____
  2. He had a helmet ____
  3. We were really scared ____
  4. Well, how would you have felt ____

284   MECHANICS   Sentences

Name _____

THINK AND REMEMBER
- Begin a sentence with a capital letter.
- End a sentence with the correct end mark.

Independent Practice

B. Writing Sentences   Write each sentence correctly.

the spaceship rises

5. The spaceship rises.

where will it go

6. _____

it moves so fast

7. _____

did you see it

8. _____

it zooms away

9. _____

Application—Writing

Journal Entry   In your journal, write about the spaceship. Use sentences that tell, ask, and show strong feeling. Use page 22 of the **Writer's Handbook** for help.

2 Names, Titles of People, I

FOCUS
- The names and titles of people begin with capital letters.
- The word I is always written as a capital letter.

The names of special people begin with capital letters. Titles of people also begin with capital letters. Most titles of people are followed by a **period (.)**.

The word I is a special word for telling about yourself. I is always written as a capital letter.

Mr. Jim Beck
Mrs. Lee
Miss Green

Guided Practice

A. Tell how to fix each sentence.

1. Mr jim Beck fights fires.
2. Our crossing guard is mrs lee.
3. I ask miss green for help.

Write the names and titles correctly.

4. _____

5. _____

6. _____

286 MECHANICS Names, Titles of People, I

Name _____

THINK AND REMEMBER

- Begin the names and titles of people with capital letters. End <u>Mr</u>., <u>Mrs</u>., <u>Ms</u>., and <u>Dr</u>. with a **period (.)**.
- Always write the word <u>I</u> as a capital letter.

Independent Practice

B. Writing Sentences   Write each sentence correctly.

ms. pell teaches me.

7. Ms. Pell teaches me.

i like dr. chin.

8. _____

My friend is mr. row.

9. _____

Is miss lind your friend?

10. _____

mrs dell is my aunt.

11. _____

Application—Writing

Story   Write a story about a hero to share with your class. Use names, titles, and <u>I</u>. Use page 24 of the **Writer's Handbook** for help.

MECHANICS   Names, Titles of People, <u>I</u>   **287**

Name _____

3 Names of Special Places

◆ **FOCUS** The name of a special place begins with a capital letter.

Each important word in the name of a special place begins with a capital letter.

Nouns	Proper Nouns
state →	**C**olorado
building →	**S**unrise **S**chool

Guided Practice

A. Tell how to fix each sentence.
1. Our dog got lost in chicago.
2. We looked in oak park.
3. Our dog was not on lake road.
4. Our dog was near red river.

Write the name of each special place correctly.

5. _____ 6. _____

7. _____ 8. _____

288   MECHANICS   Names of Special Places

Name _____

THINK AND REMEMBER
◆ Begin the names of special places with capital letters.

I go to Pine Elementary School.

Independent Practice

B. Writing Names of Places Write the name of your town, state, street, and school.

9. town _____

10. state _____

11. street _____

12. school _____

Application—Writing

Directions Write directions to tell a friend how to get from your school to your home. Use names of places and streets.

MECHANICS Names of Special Places **289**

4 Days of the Week

◆ **FOCUS**   The name of each day of the week begins with a capital letter.

Things to Do

Sunday —
Monday —
Tuesday —
Wednesday —
Thursday —
Friday —
Saturday —

Remember that the name of each day of the week begins with a capital letter.

1. Friday   2. Saturday

Look at the names of the days in the picture. Did the knight write them correctly? Tell why.

Guided Practice

A. Tell how to fix each underlined word. Write the name of each day correctly.

1. I will fight a dragon on monday.

2. On tuesday I will help a princess.

3. Can I save a kingdom on friday?

4. On sunday I will find a treasure.

290 MECHANICS   Days of the Week

Name _____

THINK AND REMEMBER
♦ Begin the name of each day of the week with a capital letter.

Independent Practice

B. Writing Days of the Week Write a day of the week to finish each sentence.

5. We have gym on  _____.

6. On _____ I help at home.

7. Is your art class on _____?

8. We go to the library on _____.

9. Tara plays ball on _____.

10. On _____ I cut the lawn.

Application—Writing and Speaking

Letter Pretend that you are the knight. Write a letter to another knight about your week. Use the names of days. Use page 28 of the **Writer's Handbook** to help you write a friendly letter.

MECHANICS Days of the Week **291**

Name _____

5 Months of the Year

◆ **FOCUS** The name of each month of the year begins with a capital letter.

Remember that the name of each month of the year begins with a capital letter.

1. January   2. September

Find your birthday month in the picture. How does the name of the month begin?

Guided Practice

A. Tell how to fix the mistake in each sentence.
1. In may I pick flowers.
2. I enjoy sunny days in june.
3. In august I collect seashells.
4. I buy a pumpkin in october.

Write the names of the months correctly.

5. _____   6. _____

7. _____   8. _____

292 MECHANICS Months of the Year

Name _____

THINK AND REMEMBER

◆ Begin the name of each month of the year with a capital letter.

Independent Practice

B. Writing Names of Months Write the name of a month to finish each sentence.

9. Thanksgiving is in  November _____ .

10. In _____ school starts.

11. My birthday is in _____ .

12. _____ begins the year.

13. We go on vacation in _____ .

14. In _____ I play in the snow.

Application—Writing and Speaking

Ad What is your favorite month? Make an ad to show to younger students. Draw pictures to show why your month is the best. Write why the students should like this month.

MECHANICS Months of the Year

Name _____

6 Holidays

◆ **FOCUS** The name of a holiday begins with a capital letter.

Remember that holidays are special days of the year. Each important word in the name of a holiday begins with a capital letter.

1. **M**emorial **D**ay   2. **F**ourth of **J**uly

What other holidays are shown in the pictures? Name other holidays you know. Tell how to write the names.

Guided Practice

A. Tell how to write each sentence correctly.
1. On veterans day I went to a parade.
2. Will he wear a halloween costume?
3. Amy picked flowers for mother's day.
4. On arbor day we planted a tree.

Write the names of the holidays correctly.

5. _____   6. _____

7. _____   8. _____

Name _____

THINK AND REMEMBER
◆ Begin each important word in the name of a holiday with a capital letter.

Independent Practice

B. Writing Names of Holidays   Write the name of a holiday to finish each sentence.

9. On Columbus Day our school is closed.

10. Dad's special day is _____.

11. _____ is our country's birthday.

12. My favorite holiday is _____.

Application—Reading, Writing, and Speaking

Riddle   Fold a piece of paper in half. Write the name of a holiday inside. Write clues about the holiday on the front. Read your clues to your classmates. Can they guess your holiday?

MECHANICS Holidays **295**

Name _____

7 Titles of Books, Stories, and Poems

◆ **FOCUS** Each important word in a title begins with a capital letter.

A title tells what a book, story, or poem is about. The first word, last word, and each important word in a title begin with capital letters. Short words such as <u>a</u>, <u>an</u>, <u>and</u>, <u>the</u>, and <u>of</u> do not begin with capital letters unless they are the first word of a title.

<u>T</u>he Heart of the <u>W</u>oods

Guided Practice

A. Tell how to write each title correctly.
1. We wrote a book called the giant balloon.
2. Did you read a mouse goes to school?
3. I wrote a book called a trip to the moon.

Write the titles correctly.

4. _____

5. _____

6. _____

Name _____

THINK AND REMEMBER
◆ Begin the first word, last word, and each important word in a title with capital letters.

Independent Practice

B. Writing Titles   Write your own title to finish each sentence.

7. Did you write The Big Surprise ?

8. My favorite story is _____.

9. I read a poem called _____.

10. I would like to write a book called _____.

Application—Writing and Speaking

Story List   Pick three stories. Write a sentence about each story that will make a friend want to read it. Write the titles correctly. Share your list.

MECHANICS   Titles of Books, Stories, and Poems

Name _____

8 Friendly Letter

◆ **FOCUS** Commas and capital letters are needed in a friendly letter.

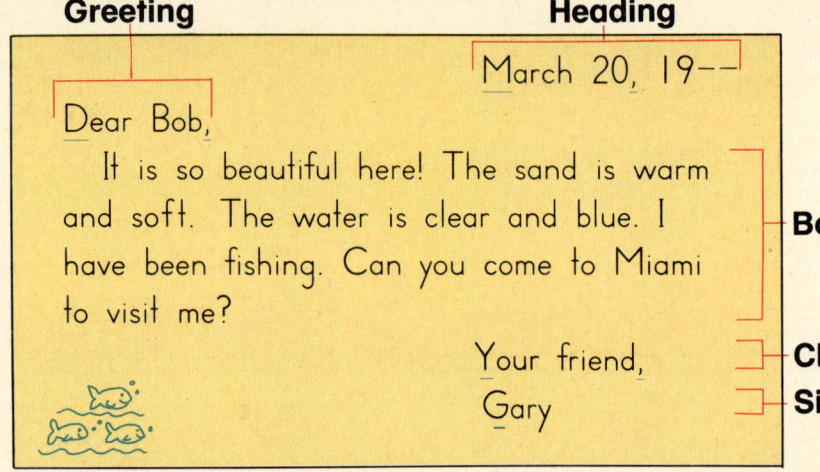

Commas and capital letters are used in a friendly letter. A **comma (,)** is used between the day and the year in the heading. A comma is used after the greeting and after the closing. The heading, greeting, and closing begin with capital letters.

How are commas and capital letters used in Gary's letter to Bob?

Guided Practice

A. Tell how to fix each letter part. Then write the part correctly.

1. may 1 1990

2. dear Ann

3. your pal

298 MECHANICS Friendly Letter

Name _____

> **THINK AND REMEMBER**
> ◆ Use a comma in the heading, the greeting, and the closing of a letter.
> ◆ Begin the heading, the greeting, and the closing with capital letters.

Independent Practice

B. Proofreading a Letter Read the letter. Mark each letter that should be a capital letter. Use this mark ≡. Add the missing commas. Then write each part correctly.

(march 2 1990)

4. _____

(dear Gary)

5. _____

   I would love to visit you in Miami. I will come next Tuesday. I'll bring my fishing pole. See you soon!

(your friend)

6. _____

Bob

Application—Writing

Letter Write a letter to a friend. Use commas and capital letters correctly. Use page 28 of the **Writer's Handbook** for help. Save your letter to mail later.

MECHANICS Friendly Letter

Name _____

9 Envelope

◆ **FOCUS** Commas and capital letters are needed in the addresses on an envelope.

Return Address

Bob Reed
145 Ginger Lane
Jackson, Wyoming 83001

Stamp

Mailing Address

Gary Ortiz
17 Second Street
Miami, Florida 33139

An envelope is used to send a letter. The **return address** names who is sending the letter. The **mailing address** names who will get the letter.

Begin special names with capital letters. Use a **comma (,)** between the names of a city and a state.

Read the envelope in the picture. Where are the commas? Which words begin with capital letters?

Guided Practice

A. Write this address correctly.

1. sharon ursino

2. 202 cotton road

3. dallas texas 75227

Name _____

THINK AND REMEMBER

♦ Begin the names of special people and places with capital letters.
♦ Use a comma between the names of a city and a state.

Independent Practice

B. Proofreading an Envelope   Read the envelope. Write the parts correctly.

Dan Tracy
387 fair Lane

4. _____

akron iowa 51001

5. _____

helen quinn

6. _____

12 Dover Way

Seattle, Washington 98109

Application—Writing

Envelope   Put the letter you wrote in Lesson 8 in an envelope. Write the addresses. Use page 31 of the **Writer's Handbook** for help. Put a stamp on the envelope. Mail your letter.

MECHANICS Envelope **301**

Building Vocabulary
Suffixes

A **suffix** is a group of letters added to the end of a word. A suffix changes the meaning of a word. <u>Less</u> and <u>ful</u> are suffixes.

Suffix	Meaning	Example
less	without	useless
ful	full of	useful

use<u>ful</u>   use<u>less</u>

Reading Practice

Name the word in each sentence with the suffix <u>less</u> or <u>ful</u>. Tell the meaning of the word.

1. I lost my money because I was careless.
2. When I found my money, I was cheerful.

Writing Practice

Add <u>less</u> or <u>ful</u> to each word in the box. Use the new words to write a story.

care	hope
color	rest
fear	thank

Project

Make a class Suffix Chart.
- Write <u>less</u> and <u>ful</u> on a sheet of paper.
- Collect words with <u>less</u> and <u>ful</u>.
- List the words under the right suffix.

less	ful
spotless	playful
fearless	hopeful
harmless	joyful

Listening and Speaking
Poetry

Listen to this poem about the days of the week.

The Cheerful Child's Week
by Beatrice Schenk de Regniers

> Super Sunday
> Marvelous Monday
> Terrific Tuesday
> Wonderful Wednesday
> Thrilling Thursday
> Fabulous Friday
> Swell Saturday

Name _____

Language Enrichment
Mechanics

Use what you know about capital letters, end marks, and commas to do these activities.

 ### Memories

Make a page for a class Memory Book. Write about the best thing you remember from this school year. Use some of these names.

- your teacher's name
- your classmates' names
- your school's name
- special places

Draw pictures on your page. Then put it into a class book. Help make a cover. Read the book.

 ### Puppet Play

Give a puppet show for your class. Work with two classmates.

- Make three puppets like the ones shown. Each one shows an end mark.
- Write a story for your puppets. The question mark asks questions. The period tells things. The exclamation point shows strong feelings.
- Give your puppet show.

front

back

Name _____

CONNECTING
LANGUAGE AND WRITING

In this unit you learned to begin sentences with capital letters and to end them with special marks. You also learned to use capital letters when you write proper nouns and titles.

◆ **Using Capital Letters and End Marks in Your Writing**   Understanding capital letters and end marks will help you write. Use them as you do the activities.

Book News

Write a letter to someone you know. Tell about your favorite book. Tell the title. Say why you like the book. Use sentences that ask, tell, and show strong feeling. Then address an envelope. Add a stamp and mail your letter.

What a Week!

Use what you learned about suffixes in **Building Vocabulary** to write sentences. Add <u>ful</u> or <u>less</u> to a word in the box to tell about an animal you met on each day of the week. Read your writing to a friend.

care	help	use
cheer	play	fear
color	spot	thank

On Monday I raced a colorful kangaroo.

Name _____

6 Unit Checkup

How-to Paragraph pages 266–267
Read Mario's how-to paragraph. Follow the directions.

> Surprise your dad with a letter holder. First, get a large wire spring, some clay, a paint brush, and paint. Next, shape the clay into a big square. Then, push the wire spring into the square. Let the clay dry. Last, paint the clay.

1. Draw a line under the words that tell what you need to make a letter holder.
2. Draw a line around the time-order words that help tell the order of the steps.

Connecting Ideas in Sequence page 268
Here are some steps for making fresh orange juice. Number the steps to show the correct order.

3. _____ Ask someone to cut the oranges in half.

   _____ Pour the juice into a glass.

   _____ Get four oranges, an orange juicer, and a glass.

   _____ Put the orange halves onto the juicer and squeeze.

Getting the Reader's Interest page 269
Draw a line under the better beginning sentence for a paragraph about making puppets.

4. **a.** Make a puppet.   **b.** You can make a puppet for a gift.

Name _____

Write a good beginning sentence about making a sand castle.

5. _____

The Writing Process pages 270–279

Draw a line around the answer to each question.

6. What should you do first to plan a how-to paragraph?

    a. Write the steps in order.   **b.** Make a list of topic ideas.

7. Suppose that you are checking your paragraph. You find a step out of order. What should you do?

    a. Choose a new topic and start over.

    b. Move the step to the correct part of the paragraph.

Sentences pages 284–285

Draw a line around each letter that should be a capital letter. Add the end mark to each sentence.

8. we see a horse ____   9. what color is it ____

10. where does it live ____   11. it runs so fast ____

Names, Titles of People, I pages 286–287

Draw a line around the mistakes in each sentence.

12. mrs. dee is a nurse.   13. She works with dr. wells.

14. My aunt ida knows her.   15. i will meet her tomorrow.

UNIT CHECKUP Unit 6 **307**

Name _____

Names of Special Places pages 288–289
Write the names of the special places correctly.

16. I live in brave town.

17. My house is on hero road.

Days of the Week pages 290–291
Draw a line around each letter that should be a capital letter.

18. Meg of Grundy was born on monday.
19. On tuesday, Meg marched off to play.
20. On friday, Meg marched back to Grundy.
21. Then she sneezed and slept until sunday.

Months of the Year pages 292–293
Write the name of a month to finish each sentence.

22. Autumn leaves are lovely in _____.

23. Spring rains come in _____.

Holidays pages 294–295
Draw a line around the words that are not written correctly.

24. We remember heroes on Veterans day.
25. There is no school on washington's Birthday.
26. I hug my father on father's day.

308 Unit 6 UNIT CHECKUP

Name _____

Titles of Books, Stories, and Poems   pages 296–297
Write each book title correctly.

27. crow boy

28. once a mouse

Friendly Letter   pages 298–299
Draw a line under each letter part that is written correctly.

29. May 6, 1990   **30.** dear Kathy   **31.** Love,

Envelope   pages 300–301
Write this return address correctly.

32. tim cory

33. 62 elm street

34. provo utah 84604

Suffixes   page 302
Add <u>less</u> or <u>ful</u> to a word in the box.
Use the word in a good sentence.

| color   help |

35. _____

UNIT CHECKUP Unit 6 **309**

Name _____

1–5 Cumulative Review

Naming and Telling Parts of a Sentence pages 30–33
Write a naming part or a telling part to finish each sentence.

1. _____ opens a big box.

2. The box _____.

3. _____ find some old pictures.

4. The pictures _____.

Kinds of Sentences pages 36–43
Read each sentence. Draw a line around the word that tells what kind of sentence it is.

5. I wish I had a pet!   statement   question   exclamation

6. Do you have a pet?   statement   question   exclamation

7. Our pet is a hamster.   statement   question   exclamation

Nouns pages 78–81
Draw a line under each noun. Then draw a line around each noun that names an animal.

8. The driver takes the family to the zoo.

9. The boys see a tiger and a giraffe.

10. The girls watch a woman feed the bear.

310   CUMULATIVE REVIEW   Units 1–5

Name _____

Nouns That Name More Than One pages 82–87
Make the nouns in the ( ) mean more than one.
Add s, add es, or change the spelling.

11. We pick _____(bunch)_____ of _____(carrot)_____.

12. The _____(child)_____ drink _____(glass)_____ of juice.

13. The _____(man)_____ put _____(box)_____ on a truck.

Proper Nouns pages 88–93
Draw a line under each proper noun. Draw a line around each proper noun that names a special place.

14. On Tuesday, Sam shops at a store in Milltown.

15. Later, he walks his dog Max in River Park.

Pronouns pages 94–97
Draw a line under the pronoun that can take the place of the underlined word or words.

16. Laura went hiking with her friends.   He   She   It   They

17. The children really had fun!   He   She   It   They

Draw a line under the correct word or words in the ( ).

18. Can you play ball with (I, me)?

19. (Billy and I, I and Billy) play ball in the park.

CUMULATIVE REVIEW Units 1–5   **311**

Name _____

Action Verbs pages 132–133
Write an action verb to finish each sentence. Use the words in the box.

| play | bounces |
| rolls | jump |

20. We _____ a game called Jump Ball.

21. Tommy _____ a ball toward the wall.

22. We _____ over the ball.

23. The ball _____ back to Tommy.

Verbs That Tell About Now or the Past pages 234–235
Write a verb from the box to finish each sentence.
Add <u>s</u> if it is needed to tell about now.
Add <u>ed</u> to tell about the past.

| rest |
| play |
| walk |
| look |

24. Last week we _____ to the beach.

25. Now Maria _____ for the baby sea lion.

26. Today many sea lions _____ on a huge rock.

27. Yesterday one sea lion _____ in the water.

Name _____

The Verbs Is, Are, Was, and Were   pages 236–237
Write the correct verb for each sentence.

28. The clowns at this circus (is, are) short.

29. Last year they (was, were) taller.

30. At that circus, a clown named Jo (was, were) as tall as a giant.

31. The new clown (is, are) small.

Describing Words   pages 178–187
Draw a line around each describing word. Draw a line under the noun it tells about.

32. Proud animals march in the long parade.

33. Two elephants carry a square sign.

34. The big bear plays a loud drum.

35. A brown monkey holds a sweet apple.

Describing Words with er and est   pages 188–189
Draw a line under the correct describing word for each sentence.

36. That parakeet is (smaller, smallest) than mine.

37. Its wings are (softer, softest) than cotton.

38. This bird chirps the (louder, loudest) of all the birds.

39. The parakeet lives in the (taller, tallest) cage of all.

CUMULATIVE REVIEW   Units 1–5   **313**

Name _____

The Verbs Has, Have, and Had pages 238–241
Write the correct verb for each sentence.

has, have
40. The neighbors _____ a problem.

has, have
41. Tom _____ a way to help.

had, have
42. Yesterday, a tiny kitten _____ climbed up a tree.

have, had
43. It _____ trouble getting down.

has, had
44. The neighbors _____ watched Tom save the cat.

The Verbs Come and Run pages 242–243
Draw a line under the correct verb in the ( ).

45. Dad and I (run, ran) every day.
46. Last week he (runs, ran) six miles.
47. Now Dad (came, comes) home feeling tired.
48. Yesterday Dad and I (come, came) home together.

314 CUMULATIVE REVIEW Units 1–5

Name _____

The Verbs Go and Do   pages 244–245
Read each sentence. Change the verb to tell about the past.

       do
      ―――――

49. Mike and Ed _____ many things at the museum.

       does
      ―――――

50. What _____ Mike see in the dinosaur room?

       goes
      ―――――

51. Later Mike _____ to the gift shop.

The Verbs See and Give   pages 246–247
Draw a line under the correct verb for each sentence.

52. We (give, gave) Chris a surprise party last week.

53. Chris (sees, saw) his friends at that party.

54. Now Chris and his friends (see, saw) a football game.

55. Jim (gives, gave) Chris a football now.

Contractions   pages 248–249
Write a contraction to take the place of the underlined words.

56. The pilot <u>did</u> <u>not</u> get in the plane.

57. The airplane <u>was</u> <u>not</u> ready.

CUMULATIVE REVIEW   Units 1–5   **315**

STUDY SKILLS

Contents

1	Using ABC Order	319
2	Finding Words in a Dictionary	320
3	Using a Dictionary Entry	321
4	Using the Parts of a Book	323
5	Using an Index	324
6	Understanding Kinds of Books	325
7	Writing a Book Report	326
8	Taking a Test	327
9	Using Charts	328
10	Using Bar Graphs	330
11	Using Pictographs	332
12	Using Maps	334
13	Writing Telephone Messages	336
14	Filling Out Forms	337

HBJ material copyrighted under notice appearing earlier in this work.

Name _____

1 Using ABC Order

The letters in the alphabet are in a special order. It is called **ABC order.**

> a b c d e f g h i j k l m n o p
> q r s t u v w x y z

Words can be put in ABC order. Use the first letters of words to put them in ABC order. These words are in ABC order.

    apple   **h**at   **p**aint

The words blue, bat, and bottle begin with the same first letter. Use their second letters to put them in ABC order. These words are in ABC order.

    bat   blue   bottle

Practice

Read each set of words. Write them in ABC order.

1. deep, lamp, corn

   corn   deep   lamp

2. zoo, bat, orange

3. boat, banana, bike

4. run, race, rib

STUDY SKILLS ABC Order

Name _____

2 Finding Words in a Dictionary

A **dictionary** is a book that lists words and their meanings. The words are in ABC order. **Guide words** help you find the words. They are at the top of each dictionary page. The guide word on the left is the same as the first word on the page. The guide word on the right is the same as the last word on the page. All other words on the page are in ABC order between the guide words.

---

choose   **cry**

choose   To decide between two or more things: I like to <u>choose</u> my own clothes.
chum   A close friend: My <u>chum</u> and I play games.

city   A large town with many people and buildings: We saw a big building in the <u>city</u>.
clam   An ocean animal that has a shell with two parts: We gather <u>clams</u> at the beach.

Practice

Draw a line under the word in each group that could be on the dictionary page above. Use the guide words.

1. cart   fish   <u>chunk</u>
2. climb   cat   balloon
3. dog   circus   certain
4. cabbage   clear   aunt

Name _____

3 Using a Dictionary Entry

The words in a dictionary are called **entry words.** Entry words are in ABC order. Usually they are in dark print. An entry word can have this information.

Entry word — join   1. To put together: Glue can join two pieces of wood. 2. To become part of a group: Sarah wants to join our team. — Example sentence (Meaning)

Some words have more than one meaning. When a word has more than one meaning, the meanings are numbered. Sometimes an entry word has one or more example sentences to make the meanings clear.

---

join   **jumper**

join   1. To put together: Glue can join two pieces of wood. 2. To become part of a group: Sarah wants to join our team.

jot   To write quickly: Let me jot down your name.

juice   Liquid that comes from fruit: We drink orange juice for breakfast.

July   The seventh month of the year: June comes before July.

jump   To hop up in the air: Chan jumps to reach the ball.

jumper   1. A person, animal, or thing that jumps: A frog is a good jumper. 2. A kind of dress: Patty wore a blue jumper to school.

STUDY SKILLS Entry Words **321**

Name _____

Practice

A. Use the example dictionary page on page 321. Write the answers.

1. Which entry word comes after join?   jot

2. Which entry words have more than one meaning?

3. Write another word that could be on the dictionary page.

4. What is the second meaning of join?

B. Use the dictionary page. Write **1** or **2** to show which meaning of the underlined words fits each sentence.

5. Pam wants to join the baseball team.   2

6. The class will join hands to make a big circle. ____

7. Do you want to join our club? ____

8. That kangaroo is a good jumper. ____

9. Did Mary wear her new jumper to the party? ____

10. Pat is a better jumper than I am. ____

Name _____

4 Using the Parts of a Book

Most books have special pages that give information about what is inside the books. Look at these special pages.

Title Page

> Picnic on the Moon
>
> by Carole Roberts

The **title page** is at the front of the book. It shows the **title,** or name of the book. It gives the author's name. The **author** is the person who wrote the book.

Table of Contents

Chapter	Table of Contents	Page
1	The Rocket Trip	9
2	A Picnic Surprise	16
3	Fun and Games	24

The **table of contents** comes after the title page. It shows the **chapters,** or parts, of a book. It shows the page number of the beginning of each chapter.

Practice

Use the example pages to answer these questions.

1. Who wrote the book <u>Picnic on the Moon</u>?

2. On what page does Chapter 2 begin? _____

3. What is the title of Chapter 1?

STUDY SKILLS Parts of a Book

Name _____

5 Using an Index

Some books have an index at the back. An **index** lists people, places, and things that are in the book. These are in ABC order. The index shows the page numbers on which you can read about each person, place, or thing.

Part of an index of a book about the seashore might look like this. In this book, you can read about seagulls on page 25.

```
seagulls ........................... 25
seals ............................. 114
seaweed .......................... 38
starfish ........................... 57
```

Practice

1. Where would you find the index of a book?
   _____
   _____

Use the index above to answer the questions.

2. On which page would you find information about seals?

3. On which page would you find information about starfish?

4. What would you learn about by reading page 38?

Name _____

6 Understanding Kinds of Books

There are two main kinds of books. They are called fiction books and nonfiction books. **Fiction books** are made-up stories. Some fiction books are about things that could never happen. **Nonfiction books** are about real people, places, and things.

Fiction Book   Curious George Goes to the Hospital
This is a story about a talking monkey.

Nonfiction Book   The World of Living Things
This book is about real plants and animals.

A library has fiction books and nonfiction books. Fiction books are kept in one part of the library. Nonfiction books are kept in another part.

Practice

Use what you have learned to answer the questions.

1. What are books about made-up events or people called?

2. Write the name of a fiction book you have read.

3. What are books about real things called?

4. Write the name of a nonfiction book you have read.

STUDY SKILLS   Kinds of Books   **325**

Name _____

7 Writing a Book Report

A **book report** tells what a book is about. It names the title and author of the book. It also tells what someone thinks about a book. Read this book report.

> **Title** Four on the Shore
>
> **Author** Edward Marshall
>
> **About the Book** This book is about four friends on a camping trip. They tell stories on the trip. The stories are supposed to be scary, but they are really very funny.
>
> **What I Think** The book made me laugh a lot. I really liked it. You should read it.

When you write a book report, be sure to tell what the story is about. Write about the important people, places, and things. Then, tell what you think about the book. You might say why you like the book. You might tell what you learned from the book.

Practice

Write a book report. Follow these steps.

1. Write the name of the book.
2. Write the name of the author.
3. Write what the book is about.
4. Write what you think about the book.

Name _____

8 Taking a Test

Following directions is a very important part of taking a test. Before you start a test, read or listen to all the directions. Pay attention to directions that tell how to mark answers.

Practice

A. Read the directions for numbers **1** and **2**. Mark the answers.

B. Read the directions for numbers **3** and **4**. Mark the answers.

Fill in the circle next to the correct answer.

1. How many legs does a cat have?
   - A. one   ○
   - B. four   ●
   - C. two   ○

2. How many legs does a bird have?
   - A. two   ○
   - B. three   ○
   - C. four   ○

Fill in the circle that finishes the sentence and makes the most sense.

3. The squirrel ran up the ____.
   - A. tree   ○
   - B. dog   ○
   - C. nut   ○

4. Squirrels eat ____ for food.
   - A. hot dogs   ○
   - B. candy   ○
   - C. nuts   ○

STUDY SKILLS Tests

Name _____

9 Using Charts

A **chart** shows information in a way that is easy to read.

When you use a chart, read the title first. It tells you the kind of information the chart shows.

Wild Animals

Name of the Animal	Where the Animal Lives	What the Animal Eats
fox	den	mice
spider monkey	trees	fruit and leaves
rabbit	hole in the ground	plants
giraffe	grasslands	leaves, twigs, and fruit

Use the chart to find out what a rabbit eats.

- Find the word <u>rabbit</u> under <u>Name of the Animal</u>. Put your finger on the word.
- Move your finger to the right. Stop when your finger is under <u>What the Animal Eats</u>.
- The word in the box tells what a rabbit eats.

Name _____

Practice

Use the information in the chart to answer the questions.

1. What is this chart about?

2. Read the words in dark print. What does the chart tell about wild animals?

3. Where does a fox live?

4. What does a rabbit eat?

5. Where does a giraffe live?

6. Where do spider monkeys live?

7. What does a fox eat?

8. What does a giraffe eat?

9. Where does a rabbit live?

STUDY SKILLS Charts

Name _____

10 Using Bar Graphs

A **bar graph** is a picture that tells a story about numbers. It is used to compare things.

Read the title of a graph first. It tells you what the graph is about. Then read the words at the side and bottom of the graph.

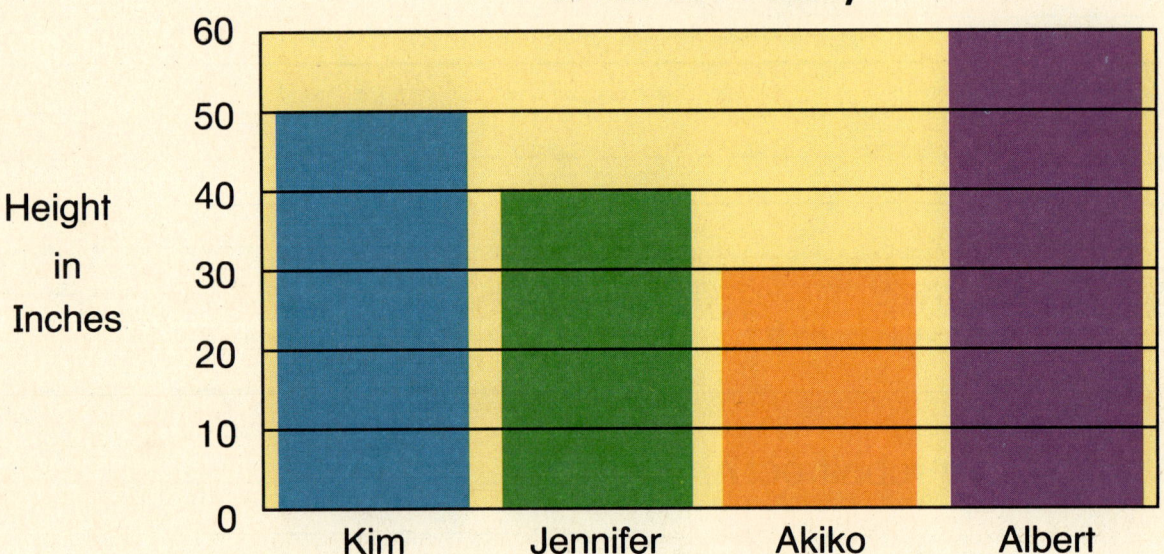

This graph shows how tall each child in the Lee family is. The name of each child is at the bottom of the graph. The height in inches is shown by the numbers along the side.

To find how tall a person is, do these things.

- ◆ Choose the name of the person.
- ◆ Move your finger up the bar. Stop at the top of the bar.
- ◆ Then move your finger to the left. Stop at the number. The number tells how many inches tall the person is.

STUDY SKILLS

330   STUDY SKILLS   Bar Graphs

Name _____

Practice

Use the information on the bar graph to answer the questions.

1. Look at the title of the bar graph. What is being compared in the bar graph?
   _____
   _____

2. How many children are in the Lee family? _____

3. How tall is Kim? _____

4. Who is the shortest? _____

5. Whose height is 40 inches? _____

6. Who is taller, Jennifer or Kim? _____

7. Who is the tallest child in the Lee family? _____

8. How tall is Akiko? _____

9. How tall is Albert? _____

STUDY SKILLS   Bar Graphs   **331**

Name _____

11 Using Pictographs

A **pictograph** is a graph that uses pictures to show how many. A **key** tells you how many each picture stands for. A pictograph helps you compare things.

To use a pictograph, read the title first. Next, look at the key. Then, look carefully at the graph.

Number of Books Read by Mr. Linotti's Students

Wendy	📖 📖
Mario	📖 📖 📖
Van	📖
Mitsuko	📖 📖
Helen	📖 📖 📖 📖
Harry	📖 📖 📖 📖 📖

KEY: 📖 = 1 book

To find out how many books someone has read, do these things.

◆ Look at the key to see how many each picture stands for.
◆ Then choose a name. Count the number of pictures next to the name.
◆ The number of pictures tells you the number of books the person read.

Name _____

Practice

Use the information on the pictograph to answer the questions.

1. What is the graph about?

2. How many students are shown on the graph?

3. How many books did Mario read?

4. Who read the most books?

5. Which student read four books?

6. Who read the same number of books as Wendy?

7. Which student read the least number of books?

8. How many more books did Helen read than Mitsuko?

9. How many books did the students read altogether?

STUDY SKILLS Pictographs **333**

Name _____

12 Using Maps

A **map** is a drawing that shows a place. It may show a neighborhood, a city, a state, or a country. You use a map to find out where places are. A map does not have room to show things the way they really look. A map uses small pictures to stand for some places. A **map key** tells you what the small pictures mean.

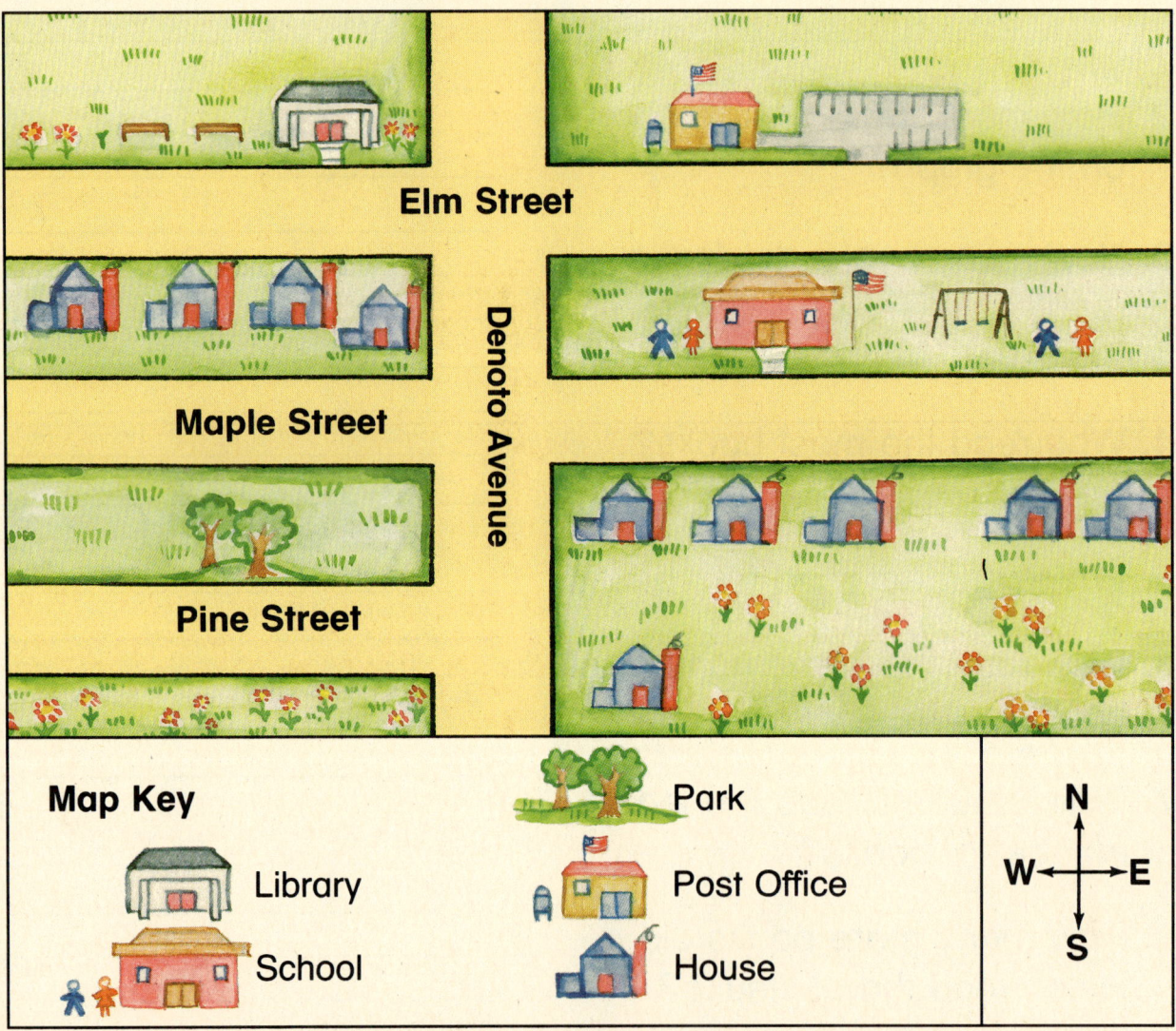

Maps also have a drawing that shows which way north (**N**), south (**S**), east (**E**), and west (**W**) are. The drawing is called a **compass rose.** On most maps, north is toward the top of the map.

Name _____

To find a park on this map, first look at the map key. Find the drawing that stands for a park. Then look at the map and find that same drawing. Did you find the park on Pine Street?

Practice

Use the map to answer the questions.

1. How many houses are shown?   10

2. What does this picture mean ?

3. Is the library north or south of Pine Street?

4. On which street would you find the school?

5. If you are at the post office, which direction do you go to get to the library?

6. Which two buildings are on Elm Street?

7. Is the school north or south of the post office?

STUDY SKILLS Maps 335

Name _____

13 Writing Telephone Messages

A **telephone message** is a note you write to let a person know that someone called him or her. A telephone message should have certain information. This telephone message shows that information.

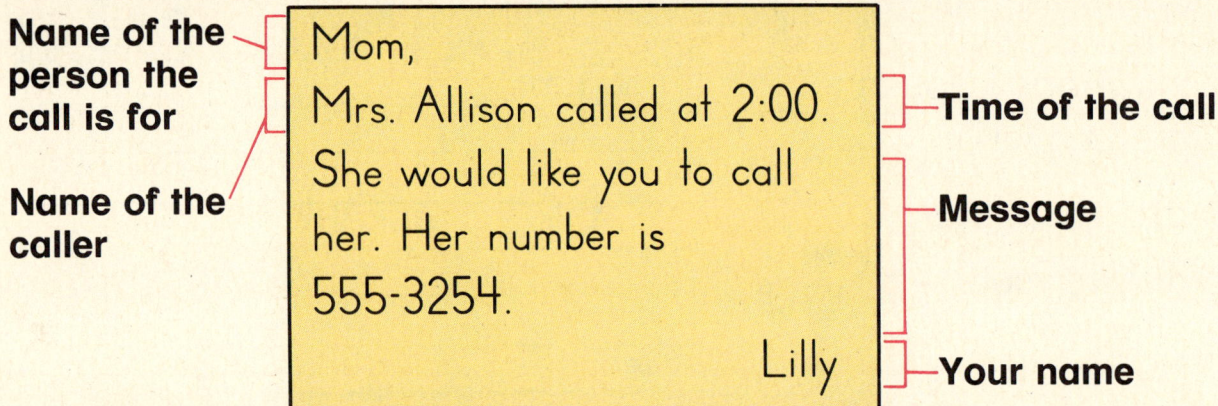

- Name of the person the call is for
- Name of the caller
- Time of the call
- Message
- Your name

When you write a telephone message, follow these steps.

1. Write the name of the person the call is for.
2. Write the name of the caller.
3. Write the time of the call.
4. Write the message. Be sure to write the phone number of the caller.
5. Read the message back to the caller to check it.
6. Sign your name.

Practice

On another piece of paper, write Bill a message to tell him about this call.

> Simon called for Bill at ten o'clock in the morning. He said that he wants to borrow Bill's baseball glove. Simon's phone number is 555-3831.

Name _____

14 Filling Out Forms

To get a library card, enter a contest, or order something, you may need to fill out a form. A **form** asks for information about you. Always read the directions on a form carefully before you write. Look at this form.

Mapletown Library Card Application

To apply for a card at the Mapletown Library, please print the following information in the spaces given.

Date: _____

Name: _____

Street address: _____

City: _____

State: _____

Zip Code: _____

Telephone number: (_____) _____–_____

Name of parent: _____

Practice

Fill in the form with the correct information about yourself.

STUDY SKILLS   Forms

EXTRA PRACTICE

Contents

Unit **1:** Sentences   3
Unit **2:** Nouns   11
Unit **3:** Verbs   21
Unit **4:** Describing Words   26
Unit **5:** Verbs   32
Unit **6:** Mechanics Wrap-up   40

Name _____

UNIT 1

1 What Is a Sentence? pages 28–29

A. Finding Sentences   Read each group of words. Draw a line under <u>Yes</u> or <u>No</u> to show if the words make a sentence.

1. My friend's name is Chris.   **a.** <u>Yes</u>   **b.** No
2. Chris and I share books.   **a.** Yes   **b.** No
3. has many good books   **a.** Yes   **b.** No
4. We also like movies.   **a.** Yes   **b.** No
5. Sometimes we watch television.   **a.** Yes   **b.** No
6. Chris and his sister   **a.** Yes   **b.** No

B. Writing Sentences   Read each group of words. Add words from the box to make a sentence.

> Her letters
> She
> is my friend
> write to Sally
> writes back

7. Sally *is my friend*.

8. _____ lives in Texas.

9. I _____.

10. Then Sally _____.

11. _____ tell about Texas.

EXTRA PRACTICE

Name _____

UNIT 1

2 Naming Part of a Sentence   pages 30–31

A. Finding Naming Parts   Read each sentence. Draw a line under the naming part. Draw a line around each naming part that tells <u>who</u>.

1. ⟨The teacher⟩ reads a funny story.
2. The children listen.
3. The story is about a train.
4. The train goes to many places.

B. Writing Naming Parts   Look at the picture. Add a naming part to finish each sentence.

5. _Joseph_____ paints a picture.

6. _____ is green.

7. _____ flies in the sky.

8. _____ floats on the lake.

9. _____ likes the picture.

4   EXTRA PRACTICE

Name _____

UNIT 1

3 Telling Part of a Sentence pages 32–33

A. Finding Telling Parts Read each sentence. Draw a line around the telling part.

1. The telephone ⟨rings in the kitchen⟩.
2. Brenda answers the telephone.
3. She talks to her friend.
4. The girls talk about a camping trip.
5. Brenda hangs up the telephone.

B. Writing Telling Parts
Look at the picture. Add a telling part to finish each sentence.

6. The children _work together_ .

7. The teacher _____ .

8. The girl _____ .

9. The boy _____ .

EXTRA PRACTICE

Name _____

UNIT 1

4 Word Order in a Sentence   pages 34–35

A. Finding Sentences   Draw a line around Yes or No to show if each group of words is in the correct order.

1. Jamie has a radio.   (Yes)   No
2. music He likes much very.   Yes   No
3. He also hears the news.   Yes   No
4. He learns about the world.   Yes   No
5. enjoys his radio Jamie.   Yes   No

B. Writing Sentences   Write each group of words in the correct order.

Talia read to likes.

6. _Talia likes to read._

likes She also to write.

7. _____

She story a wrote.

8. _____

about dog her It was.

9. _____

read to She it class her.

10. _____

EXTRA PRACTICE

6 EXTRA PRACTICE

Name _____

UNIT 1

5 Statements pages 36–37

A. Proofreading Statements Read each sentence. Draw a line around the sentence if it is written correctly.

1. ⟨The children wrote a story.⟩
2. it was about Princess Amanda
3. Amanda lived in a tower.
4. An old woman tricked her.
5. the princess could not leave the tower
6. a prince came to save her
7. The old woman put the prince in the tower.
8. the princess saved the prince instead

B. Writing Statements Fix the mistakes in the sentences from **Practice A.** Begin and end each statement correctly.

9. 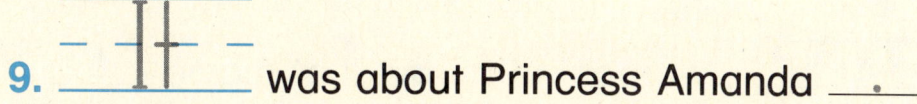 _____ was about Princess Amanda ___.

10. _____ princess could not leave the tower ____

11. _____ prince came to save her ____

12. _____ princess saved the prince instead ____

EXTRA PRACTICE **7**

Name _____

UNIT 1

6 Questions   pages 38–39

A. Finding Questions   Read each sentence. Draw a line around Yes if it is a question. Draw a line around No if it is not.

1. What was the movie about?   **[Yes]**   No
2. We saw a movie about snakes.   Yes   No
3. Some snakes hatch from eggs.   Yes   No
4. Which snake is the longest?   Yes   No
5. Can snakes climb trees?   Yes   No
6. Snakes have smooth, dry skin.   Yes   No
7. Do all snakes have teeth?   Yes   No
8. Did you like the movie?   Yes   No

B. Writing Questions   Begin and end each question correctly. Use question words from the box.

When	Who
Where	Does
	Are

9. _Are_ you going to see that movie

10. _____ is the movie theater ____

11. _____ has the tickets ____

12. _____ does the movie start ____

13. _____ your sister want to come too ____

EXTRA PRACTICE

Name _____

UNIT 1
7 Exclamations   pages 40–41

A. Finding Exclamations   Read each pair of sentences. Draw a line around the sentence that is an exclamation.

1. Those clowns are nice.   ⌈Those clowns are so funny!⌉
2. Is the bear wonderful?   The bear is wonderful!
3. The elephants are huge!   The elephants are big.
4. I like the circus.   I love the circus!

B. Writing Exclamations   Look at the pictures. Finish each exclamation in your own words.

5. I saw a real bear!

6. One bear _____

7. The alligator's teeth _____

8. The elephant's tusks _____

9. The zoo _____

EXTRA PRACTICE

Name _____

UNIT 1

8 Kinds of Sentences pages 42–43

A. Finding Different Kinds of Sentences
Read each sentence. Draw a line around S, Q, or E to show what kind of sentence it is.

S—Statement
Q—Question
E—Exclamation

1. Did you read that book?   S [Q] E
2. It is about whales.   S   Q   E
3. Some whales grow to be 60 feet long! S   Q   E
4. Do you know what they eat?   S   Q   E
5. Most whales eat tiny plants.   S   Q   E
6. Some whales eat very small fish. S   Q   E
7. Whales are very interesting animals! S   Q   E

B. Writing Sentences Use your own words to finish each sentence. Make **9** a <u>question</u>. Make **10** an <u>exclamation</u>. Make **11** a <u>statement</u>.

8. I read a good  story.

9. Do you _____

10. The book is _____

11. You can find it _____

EXTRA PRACTICE

10 EXTRA PRACTICE

Name _____

UNIT 2

1 Naming Words for People and Animals
pages 78–79

A. Finding Nouns   Read each sentence. Draw a line around each noun that names a person or an animal.

1. A ⬚boy⬚ and his ⬚mother⬚ went to the zoo.
2. The boy saw an elephant eat peanuts.
3. One man gave food to a tiger.
4. A girl laughed at a silly monkey.
5. A zookeeper fed a big brown bear.

B. Writing Nouns   Read each sentence. Write a noun from the box to finish the sentence.

ranger
sister
uncle
bird
squirrel

6. My _____uncle_____ took us to the park.

7. The _____ told us about the animals.

8. I saw a _____ climb a tree.

9. My _____ saw a turtle.

10. We heard a baby _____.

EXTRA PRACTICE **11**

UNIT 2

2 Naming Words for Places and Things
pages 80–81

A. Finding Nouns   Read each sentence. Draw a line around the noun that names a place or a thing.

1. My family likes the [beach].
2. We look for shells.
3. A man stands on the shore.
4. He takes a picture.
5. The ocean is beautiful.

B. Using Clear Nouns   Read each sentence. Choose a clearer noun to take the place of the underlined word. Use the words in the box.

| tree | forest |
| daisy | river |

This place is green.

6. 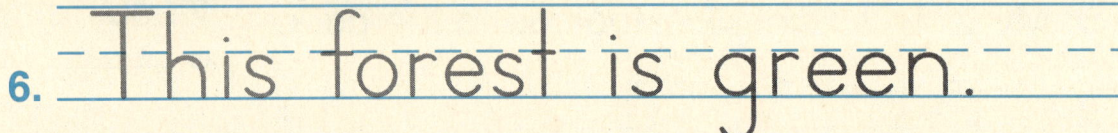 This forest is green.

I see a tall plant.

7. _____

A flower grows by a rock.

8. _____

Do you see the water?

9. _____

12   EXTRA PRACTICE

Name _____

UNIT 2

3 Nouns That Name More Than One
pages 82–83

A. Finding Nouns   Read each sentence. Draw a line around each noun that names more than one.

1. ⬚Picnics⬚ in the park are fun.
2. Ask your friends to go with you.
3. Take some apples and oranges to eat.
4. Remember to take plates and napkins.
5. Bring some cups for lemonade, too.

B. Revising Nouns   Write a noun from the box to finish each sentence. Make the noun mean more than one.

> plant
> duck
> wing
> animal
> feather

6. Many _____animals_____ live by the pond.

7. We watch the _____ swim.

8. Their _____ are different colors.

9. The ducks flap their _____ to fly!

10. They hide in the _____ by the water.

EXTRA PRACTICE 13

Name _____

UNIT 2

4 More Nouns That Name More Than One
pages 84–85

EXTRA PRACTICE

A. Finding Nouns   Draw a line around the noun that names more than one.

1. Mom shops for two (lunches, lunch).
2. She buys lettuce for (sandwich, sandwiches).
3. She picks fresh (radishes, radish) for Andy.
4. The (peach, peaches) are fresh too.
5. Then we pack our lunch (boxes, box).

B. Proofreading Nouns   Write a noun from the box to finish each sentence. Make the noun mean more than one.

class	box
bench	bush
bus	

6. Two ___classes___ cleaned the park.

7. We raked under the _____.

8. We threw old papers into _____.

9. Then we cleaned off the _____.

10. Soon the _____ came to take us home.

14   EXTRA PRACTICE

Name _____

UNIT 2

5 Other Nouns That Name More Than One
pages 86–87

A. Choosing Nouns   Read each sentence. Draw a line around the noun that goes with the sentence and names more than one.

1. The ____ listen to a talk about climbers.   a. child   b. (children)
2. These ____ climb snowy mountains.   a. men   b. man
3. The ____ climb mountains too.   a. woman   b. women
4. The cold air makes their ____ chatter.   a. teeth   b. tooth
5. They wear warm boots on their ____.   a. foot   b. feet

B. Writing Sentences   Read each sentence. Write the sentence again. Make the underlined noun mean more than one.

The <u>woman</u> had maps.

6.  The women had maps.

The <u>man</u> showed pictures.

7. _____.

The <u>child</u> clapped.

8. _____.

EXTRA PRACTICE 15

Name _____

UNIT 2

6 Nouns That Name Special People and Animals   pages 88–89

A. Finding Proper Nouns   Read each sentence. Draw a line around the proper noun that takes the place of the underlined words.

1. The bear is big and brown.
   a. John   b. Henry

2. The bike belongs to the girl.
   a. Bonnie   b. Fluffy

3. The rabbit has long ears.
   a. Henry   b. Fluffy

4. The boy writes a story.
   a. John   b. Bonnie

Henry

John

Bonnie

Fluffy

B. Writing Proper Nouns   Read each sentence. Finish the sentence with your own proper noun.

5. Do you have a dog named ___Sasha___ ?

6. If I had a pet, I would name it _____ .

7. My favorite singer is _____ .

8. My teacher's name is _____ .

Name _____

UNIT 2

7 Nouns That Name Special Places
pages 90–91

A. Finding Proper Nouns   Read each sentence. Draw a line around the noun that names a special place.

1. ⟨New York⟩ is a busy city.
2. Times Square has many bright lights.
3. You can shop on Fifth Avenue.
4. You can see the Statue of Liberty.
5. It is on an island called Liberty Island.
6. There is a big zoo in Central Park.

B. Proofreading Proper Nouns   Use the noun above the line to finish each sentence. Write the proper noun correctly.

7. My grandmother lives in ___Salem_____.
   (salem)

8. Salem is in a state called _____.
   (oregon)

9. Grandma's house is on _____.
   (palm street)

10. It is near _____.
    (lincoln park)

EXTRA PRACTICE **17**

Name _____

UNIT 2

8 Days, Months, and Holidays pages 92–93

A. Choosing Proper Nouns   Read each sentence. Draw a line under the noun that is written correctly.

1. Our picnic is on ____.
   <u>Thursday</u>   thursday

2. It is the last day in ____.
   June   june

3. The next picnic is on the Fourth of ____.
   july   July

4. That day is also called ____.
   Independence Day   independence day

B. Writing Proper Nouns   Read each sentence. Write the proper noun correctly.

labor day
_____

5. __Labor Day_____ is in September.

monday
_____

6. It is always on a _____.

october
_____

7. I like _____ best.

columbus day
_____

8. _____ is in October.

Name _____

UNIT 2

9 Words That Take the Place of Nouns
pages 94–95

A. Using Pronouns Read each sentence. Write a pronoun from the box to take the place of the underlined word or words.

| they | it |
| She | He |

1. <u>Mike</u> watches the spaceship.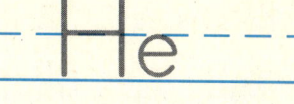

2. Do you see <u>the rocket</u>?

3. Look how big <u>the engines</u> are!

4. <u>That woman</u> is an astronaut. _____

B. Writing Pronouns Write the sentences. Use <u>he</u>, <u>she</u>, <u>it</u>, or <u>they</u> in place of the underlined words.

<u>The astronaut</u> is in the spaceship.

5.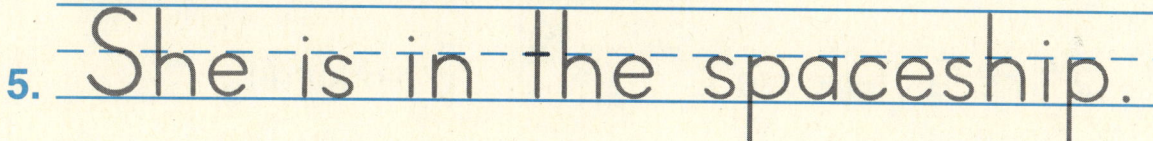

Do you see <u>the large planet</u>?

6. _____

<u>The stars</u> are so bright!

7. _____

EXTRA PRACTICE **19**

Name _____

UNIT 2

10 The Pronouns I and Me   pages 96–97

A. Choosing Pronouns   Read each sentence. Draw a line around the correct pronoun that finishes each sentence.

1. My friend and ____ have a garden.   ⒤   me
2. My friend gives seeds to ____ .   I   me
3. He helps ____ plant them.   I   me
4. ____ like to grow carrots.   I   me
5. The leafy tops seem pretty to ____ .   I   me
6. ____ like our garden!   I   me

B. Writing Pronouns   Read each sentence. Use <u>I</u> or <u>me</u> to finish the sentence.

7. Lisa and ____I____ went to a farm.

8. _____ petted a little calf.

9. The farmer gave _____ a kitten.

10. He taught _____ to milk a cow!

11. Lisa and _____ fed some pigs.

12. _____ had a wonderful time!

20   EXTRA PRACTICE

Name _____

UNIT 3

1 Action Verbs   pages 132–133

A. Finding Action Verbs   Read each sentence. Draw a line around the action verb.

1. My hat ⟨falls⟩ on the grass.
2. My dog Bandit creeps up to it.
3. Bandit growls at the hat.
4. Bandit crawls under the hat.
5. The hat moves across the grass!

B. Revising Action Verbs   Finish each sentence. Write a strong verb to take the place of the verb above the line. Use words from the box.

| cooks   pours   flips   plops |

6. Dad ~~makes~~ **cooks** pancakes for Kim.

7. He ~~places~~ _____ pancake batter into a pan.

8. Dad ~~turns~~ _____ the pancakes.

9. One pancake ~~falls~~ _____ to the floor!

EXTRA PRACTICE 21

Name _____

UNIT 3

2 Verbs That Tell About Now
pages 134–135

A. Choosing Verbs Read each sentence. Draw a line around the correct verb.

1. A player ____ the ball. **a.** strike   **b.** [strikes]
2. The ball ____ through the air. **a.** spin   **b.** spins
3. The coaches ____. **a.** shout   **b.** shouts
4. I ____ for the player. **a.** cheer   **b.** cheers
5. The bands ____ songs. **a.** play   **b.** plays
6. The ball ____ in a fountain! **a.** land   **b.** lands

B. Writing Verbs Write a word from the box to finish each sentence. Add <u>s</u> to the verb if it is needed.

blow	jump
race	win
	kick

7. The coach __blows__ the whistle.

8. The frogs _____ into the water.

9. The frogs _____ their legs.

10. A tiny frog _____ to the finish line.

11. It _____ the race!

22 EXTRA PRACTICE

Name _____

UNIT 3

3 Verbs That Tell About the Past
pages 136–137

A. Choosing Verbs Read each sentence. Draw a line around the verb that tells about the past.

1. We (watched, watch) a funny movie.
2. A robot (works, worked) in a house.
3. It (cleans, cleaned) the dishes in the tub.
4. It (dusted, dusts) the washing machine!
5. The robot (knocked, knocks) over chairs!
6. We (laugh, laughed) at the silly robot.

B. Revising Verbs Write a word from the box to finish each sentence. Make the verb tell about an action in the past.

paint	laugh
peek	cover
leak	

7. Pat __painted__ the doghouse.

8. Some paint _____ through the roof.

9. She _____ inside the doghouse.

10. Drops of paint _____ Jeb's fur.

11. Pat _____ at her spotted dog!

EXTRA PRACTICE **23**

Name _____

UNIT 3

4 The Verbs Is and Are   pages 138–139

A. Choosing Verbs   Read each sentence.
Draw a line around the correct verb.

1. A kiwi ____ an odd bird.   (is)   are
2. Its body ____ fuzzy.   is   are
3. Its legs ____ short.   is   are
4. Its bill ____ long and thin. is   are
5. The wings ____ very small.   is   are
6. The feathers ____ brown.   is   are

B. Writing Verbs   Finish each sentence.
Write is or are in the sentence.
Use the picture for ideas.

7. This animal _is gray all over_ .

8. Its ears _____ .

9. Its tail _____ .

10. Its skin _____ .

11. Its legs _____ .

EXTRA PRACTICE

24   EXTRA PRACTICE

Name _____

UNIT 3

5 The Verbs Was and Were   pages 140–141

A. Choosing Verbs   Read each sentence. Draw a line around the correct verb.

1. The park ____ open today.   [was]   were
2. Some of the rides ____ fun.   was   were
3. Our favorite one ____ the river raft. was   were
4. We ____ all wet!   was   were
5. It ____ funny.   was   were

B. Writing Sentences   Read each sentence. Use <u>was</u> or <u>were</u> to finish the sentence. Write the sentence.

6. The clowns ____ great.

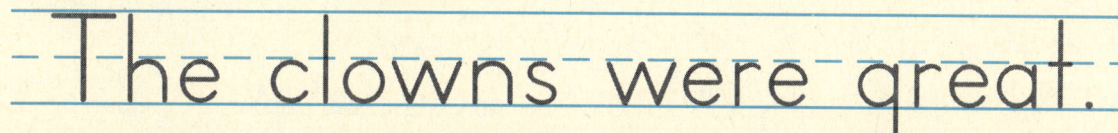

7. One clown ____ very silly.

8. A nest ____ on his head.

9. Birds ____ in the nest!

EXTRA PRACTICE 25

Name _____

UNIT 4

1 Describing Words pages 178–179

A. Finding Describing Words Read each sentence. Draw a line under the describing word.

1. A <u>long</u> road leads to a castle.
2. The castle is in a deep valley.
3. The towers are tall.
4. Some of the windows are tiny.

B. Revising Sentences Read each sentence. Use a clear describing word from the box to take the place of the underlined word. Write the sentence.

| jolly | silky |
| huge | golden |

5. We live in a <u>big</u> castle.

   We live in a huge castle.

6. The king has a <u>nice</u> smile.

7. The queen's crown is <u>bright</u>.

8. The princess has <u>soft</u> hair.

26 EXTRA PRACTICE

Name _____

UNIT 4

2 Describing Words for Shape and Color
pages 180–181

A. Finding Describing Words   Read each sentence. Draw a line around the describing word. Draw a line under the noun it tells about.

1. I saw a ⟨round⟩ <u>snowman</u> in my dream.
2. The snowman's hair was red.
3. He wore a square hat.
4. He waved his thin arms at me.
5. Then he rolled away into the green forest.

B. Writing Describing Words

Choose a describing word to finish each sentence. Use the **Word Bank.**

Word Bank
little   shiny
soft   round
long   white
orange black

6. The ___white___ snow covers the ground.

7. We roll it into _____ balls.

8. Our snowman's hair is _____!

9. We use _____ stones for his eyes.

10. His nose is a _____ carrot.

EXTRA PRACTICE

Name _____

UNIT 4

3 Describing Words for Size and Number
pages 182–183

A. Finding Describing Words   Read each sentence. Draw a line around the describing word. Draw a line under the noun it tells about.

1. Last night I had ⬚one⬚ <u>dream</u>.
2. I climbed a huge tree.
3. I sat on a tiny branch.
4. Three birds watched me.
5. One bird talked to me.
6. Then I woke up in my small bed.

B. Using Describing Words   Finish each sentence with a describing word that tells <u>size</u> or <u>how many</u>.

7. A ____small____ owl flew through the sky.

8. It saw _____ cows below.

9. A _____ barn was in a field.

10. The owl flew past _____ clouds.

11. The owl flew to its _____ nest.

EXTRA PRACTICE

Name _____

UNIT 4

4 Describing Words for Taste, Smell, Feel, and Sound   pages 184–185

A. Choosing Describing Words   Read each sentence. Draw a line to a describing word that finishes the sentence.

1. The elf picked a berry that tasted ____.   sharp
2. The thorns on the berry bush felt ____.   sweet
3. Then he made a pie that smelled ____.   fruity
4. He baked it on a fire that sounded ____.   delicious
5. The pie that the elf made tasted ____.   crackly

B. Writing Sentences   Choose a describing word from the box to finish each sentence. Write the sentence.

| roaring | bumpy |
| smoky | spicy |

6. He saw a ____ river.

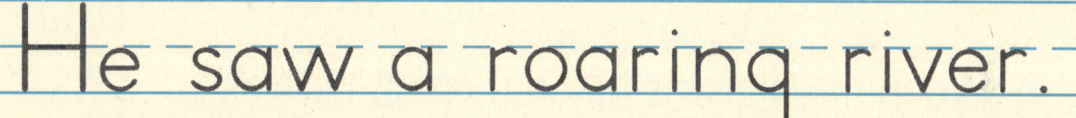

7. The fire smelled ____.

8. He sat on a ____ log.

9. He ate the ____ soup.

EXTRA PRACTICE   **29**

Name _____

UNIT 4

5 Describing Words for Feelings
pages 186–187

A. Finding Describing Words   Read each sentence. Draw a line around the describing word that names a feeling.

1. Yesterday the king was ⬚worried⬚.
2. The prince looked sad.
3. The prince felt shy at school.
4. Today he is happy.
5. He is glad to have new friends.

B. Choosing Describing Words   Finish each sentence with a describing word from the box.

| happy   amused   lonely   excited   worried   upset   angry |

6. When the prince's friend moved, he was  .

7. When he got a flying horse, he felt _____.

8. When he lost his crown, he was _____.

9. The _____, _____ queen laughed.

10. The _____, _____ king cried.

30   EXTRA PRACTICE

Name _____

UNIT 4

6 Describing Words With er and est
pages 188–189

A. Choosing Describing Words Read each sentence. Draw a line to the word that best completes the sentence.

1. Some footsteps are ____ than others. — tallest
2. Giants make the ____ sounds of all. — louder
3. Giants are the ____ people of all. — loudest
4. The tiny elf is ____ than a giant. — stronger
5. The giant is ____ than the elf. — smaller

B. Writing Describing Words Read each sentence. Add er or est to the word above the line to finish the sentence.

tall

6. John is the 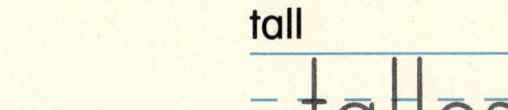 boy in the land.

short

7. I am _____ than he is.

tall

8. We climb trees that are _____ than buildings.

strong

9. We find the _____ of all the branches.

EXTRA PRACTICE **31**

Name _____

UNIT 5

1 Verbs That Tell About Now or the Past
pages 234–235

A. Choosing Verbs Read each sentence. Draw a line around the verb that completes the sentence.

1. Jill and Jim ____ in a big house.   ⬚live⬚   lives
2. One day Jill ____ a secret room.   find   finds
3. The children ____ the room.   explore   explores
4. Jim ____ some old clothes in a box.   see   sees

B. Revising Verbs Read each sentence. Make the verb tell about the past. Write the sentence.

The wind howls.

5. The wind howled.

Cold rain pours down.

6. _____

A dog barks excitedly.

7. _____

I look out the window.

8. _____

Then I crawl into bed.

9. _____

32 EXTRA PRACTICE

Name _____

UNIT 5

2 The Verbs Is, Are, Was, and Were
pages 236–237

A. Choosing Verbs   Read each sentence. Draw a line around was or were to show which verb is correct.

1. The submarine ride ____ fun.   a. (was)   b. were
2. The bottom of the sea ____ dark. a. was   b. were
3. All the plants ____ beautiful.   a. was   b. were
4. Many fish ____ in the sea.   a. was   b. were
5. Some fish ____ tiny.   a. was   b. were
6. One shark ____ huge.   a. was   b. were

B. Writing Verbs   Read each sentence. Choose is or are to finish the sentence. Write the verb.

7. The mountain ____ big.   is

8. The cliffs ____ high.

9. Every path ____ narrow.

10. The rocks ____ sharp.

11. Some trees ____ huge.

12. The top ____ far away.

EXTRA PRACTICE **33**

Name _____

UNIT 5

3 The Verbs Has, Have, and Had
pages 238–239

A. Choosing Verbs   Read each sentence. Draw a line under the correct verb.

1. Last year I (had, have) fun going to baseball games.
2. This year we (have, has) tickets for every game.
3. We (has, have) good seats at today's game.
4. Our team (has, have) red caps.
5. The other players (has, have) blue caps.
6. Last week we (have, had) a great time.

B. Writing Verbs   Read each sentence. Write has or have to finish the sentence.

7. The players ____have____ bats.

8. Who _____ the ball?

9. The catcher _____ the ball.

10. Our players _____ blue shirts.

11. We all _____ blue and white caps.

12. One player _____ red sneakers.

34   EXTRA PRACTICE

Name _____

UNIT 5

4 Helping Verbs   pages 240–241

A. Finding Verbs   Read each sentence. Draw a line under each pair of verbs. Draw a line around the helping verb.

1. The adventure ⬚has⬚ started.
2. We have lifted the anchor.
3. We had sailed at dawn.
4. The captain has looked at the map.

B. Writing Helping Verbs   Read each sentence. Write the correct helping verb.

(had, have)

5. The wind ____had____ howled all night.

(has, have)

6. Waves _____ crashed against the ship.

(had, have)

7. Water _____ covered the deck.

(has, have)

8. The storm _____ ended.

(has, have)

9. The men _____ sighted land.

EXTRA PRACTICE

Name _____

UNIT 5

5 The Verbs Come and Run   pages 242–243

A. Choosing Verbs   Read each sentence.
Draw a line around the correct verb.

1. A fox ____ to a stream.   a. come   b. (comes)
2. Some squirrels ____ away.   a. run   b. runs
3. Two raccoons ____ to the water.   a. come   b. comes
4. One raccoon ____ after the other one. a. run   b. runs
5. The fox ____ toward the raccoons.   a. come   b. comes
6. Both raccoons ____ away.   a. run   b. runs

B. Revising Verbs   Read each sentence.
Make the underlined verb tell about the past.
Write the verb.

7. Two dogs <u>come</u> to the stream.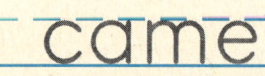

8. The fox <u>runs</u> away.

9. A bear <u>comes</u> from the woods.

10. The dogs <u>run</u> off.

11. The fox <u>comes</u> out again.

36   EXTRA PRACTICE

Name _____

UNIT 5
6 The Verbs Go and Do   pages 244–245

A. Choosing Verbs   Read each sentence. Draw a line around the correct verb.

1. We (go, goes) to an island.
2. We (do, does) many things there.
3. Mom (do, does) some fishing.
4. Dad (do, does) some hiking.
5. We (go, goes) to the beach.
6. Everyone (go, goes) to sleep early.

B. Revising Sentences   Write each sentence from Practice A. Change the verb to tell about the past.

7. We went to an island.
8. _____
9. _____
10. _____
11. _____
12. _____

EXTRA PRACTICE **37**

Name _____

UNIT 5

7 The Verbs See and Give   pages 246–247

A. Choosing Verbs   Read each sentence. Draw a line under the correct verb.

1. We (see, sees) the desert.
2. Mark (see, sees) the hot sun.
3. He (give, gives) them some fruit.
4. They (give, gives) him some water.
5. We (see, sees) a small tree.
6. The tree (give, gives) us shade.

B. Revising Sentences   Read each sentence. Change the verb above the line to tell about the past. Write the verb.

7. Our horses <u>see → saw</u> a stream.

8. We <u>give → _____</u> the horses a drink.

9. Mark <u>gives → _____</u> each horse an apple.

10. He <u>sees → _____</u> a town far away.

38   EXTRA PRACTICE

Name _____

UNIT 5
8 Contractions pages 248–249

A. Finding Word Pairs   Read each sentence. Draw a line to the two words that make up the underlined contraction.

1. The scouts <u>don't</u> feel tired.   were not
2. The hiking trail <u>wasn't</u> long.   does not
3. The mountains <u>weren't</u> too high.   do not
4. The river <u>isn't</u> wide.   are not
5. Snow <u>doesn't</u> fall.   is not
6. Their friends <u>aren't</u> far away.   was not

B. Writing Contractions   Read each sentence. Draw a line around the two words that can be joined to make a contraction. Write the contraction.

7. The children (are not) sleepy.

8. They do not want to go to bed.

9. Mom does not want them to be tired.

10. The children did not stay awake.

11. It was not long before they fell asleep.

EXTRA PRACTICE **39**

Name _____

UNIT 6

1 Sentences   pages 284–285

A. Finding Kinds of Sentences   Read each sentence. Draw a line around S, Q, or E to show if it is a statement, a question, or an exclamation.

1. Wow, the knights are riding by!   S   Q   [E]
2. They ride white horses.   S   Q   E
3. How I wish I could join them!   S   Q   E
4. Where are they going?   S   Q   E
5. They are riding to the forest.   S   Q   E
6. Is the forest far away?   S   Q   E

B. Writing Sentences   Read each sentence. Write the sentence correctly.

They are on a hunt

7. They are on a hunt.

what will they find

8. _____

They will find dragons

9. _____

the hunt sounds so exciting

10. _____

40   EXTRA PRACTICE

Name _____

UNIT 6

2 Names, Titles of People, I pages 286–287

A. Choosing Names and Titles   Read each sentence. Draw a line around the names and titles that are written correctly.

1. (ms win, Ms. Win) read a book to us.
2. It was about (George Washington, george washington).
3. (mr. washington, Mr. Washington) was our first President.
4. The book was written by (Jean Fritz, jean fritz).
5. (i, I) liked the story.

B. Writing Names and Titles   Write the names and titles to finish each sentence. Use the words in the box.

| Dr. Kirk   Mike   June Tracy   Mrs. Tracy |

6. A girl named _June Tracy_ found a baby robin.

7. Her brother _____ saw its broken wing.

8. They took the bird to _____ at the pet hospital.

9. Their mother, _____, was proud of them.

EXTRA PRACTICE

Name _____

UNIT 6

3 Names of Special Places   pages 288–289

A. Choosing Names of Places   Read each sentence. Draw a line under the names of places that are written correctly.

1. Amelia Earhart is famous in the (united states, <u>United States</u>).
2. She flew over the (Atlantic Ocean, atlantic ocean).
3. This pilot was born in (Kansas, kansas).
4. She lived in the city of (atchison, Atchison).
5. Amelia Earhart once flew to (ireland, Ireland).
6. She also flew to (Hawaii, hawaii).

B. Writing Names of Places
Write the name of a place to finish each sentence. Use the words in the box.

> Angel Island
> San Francisco
> California
> Golden Gate Bridge

7. We like the city of San Francisco.

8. The city is in _____.

9. We saw the _____.

10. We sailed to _____.

EXTRA PRACTICE

42 EXTRA PRACTICE

Name _____

UNIT 6

4 Days of the Week   pages 290–291

A. Finding Days of the Week   Read each sentence. Draw a line around the day of the week that is written correctly.

1. Susie found a library book on (Monday, monday).
2. On (tuesday, Tuesday) she read about Christopher Columbus.
3. She wrote her book report on (Wednesday, wednesday).
4. On (thursday, Thursday) she read it to her class.
5. Susie returned the book on (friday, Friday).

B. Writing Days of the Week   Write a day of the week to finish each sentence.

6. My friend lost her dog on  .

7. On _____ she put up a "Lost Dog" sign.

8. I saw the sign on _____ .

9. On _____ I found the dog.

10. I took the dog to its home on _____ .

EXTRA PRACTICE   43

Name _____

UNIT 6

5 Months of the Year pages 292–293

A. Choosing Names of Months Read each sentence. Draw a line around the name of the month that is written correctly.

1. In (August, august) the Pilgrims left England.
2. They sailed to America in (september, September).
3. In (October, october) the Pilgrims talked about America.
4. In (november, November) they first saw land.
5. They landed at Plymouth Rock in (December, december).
6. In (January, january) they built new homes.

B. Writing Names of Months Finish each sentence. Write the name of the month correctly.

7. The Pilgrims ate dried corn in __February__.

   february

8. They planted corn in _____.

   march

9. The corn was tall by _____.

   july

10. They picked the corn in _____.

    october

44 EXTRA PRACTICE

Name _____

UNIT 6
6 Holidays pages 294–295

A. Choosing Names of Holidays   Read each sentence. Draw a line under the name of the holiday that is written correctly.

1. Hearts are for (valentine's day, <u>Valentine's Day</u>).
2. On (Halloween, halloween) I wear a costume.
3. On (Independence Day, independence day) we watch fireworks.
4. We fly the flag on (Flag Day, flag day).
5. January 1 is (new year's day, New Year's Day).

B. Writing Names of Holidays   Write the name of a holiday to finish each sentence.

6. Mom's special day is Mother's Day .

7. I like _____ best.

8. School is closed for _____.

9. We eat special food on _____.

10. There is a parade on _____.

11. We see fireworks on _____.

EXTRA PRACTICE 45

Name _____

UNIT 6

7 Titles of Books, Stories, and Poems
pages 296–297

A. Proofreading Titles Draw a line around each letter that should be a capital letter.

1. (t)he (l)ittle (p)ainter
2. The knight of the golden plain
3. the golden bird
4. jethro and the jumbie
5. the bravest babysitter
6. afraid of the dark
7. strange bumps
8. the fisherman under the sea
9. a bell for ursli
10. the boy who fooled the giant

B. Writing Book Titles Write your own book title to finish each sentence.

11. The librarian shared 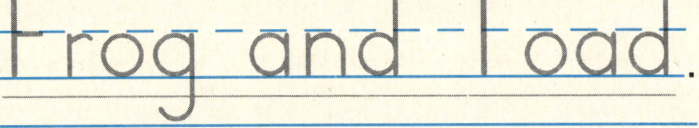 Frog and Toad.

12. An exciting book is _____.

13. Our teacher read _____ to us.

Name _____

UNIT 6
8 Friendly Letter   pages 298–299

A. Proofreading Parts of a Letter   Read each item. Mark each letter that should be a capital letter. Use this mark ≡ . Add the missing commas.

1. dear Aunt Sylvia,
2. dear Pat
3. august 10 1990
4. july 27 1990
5. yours truly
6. love,
7. december 18 1990
8. january 1 1990
9. your friend,
10. your son
11. dear Mr. Smith
12. dear Miss Tate

B. Writing Parts of a Letter   Write each heading, greeting, and closing correctly.

13. May 2 1990   May 2, 1990

14. october 15 1990

15. dear Nicky

16. best wishes

17. your pal

EXTRA PRACTICE 47

Name _____

UNIT 6

9 Envelope pages 300–301

A. Proofreading Addresses Read each address. Draw a line around the mistakes. Then write each address correctly on the envelope below.

1. (Return address)

   (ann) (k)irk
   2 rio road
   alta, iowa 51002

2. (Mailing address)

   jim king
   21 high lane
   ogden, utah 84401

3. Ann Kirk

4.

5.

6.

7.

8.

B. Addressing an Envelope Draw an envelope on a piece of paper. Address the envelope correctly. Use your address for the return address. Use a classmate's address for the mailing address.

48 EXTRA PRACTICE

WRITER'S HANDBOOK

Contents

Grammar	3
Mechanics	10
Usage	13
Composition	16
Vocabulary	32
Spelling	33

Name _____

GRAMMAR

Sentences

- A **sentence** is a group of words that tells a complete thought. The words are in an order that makes sense. Every sentence begins with a capital letter and ends with an end mark.

      The children go to school.

  sentence

- A **statement** is a sentence that tells something. It ends with a **period (.)**.

      The girl draws a picture.

  statement

- A **question** is a sentence that asks something. It ends with a **question mark (?)**.

      Where do you live?

  question

- An **exclamation** is a sentence that shows strong feeling. It ends with an **exclamation point (!)**.

      I love to swim!

  exclamation

- A sentence has a **naming part** that names who or what the sentence is about.

      The boy rides his bicycle.

  naming part

- A sentence has a **telling part** that tells what someone or something is or does.

      The boy rides his bicycle.
      This puppy is very playful.

  telling part

WRITER'S HANDBOOK   Grammar   **3**

GRAMMAR

Nouns

people
- A word that names a person is called a **noun.**

    The baby is crying.

animals
- A word that names an animal is called a **noun.**

    The dog is barking.

places
- A word that names a place is called a **noun.**

    I went to the park today.

things
- A word that names a thing is called a **noun.**

    I like to ride my bicycle.

more than one
- Some nouns name more than one. Add the letter s to most nouns to name more than one.

    tiger—tigers

- Some nouns end with es to name more than one. Use the Spelling part of this **Writer's Handbook** for help spelling other nouns that name more than one.

    peach—peaches

- Some **nouns** change spelling to name more than one.

    child—children

GRAMMAR

Proper Nouns

- Some **proper nouns** are the names of special people. Names of special people begin with capital letters. — **people**

    Dave Thomas is my best friend.

- Some **proper nouns** are the names of special animals. Names of special animals begin with capital letters. — **animals**

    There is a famous dog named Benji.

- Some **proper nouns** are the names of special places. Names of special places begin with capital letters. — **places**

    I was born in Florida.

- The names of days are **proper nouns**. The names of days begin with capital letters. — **days of the week**

    Sunday, Monday, Tuesday, Wednesday, Thursday, Friday, Saturday

- The names of holidays are **proper nouns**. All important words in the names of holidays begin with capital letters. — **holidays**

    We go on a picnic every Labor Day.

- The names of months are **proper nouns**. The names of months begin with capital letters. — **months of the year**

    January, February, March, April, May, June, July, August, September, October, November, December

WRITER'S HANDBOOK Grammar 5

GRAMMAR

Verbs

action verb
- An **action verb** is a word that tells what someone or something does.

    They jump over the big rock.

action that happens now
- Add s to an action verb that tells what one person, animal, or thing does.

    The boys climb the rope.
    The boy climbs the rope.

action that happened in the past
- Many verbs end with ed to tell about something that happened in the past. Use the Spelling part of this **Writer's Handbook** to help you spell verbs that tell about the past.

    Yesterday Kim walked to school.

is and are
- The verbs is and are tell what someone or something is like. They tell about now.

    He is very tall.
    They are short.

was and were
- The verbs was and were tell what someone or something was like. They tell about the past.

    She was cheerful yesterday.
    They were busy last night.

has, have, had
- The verbs has and have tell about now. The verb had tells about the past.

    She has a pet hamster.
    They have a pet hamster.
    They had a pet hamster last spring.

GRAMMAR

- The verbs come and run tell about now. The verbs came and ran tell about the past.

    Come to my birthday party today.

    I run home from school now.

    She came to my party last week.

    Yesterday he ran home from school.

come and run

- The verbs go and do tell about now. The verbs went and did tell about the past.

    I go to school today.

    Do your homework now.

    We went to a movie last night.

    I did my homework yesterday.

go and do

- The verbs see and give tell about now. The verbs saw and gave tell about the past.

    I see a squirrel in that tree.

    Give me your ticket now, please.

    She saw a bird this morning.

    I gave her a present last year.

see and give

- Has, have, and had can be **helping verbs.** They can work with other verbs to show action that happened in the past.

    The rain has watered the flowers.

    The snow had covered the trees.

    The boys have finished the snowman.

helping verbs

- A **contraction** is a short way to write two words. An **apostrophe** (') takes the place of one or more letters that are left out.

    I do not want a snack.

    I don't want a snack.

contraction

WRITER'S HANDBOOK   Grammar   7

GRAMMAR

Pronouns

pronoun
- A **pronoun** is a word that takes the place of a noun. <u>He</u>, <u>she</u>, <u>it</u>, <u>they</u>, <u>I</u>, and <u>me</u> are pronouns.

> James ran home.
> He ran home.

I
- The word <u>I</u> takes the place of some nouns. Use <u>I</u> in the naming part of a sentence.

> I went to the store.

me
- The word <u>me</u> takes the place of some nouns. Use <u>me</u> in the telling part of a sentence.

> My mom drove me to school.

Describing Words

describing word
- A **describing word** tells about a noun.

> The sun is bright.

shape
- Some describing words tell about shape.

> The ball is round.

color
- Some describing words tell about color.

> The sky is blue.

size
- Some describing words tell about size.

> The tiny mouse is in my pocket.

number
- Some describing words tell <u>how many</u>.

> There are five fish in the pond.

WRITER'S HANDBOOK Grammar

GRAMMAR

- Some describing words tell how something tastes.   **taste**

    Lemons are sour .

- Some describing words tell how something smells.   **smell**

    Flowers smell fresh .

- Some describing words tell how something feels.   **feel**

    The baby's skin is smooth .

- Some describing words tell how something sounds.   **sound**

    She speaks in a quiet voice.

- Some describing words tell about feelings.   **feelings**

    Susan is happy .

- A describing word that ends with <u>er</u> compares two things.   **er**

    John is taller than Bill.

- A describing word that ends with <u>est</u> compares more than two things.   **est**

    John is the tallest boy in the class.

MECHANICS

Capital Letters

sentences
- A sentence begins with a capital letter.

  We went to the park yesterday.

names of people and animals
- The names of special people and animals begin with capital letters.

  My sister's name is Pam.

  I read a book about Koko the ape.

I
- The word I is always written as a capital letter.

  John and I play baseball together.

titles of people
- The title of a person, such as Mr., Mrs., Ms., Miss, or Dr., begins with a capital letter.

  Our teacher's name is Mr. Jones.

places
- The name of a special place begins with a capital letter.

  I live on Elm Street.

days of the week
- The name of each day of the week begins with a capital letter.

  Mary goes to ballet class every Tuesday.

  Sunday, Monday, Tuesday, Wednesday, Thursday, Friday, Saturday

months of the year
- The name of each month of the year begins with a capital letter.

  My birthday is in August.

MECHANICS

January, February, March, April,
May, June, July, August, September,
October, November, December

- Each important word in the name of a holiday begins with a capital letter.   **holidays**

  We see fireworks on the Fourth of July.

- Capital letters are used in the <u>heading</u>, the <u>greeting</u>, and the <u>closing</u> of a letter.   **parts of a letter**

> Dear Sharon,
>   I had a great time at your party!
>   Your friend,
>   David

- The first word, the last word, and each important word in a title begin with capital letters.   **titles of books, stories, and poems**

  I read <u>Secret of the Cave</u>.

End Marks

- A statement tells something. It ends with a **period (.)**.   **sentences**

  The party is on Saturday.

- A question asks something. It ends with a **question mark (?)**.

  How tall are you?

MECHANICS

- An exclamation shows strong feeling. It ends with an **exclamation point (!)**.

    I love going to the beach!

titles of people
- Most titles of people are followed by a **period (.)**.

    Mrs. Smith   Ms. Douglas
    Mr. Glinos   Dr. Trent

Commas

envelope
- Use a **comma (,)** between the city and the state in an address.

    Mark Reed
    5 Lee Road
    Orlando, Florida 32803

friendly letter
- Use a **comma (,)** between the day and the year in the heading of a letter.

    April 12, 1990

- Use a **comma (,)** after the greeting and the closing of a letter.

    Dear Jane,   Your friend,

Apostrophe

contraction
- Use an **apostrophe (')** in a contraction to take the place of a letter or letters that are left out.

    are not—aren't   did not—didn't

USAGE

Troublesome Words

- The words <u>I</u> and <u>me</u> take the place of your name. Use <u>I</u> in the naming part of a sentence. Use <u>me</u> in the telling part of a sentence.

    <u>I</u> like to skate.

    Julie went skating with <u>me</u>.

    I and me

- When you tell about another person and yourself, name yourself last.

    Mom and <u>I</u> went to the store.

    Billy played with Terry and <u>me</u>.

- The words <u>there</u>, <u>their</u>, and <u>they're</u> sound the same, but they have different meanings.

    <u>There</u> is a bird in the tree.

    I went to <u>their</u> house for dinner.

    <u>They're</u> going on a trip.

    there, their, they're

- The words <u>to</u>, <u>too</u>, and <u>two</u> sound the same, but they have different meanings.

    I wanted <u>to</u> bake something.

    I baked the biscuits <u>too</u> long.

    I ate <u>two</u> biscuits for breakfast.

    to, too, two

WRITER'S HANDBOOK

USAGE

Agreement

pronouns
- A **pronoun** is a word that takes the place of a noun. He, she, it, and they are pronouns. He and she tell about people. It tells about animals and things. They tells about more than one.

>He ran to the bus stop.
>
>She rode the bus.
>
>It was yellow.
>
>They went to school.

nouns and verbs
- Add s to an action verb that tells what one person, animal, or thing does. Do not add s to an action verb that tells about more than one.

>One frog hops away.
>
>Six frogs hop away.

is and are
- The verbs is and are tell about now. Use is with nouns that tell about one. Use are with nouns that tell about more than one.

>She is happy today.
>
>Her friends are happy, too.

was and were
- The verbs was and were tell about the past. Use was with nouns that name one. Use were with nouns that name more than one.

>One bird was in the tree this morning.
>
>Many birds were in the tree yesterday.

USAGE

- Use <u>has</u> to tell about one. Use <u>have</u> to tell about more than one. Use <u>had</u> to tell about one or more than one. <u>Had</u> tells about the past.

    The boy has a bicycle.

    Bicycles have wheels.

    Yesterday he had a flat tire.

has, have, had

- The verbs <u>come</u> and <u>run</u> tell about now. Add <u>s</u> to <u>come</u> and <u>run</u> to tell about one.

    The girl runs.

    Three girls run.

come and run

- The verbs <u>go</u> and <u>do</u> tell about now. To make <u>go</u> and <u>do</u> tell about one, change them to <u>goes</u> and <u>does</u>.

    We go swimming.

    She goes swimming.

    They do the backstroke.

    He does a swan dive.

go and do

- The verbs <u>see</u> and <u>give</u> tell about now. Add <u>s</u> to <u>see</u> and <u>give</u> to tell about one.

    They see a plane.

    He sees a bird.

    They give presents to each other.

    He gives a present to me.

see and give

COMPOSITION

Sentence

sentence
- A **sentence** is a group of words that tells a complete thought. It tells what someone or something is or does. A sentence begins with a capital letter. It ends with an end mark.

> **Writer's Guide: Sentence About a Picture**
> 1. Choose an idea.
> 2. Draw a picture that shows your idea.
> 3. Write a sentence that tells the main idea of your picture.
> 4. Be sure your sentence tells a complete thought.

capital letter — I like to ride my bike with my friend. — **end mark**

COMPOSITION

Paragraph

- A **paragraph** is a group of sentences that tells about one main idea. A paragraph begins with a topic sentence. The **topic sentence** tells the main idea. The other sentences are called detail sentences. **Detail sentences** tell about the main idea.

paragraph

Writer's Guide: Paragraph

1. Write a topic sentence that tells the main idea of your paragraph.
2. Indent the first line.
3. Write detail sentences that tell about the main idea.

topic sentence — Tigers hunt for their food. They hunt at night. Tigers can see well in the dark.
detail sentences — They also hear and smell things that are far away. These things help tigers find their food. Tigers can run very fast. This helps them catch their food.

COMPOSITION

How-to Paragraph

how-to paragraph
- In a **how-to paragraph,** a writer gives directions that tell how to make or do something. The steps are in order.

Writer's Guide: How-to Paragraph

1. Write a sentence to name your topic.
2. Write a sentence that tells what things are needed. This is the first step.
3. Write steps in the correct order to tell how to make or do something.
4. Use the words <u>first</u>, <u>next</u>, <u>then</u>, and <u>last</u> to show the order of the steps.

topic sentence — How would you like to make a bird feeder? **things that are needed** — First, get a pine cone, string, peanut butter, a spoon, and birdseed. **steps** — Next, tie the string around one end of the pine cone. Put peanut butter on the pine cone. Then, roll the pine cone in birdseed. Last, hang your bird feeder in a tree. You and the birds will enjoy your bird feeder.

COMPOSITION

Paragraph That Tells How Things Are Alike

- In a **paragraph that tells how things are alike,** a writer shows how two people, animals, places, or things are alike.

paragraph that tells how things are alike

> **Writer's Guide: Paragraph That Tells How Things Are Alike**
>
> 1. Write a topic sentence. Name a way that two people, animals, places, or things are alike.
> 2. Write detail sentences. Explain how the two people, animals, places, or things are alike.

topic sentence — My sister and I look alike. We both have long, brown hair. She has blue eyes and so do I. My sister and I are both tall and thin. — **detail sentences**

WRITER'S HANDBOOK Composition

COMPOSITION

Paragraph That Tells How Things Are Different

paragraph that tells how things are different

- In a **paragraph that tells how things are different,** a writer shows how two people, animals, places, or things are different from each other.

> **Writer's Guide: Paragraph That Tells How Things Are Different**
>
> 1. Write a topic sentence. Name a way that two people, animals, places, or things are different.
> 2. Write detail sentences. Explain how the two people, animals, places or things are different.

topic sentence — A duck and a chicken look different from each other.

detail sentences — A duck has a flat bill. A chicken has a small, pointy beak. A duck has wide, webbed feet that help it swim. A chicken has thin toes with claws on the ends.

COMPOSITION

Paragraph That Describes

- In a **paragraph that describes,** a writer describes a person, an animal, a place, or a thing. The writer uses describing words that help the reader <u>see</u>, <u>hear</u>, <u>taste</u>, <u>smell</u>, and <u>feel</u>.

paragraph that describes

Writer's Guide: Paragraph That Describes

1. Write a topic sentence to tell whom or what your paragraph is about.
2. Write sentences that tell what the person, animal, place, or thing is like.
3. Use words that give a good word picture.

A rocket is ready to blast off into space. The tall rocket looks like a giant jet. There are many big engines. Suddenly they roar! The ground shakes. White smoke and yellow and orange flames come out of the engines. The rocket goes up slowly. It leaves a smoky smell behind in the air.

topic sentence

describing words in detail sentences

WRITER'S HANDBOOK Composition 21

COMPOSITION

Journal

journal
- In a **journal,** a writer tells about important things that happen.

Writer's Guide: Journal Entry

1. Write the date.
2. Write about important things that happened.
3. Tell why these things are important to you.

date — September 21, 1993

what happened — Today a new family moved in next door. They have a boy my age. His name is Jamie. He likes to play baseball and read books. I do too. I think Jamie and I are going to be good friends.

why it is important

COMPOSITION

Personal Story

- In a **personal story,** a writer tells about something that has happened in his or her life. A personal story can tell how the writer feels about something.

personal story

> **Writer's Guide: Personal Story**
>
> 1. Think of things that have happened in your life. Choose one of these things to tell about.
> 2. Write your story in the order in which things happened. Use time-order words like <u>first</u>, <u>next</u>, <u>then</u>, and <u>last</u>.
> 3. Use words like <u>I</u> and <u>me</u> to tell about yourself.

    One Saturday my sister Judy and I rode in Mr. Reed's balloon. First, we got the balloon ready. Next, we got into a basket tied to the balloon. Then, the balloon went up into the sky. I waved to my friends. They were really surprised!
    Mr. Reed helped us land the balloon in a big field. When I got out, I helped carry the lunches for a picnic. People ran over to see our big balloon.

Time-order words help show the order in which things happen.

WRITER'S HANDBOOK Composition   **23**

COMPOSITION

Story

story

- A **story** tells about real or make-believe events. A story has a beginning, a middle, and an ending.

Writer's Guide: Story

1. Write a beginning. Tell who the characters are, where the story takes place, and what the problem is.
2. Write the middle. Tell what happens to the characters. Tell what they do.
3. Write the ending. Tell how the problem is solved.
4. Write a title for your story.

title

Fox to the Rescue

beginning

Mouse and Fox lived in a beautiful forest. One evening, Fox came to visit his friend Mouse. Mouse had just woken up from her nap. She couldn't get out of her house, though. A big rock had rolled into her doorway. She pushed and puffed, but she couldn't move it.

middle

When Fox saw the big rock, he knew Mouse was trapped! Then Fox thought of a way to help.

ending

Fox gathered all his strength and pushed the rock away. Mouse was so happy! She hurried outside to play with Fox.

WRITER'S HANDBOOK   Composition

COMPOSITION

Poem

- In a **poem,** a writer paints a picture with words. A poet often describes something in an interesting way. Some poems have rhyming words. These poems often have a **rhythm,** or **beat,** that makes them fun to read.

    Other poems do not rhyme. These poems use colorful words to give a good word picture.

Writer's Guide: Poem
1. Use colorful words to write a good word picture.
2. Use rhyming words if you want to.
3. Give your poem a title.

poem that rhymes

New Shoes
When I woke up and dressed for school
I knew that it was Monday.
But when I put on my new shoes,
my feet still felt like Sunday.

poem that does not rhyme

Toad
Toad sits and sits and sits.
Sometimes he winks
and hops one hop.
Then he sits and sits and sits
again.
That's how it is with toads.

COMPOSITION

Riddle

riddle

- In a **riddle,** a writer gives clues. The clues help the reader guess who or what is being described.

Writer's Guide: Riddle

1. Write sentences that give clues about a person, animal, place, or thing.
2. Write a question at the end.
3. Write the answer on the back of your paper.

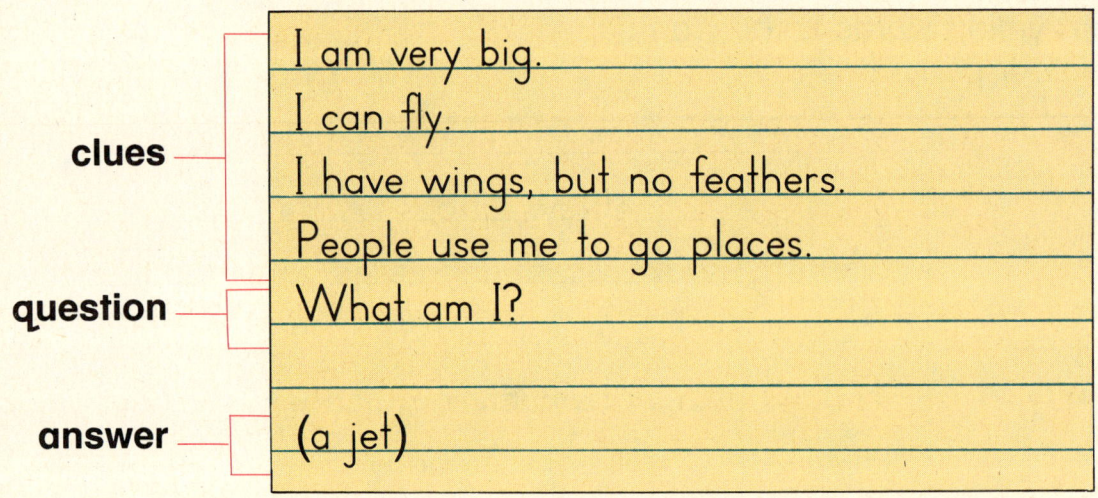

clues
- I am very big.
- I can fly.
- I have wings, but no feathers.
- People use me to go places.

question
- What am I?

answer
- (a jet)

COMPOSITION

Book Report

- In a **book report,** a writer tells what a book is about. It also tells what the writer thinks about the book.

book report

Writer's Guide: Book Report

1. Write the title of the book.
2. Write the author's name.
3. Write sentences that tell what the book is about. Tell about something that happens.
4. Write what you think about the book. Tell why you like or do not like the book.

Nate the Great and the Sticky Case — title

by Marjorie Weinman Sharmat — author

This book is about Nate and Sludge. Sludge is Nate's dog. Nate is looking for a lost stamp. His dog helps him. — about the book

This book is good because it is interesting. You will like this book if you like mystery stories. — what I think

COMPOSITION

Friendly Letter

friendly letter

- In a **friendly letter,** a writer writes to someone he or she knows. A friendly letter has five parts.

Writer's Guide: Friendly Letter

1. Write the date as the heading.
2. Write a greeting to say hello.
3. Write a friendly message in the body.
4. Write a closing to end your letter.
5. Sign your name under the closing.

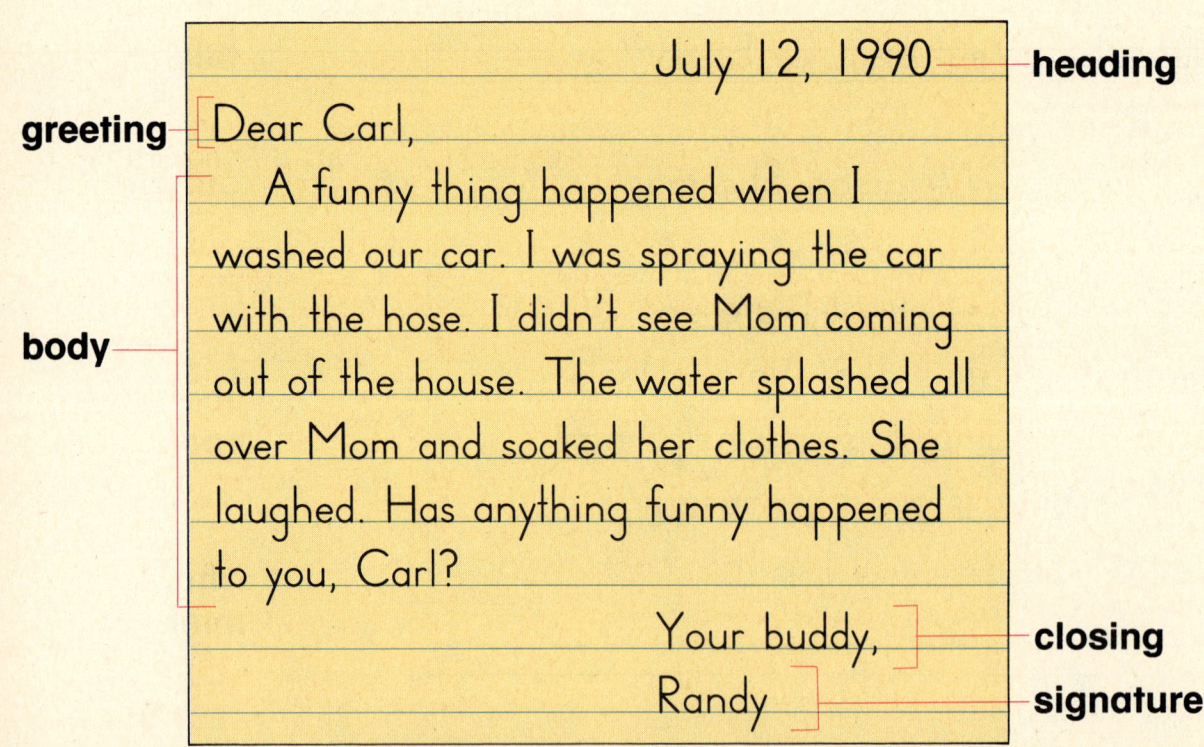

28 WRITER'S HANDBOOK Composition

COMPOSITION

Invitation

- In an **invitation**, a writer invites someone to come somewhere or to do something. An invitation has five parts.

invitation

Writer's Guide: Invitation

1. Write the date as the heading.
2. Write a greeting to say hello.
3. Write the body. Tell <u>who</u> is invited. Tell <u>what</u> the invitation is for. Tell <u>when</u> and <u>where</u> the event will take place.
4. Write a closing to end your invitation.
5. Sign your name under the closing.

---

heading: February 2, 1990

greeting: Dear Mary,

body:
I am having a Valentine's Day party. It will be on February 14. The party is at 3:00 P.M. at my house. I live at 44 Green Street. Can you come to my party?

closing: Your friend,
signature: Michelle

COMPOSITION

Thank-You Note

thank-you note
- In a **thank-you note,** a writer thanks someone for something. A thank-you note has five parts.

> **Writer's Guide: Thank-You Note**
>
> 1. Write the date as the heading.
> 2. Write a greeting to say hello.
> 3. Write the body. Tell what you are thanking the person for.
> 4. Write a closing to end your note.
> 5. Sign your name under the closing.

February 20, 1993 — **heading**

greeting — Dear Michelle,

body — Thank you for inviting me to your party. It was fun! I still have the red balloon I got at the party. I put it in my bedroom.

Your friend, — **closing**

Mary — **signature**

COMPOSITION

Envelope

- An **envelope** is used to send a letter. — envelope
- The **return address** names who is sending the letter. — return address
- The **mailing address** names who will get the letter. — mailing address

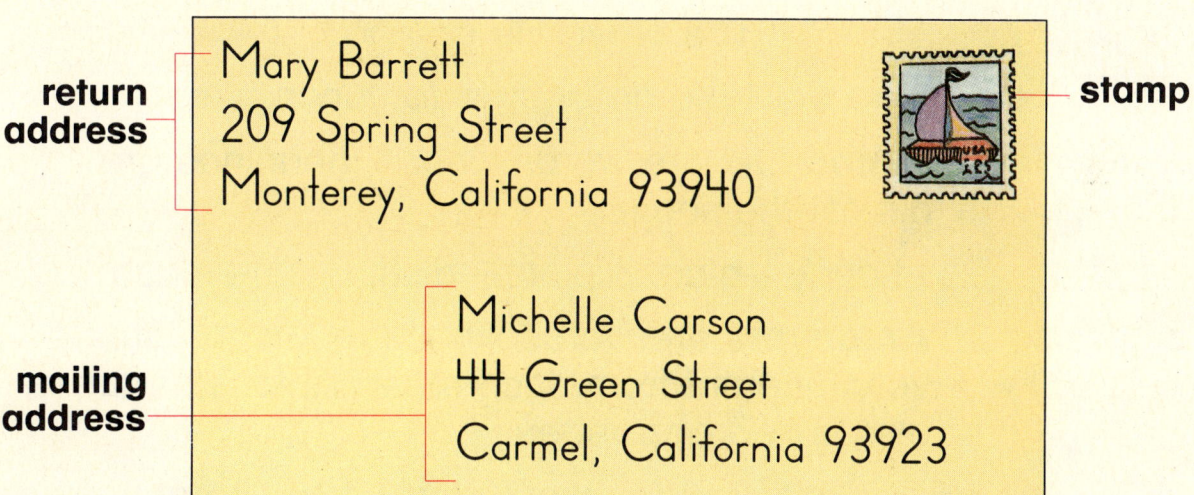

return address
- Mary Barrett
- 209 Spring Street
- Monterey, California 93940

stamp

mailing address
- Michelle Carson
- 44 Green Street
- Carmel, California 93923

VOCABULARY

Vocabulary

rhyming words
- **Rhyming words** end with the same sound.

  be—me   bat—hat   hot—pot

compound words
- A **compound word** is made up of two words. The two words together make a new word.

  foot + ball = football

words that have more than one meaning
- Some words have more than one meaning.

  The crayon is orange.

  I ate an orange for lunch.

synonyms
- **Synonyms** are words whose meanings are almost the same.

  happy—glad   plate—dish   run—dash

antonyms
- **Antonyms** are words whose meanings are very different from each other. Antonyms are also called **opposites.**

  hot—cold   wet—dry   full—empty

prefixes
- A **prefix** is a group of letters added to the beginning of a word. A prefix changes the meaning of a word. The prefix un means "not." The prefix re means "again."

  untie   retie

suffixes
- A suffix is a group of letters added to the end of a word. A suffix changes the meaning of a word. The suffix less means "without." The suffix ful means "full of."

  hopeless   hopeful

SPELLING

Study Steps to Learn a Word

Say the word. Listen to each sound. Think about what the word means.

Look at the word. See how the letters are made. Try to see the word in your mind.

Spell the word to yourself. Think about the way each sound is spelled.

Write the word. Copy the word. Check the way you made your letters. Write the word again.

Check your learning. Cover the word and write it. Did you spell it correctly? If not, do these steps until you know how to spell the word.

SPELLING

How to Keep Your Own Spelling Word List

You may want to keep your own spelling word list in a notebook. You can put your words in ABC order. You might list the same kinds of words together. Follow these steps.

1. Check your writing for words you may have spelled wrong. Draw a line around each word you are not sure about.

   > I like to (rite) stories.

2. Find out how to spell the word.
   - Look up the word in a dictionary or the **Word Book.**
   - Ask a teacher or a classmate for help.

   > write
   > I like to (rite) stories.

3. Write the word in your notebook.
   - Spell the word correctly.
   - Use the word in a sentence that shows what the word means.

   > I like to write poems.

4. Look at your spelling word list to check your spelling when you write.

   > She likes to write about animals.

SPELLING

Troublesome Words to Spell

A
afraid
again
almost
always
another
around

B
because
before
behind
better
broke
brought

C
children
could

D
daddy
dropped

E
every
everybody
everyone

F
family
far
finally
fine
friends

G
getting
goes
guess

H
hair
happened
having
helping
high
himself
hours

I
inside

K
keep
knew
know

L
laughing

M
maybe
might
minute
minutes
money
morning
mouth

P
party
people
person
please
practice
pretty
probably

Q
quick

R
ready
real
really
right
running

S
scared
shirt
sitting
sky
somebody
someone
stayed
stopped
summer

T
their
thought
threw
through
throw
throws
tired
together
tomorrow
too
tried
turned

U
until
upon

W
waiting
watch
where
while
white
woke
woman
wrong

Y
years

WRITER'S HANDBOOK

SPELLING

Vowel Sounds

short vowel sounds
- The **short vowel sounds** are usually spelled with one letter. These sounds can be spelled with a, e, i, o, or u.

    bad   net   fit   stop   cut

long vowel sounds
- **Long vowel sounds** are usually spelled with more than one letter.

long a
- Here are three ways to spell the **long a** sound.

    a-consonant-e, as in bake
    ai, as in rain
    ay, as in say

long e
- Here are four ways to spell the **long e** sound.

    e, as in me
    ee, as in free
    ea, as in each
    y, as in story

long i
- Here are four ways to spell the **long i** sound.

    i-consonant-e, as in five
    i, as in find
    igh, as in right
    y, as in sky

long o
- Here are four ways to spell the **long o** sound.

    o-consonant-e, as in bone
    o, as in no
    oa, as in toast
    ow, as in grow

SPELLING

- Here are three ways to spell the **oo** sound.

    oo, as in food
    u-consonant-e, as in rude, tube
    ew, as in blew

oo sound

Letter Combinations

- Here are three ways to spell the sound you hear at the end of father.

    ar, as in dollar
    er, as in mother
    or, as in sailor

other vowel sounds

Consonants

- A **consonant cluster** is made up of consonants that you write together. You hear the sounds of the letters together. Here are some consonant clusters.

    br, as in brother   **sm,** as in small
    fr, as in from   **sp,** as in spot and wasp
    gl, as in glad   **st,** as in stand and most
    gr, as in great   **sw,** as in swim
    pl, as in place   **tr,** as in true
    pr, as in pretty

consonant clusters

WRITER'S HANDBOOK Spelling **37**

SPELLING

Verbs

adding ed and ing

- Many verbs end with <u>ed</u> to tell about the past.
    walk—walked   climb—climbed
- If a verb ends in a short vowel and a consonant, double the final consonant. Then add <u>ed</u> or <u>ing</u>.
    stop—stopped   run—running

Nouns

- Most nouns end with <u>s</u> to mean more than one.
    cat—cats   lake—lakes
- If a noun ends in <u>s</u>, <u>x</u>, <u>ch</u>, or <u>sh</u>, add <u>es</u> to name more than one.
    bus—buses   fox—foxes
    lunch—lunches   dish—dishes
- If a noun ends in a consonant and <u>y</u>, change <u>y</u> to <u>i</u>. Then add <u>es</u> to name more than one.
    story—stories   lady—ladies

spelling changes

- Change the spelling of some nouns to name more than one.
    woman—women   child—children

Describing Words

adding er and est

- If a describing word ends in a consonant and <u>y</u>, change <u>y</u> to <u>i</u>. Then add <u>er</u> or <u>est</u>.
    happy—happier—happiest

GLOSSARY

Contents

Composition Terms — 2
Literary Terms — 8

Name _____

Composition Terms

DRAFTING You make a first try at writing when you are drafting. This boy is using a list to write his first draft.

```
Topic
 going to summer camp
Details
 3 cooked hot dogs
 1 slept in a cabin
 2 learned how to swim
```

EDITOR'S MARKS Editor's marks are the marks you use as you revise and proofread your writing.

Use these marks when you revise.

∧	Add something.
℮	Take out something.
⌒	Change something.
↺	Move something.

Use these marks when you proofread.

≡	Use a capital letter.
⊙	Add a period.
∧	Add something.
℮	Take out something.
⌒	Change something.
◯	Check the spelling.
¶	Indent the paragraph.

GLOSSARY

FINAL DRAFT   The final copy of your writing that is ready to be published is called a final draft. This example shows the final draft of the boy's story.

> I went to summer camp and slept in a cabin. I learned how to swim. We roasted hot dogs at night.

FIRST DRAFT   The first copy of your writing, in which you try to get your thoughts on paper, is called a first draft. This first draft still needs a little work.

> I like swimming. Swimming is fun. The water is cold. I don't mind.

PREWRITING   Prewriting is the part of the writing process in which you think of ideas and put them in order. These examples show ways to put ideas in order.

- **chart**   A chart can be used to write facts or ideas in groups.

Birds in My Neighborhood

Birds	Color of Feathers
robin	brown, orange
blue jay	blue, black, white
cardinal	red, brown

- **drawing** You make a drawing by writing a topic in the middle and adding details around it.

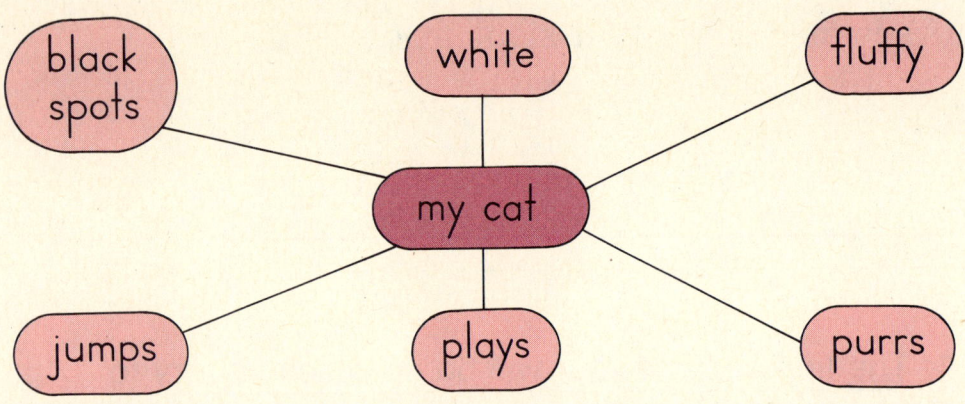

- **list** A list is a way of writing down ideas about a topic.

> Topic
> going to the zoo
> Details
> heard the lions
> saw some monkeys
> rode an elephant
> saw some snakes

- **story map** You can use a story map to put the parts of a story in order. A story map shows what happens in the beginning, the middle, and the ending.

Beginning	
Who:	an elf, a dragon, a hunter
Where and when:	deep in the forest, long ago
Problem:	The dragon gets caught by the hunter.

Middle
What happens: The hunter ties up the dragon with rope. The elf sees his friend the dragon. The elf goes to get help.

Ending
How the problem is solved: All the elves in the forest come to help the dragon. They cut the ropes while the hunter sleeps. The dragon flies away.

- **word map** A word map is a picture with words that helps a writer remember just how something looked. A word map helps a writer write a clear word picture.

GLOSSARY 5

PROOFREADING When you check your writing to correct mistakes in capital letters, end marks, and spelling, you are proofreading. Look at the change in the first letter.

PUBLISHING When you share with others a final draft of what you have written, you are publishing. This boy is sharing his story by reading it aloud.

RESPONDING Responding is thinking about your writing and talking about it with others. It is a way to get ideas for making your writing better. The boy is telling the girl why he likes her story.

RESPONSE GROUP A response group is a group of students who help make each other's work better by asking and answering questions about it. These children are responding to a question about a story.

REVISING You think about how to put ideas in order and how to make the writing clearer when you are revising. Look at how this change makes the story clearer.

> I went to lunch with John and Alicia. We ate cheeseburgers. John paid for the lunches. Alicia had salad too. ⎤—Move

TOPIC The idea you choose to write about is called a topic. Look at the list of story ideas. One of these will be the topic for a story.

> 1. riding in a balloon
> 2. winning my baseball game
> 3. having lunch with my friends

WRITING PROCESS The writing process is a way to write by following certain stages. The stages are prewriting, drafting, responding and revising, proofreading, and publishing. A writer can go back and forth between the stages to write a final draft.

Literary Terms

CHARACTERS The people or animals in a story, poem, or play are called characters. Writers can make their characters seem real. How the characters think, feel, and act is important. In the story "Carmen's Surprise," Carmen misses her grandfather. This causes her to make something special for her grandfather.

RHYME A rhyme is a short poem. The lines end with words that have the same ending sounds. These two lines make a rhyme.

> **The Hummingbird**
> A hummingbird can zip and zoom.
> This tiny bird needs lots of room!

RHYMING WORDS Rhyming words are words that end with the same sounds. In the rhyme about the hummingbird, zoom and room are rhyming words.

SETTING The setting is when and where a story takes place. Writers use words and pictures to tell us the setting of a story. In the story "Going to the Museum," James Ramsey writes the words "when I lived in New York." These words tell us that James's story happened some time ago in New York. The pictures he drew show what the museum looks like.

WORD PICTURE A word picture is a way of using words that helps you see exactly what something looks like. In the book Cat and Canary, Michael Foreman tells us that "All the birds flocked to his roof. Most days his roof was a blizzard of birds." You can picture a lot of birds in your mind as you read these words.

WORD BOOK

Contents

What Is a Word Book?   2
How to Use Your Word Book   3

Name _____

What Is a Word Book?

The **Word Book** is a list of words. The words are in ABC order. Each of these words is called an **entry word**. The Word Book lists words that have almost the same meaning. Sometimes the Word Book lists opposites.

Look at this example from the Word Book.

The entry word is in color. It is used in a sentence to show what it means.

| little | Large trees grow from little seeds. |

Words that mean almost the same as the entry word are in a list. Each word is used in a sentence.

short	The short person could not reach the top shelf.
small	A small child was going to school for the first time.
tiny	The tiny ant eats a bread crumb.

Opposites are also listed.

OPPOSITES: big, giant, huge, large, tall

How to Use Your Word Book

Pretend that you write some sentences about a baby animal. You read your sentences. You see that you used the word little too many times. You can use the **Word Book** to find words that mean almost the same as little. Follow these steps.

1. Find the word little. Remember that words in the Word Book are in ABC order. To find little, look under the letter L.

2. Read the entry carefully. Choose the words from the list that will make your writing clearer and stronger.

Remember: Not every word in the list will have the meaning you want. Look at the example on page 10. Which words from the list for little fit best in sentences about a kitten? Tell why.

afraid — bright

A

afraid — Sue is afraid to go into the dark room.
frightened — Ed is not frightened of the big spider.
scared — The dog barked, and the mail carrier was scared.

OPPOSITES: brave, fearless, unafraid

B

bad — We cannot have a picnic because the weather is bad.
awful — The trash has an awful smell.
dreadful — I caught a dreadful cold last winter.
naughty — The naughty child took his friend's toy.
terrible — There was a terrible storm last night.

OPPOSITES: good, nice, wonderful

big — The dog digs a big hole.
great — A great number of people watch the parade.
huge — The huge wagon holds many things.
large — The large man weighs 200 pounds.

OPPOSITES: little, short, small, tiny

brave — The brave fire fighters put out the fire.
bold — The deer was bold to eat from my hand.
daring — The boy made a daring leap over the big hole.

OPPOSITES: afraid, cowardly, timid

bright — We close our eyes because the sun is so bright.
brilliant — A rainbow has brilliant colors.
shiny — The moonlight makes the lake look shiny.

OPPOSITES: dim, dull

C

call	I **call** to Sara to come out to play.
cry	They cry to the fire fighter for help.
scream	We scream loudly at the game.
shout	Shout to your friend across the street.
yell	We yell for our team to win.

OPPOSITES: mumble, whisper

catch	**Catch** a football with your hands.
grab	Grab the vase before it falls.
grasp	They easily grasp the large rubber ball.

OPPOSITES: drop, miss, throw

cold	The **cold** ice cream hurts my teeth.
chilly	The chilly air makes me shiver.
cool	Jimmy feels cool without his coat.
icy	I rub my icy hands together to warm them.
unheated	The unheated water is cold.

OPPOSITES: heated, hot, warm

collect	Joey likes to **collect** stamps.
gather	We gather flowers from the garden.
get	I get the eggs the hens lay.

OPPOSITES: leave, scatter

cook	Dad and I **cook** the peas for dinner.
bake	Mother and Sara bake a cake.
boil	Boil the eggs in water for three minutes.
fry	We fry eggs in a pan.
roast	We always roast a turkey for Thanksgiving.

cry	The babies **cry** for their mothers.
sob	Lucy and Danny sob at the bad news.
weep	They weep at the sad story.

OPPOSITES: chuckle, giggle, laugh

cut   fast

cut	Tony and Jerry cut the cake.
carve	Carve a toy out of wood.
chop	Chop the wood with an ax.
slice	I slice the bread for dinner.
split	I split the pie seven ways.
trim	We trim the bushes once a month.

E

| easy | Our spelling test was easy. |
| simple | It is simple to learn how to use a telephone. |

OPPOSITES: difficult, hard, tough

eat	We eat when we are hungry.
feast	We always feast at Thanksgiving.
gobble	The dogs gobble the food.
nibble	Rabbits nibble on carrots.
taste	Taste the warm tomato soup.

| exciting | The boat ride is exciting. |
| thrilling | We think the roller coaster is thrilling! |

OPPOSITES: boring, dull

F

fall	Snowflakes fall softly from the sky.
drop	Apples drop from the tree before they are picked.
sink	The pennies sink to the bottom of the pool.
trip	The children trip on the bus step.
tumble	The clowns tumble over each other.

OPPOSITES: climb, rise

fast	The fox ran fast to get away from the farmer.
quick	The magician was so quick that we didn't see the trick.
speedy	The speedy car won the race.
swift	The swift cat caught the mouse.

OPPOSITE: slow

WORD BOOK

fat	We bought a **fat** turkey for Thanksgiving.	**fly**	Some squirrels **fly** through the air.
chubby	The baby has <u>chubby</u> cheeks.	glide	Hawks <u>glide</u> through the air without flapping their wings.
stout	Winnie-the-Pooh is <u>stout</u> because he eats a lot of honey.	soar	The planes <u>soar</u> out of sight.

OPPOSITES: skinny, slender, thin

		frighten	Loud noises **frighten** some birds.
favorite	My **favorite** fruit is a ripe peach.	scare	We <u>scare</u> each other on Halloween.
special	Going to the beach is a <u>special</u> treat.	startle	The dogs <u>startle</u> the sleeping cat.
find	Please **find** my old skates.	**full**	When everyone is home, our house is **full**.
discover	We <u>discover</u> a secret door in our house.	crowded	There are no seats on the <u>crowded</u> bus.
uncover	We <u>uncover</u> a lost watch in the sand.	filled	The heavy bucket is <u>filled</u> with water.

OPPOSITES: bury, hide, lose

		loaded	The dump truck is <u>loaded</u> with dirt.
flat	The tabletop is **flat**.	packed	My suitcase is <u>packed</u> with clothes.
even	A pilot must land his plane on <u>even</u> ground.	stuffed	The pillow is <u>stuffed</u> with feathers.
smooth	The window glass feels <u>smooth</u>.		

OPPOSITES: bumpy, uneven   **OPPOSITE: empty**

fun

fun	There were **fun** games to play at the fair.
amusing	The amusing clown does funny tricks.
enjoyable	We had an enjoyable visit with my uncle.
exciting	There are many exciting things to do in New York City.

OPPOSITES: boring, dull

G

get	I hope I **get** a present for my birthday.
capture	The police capture the bank robber.
earn	They earn money for each tomato they pick.
receive	We receive letters in the mail.

OPPOSITES: give, lose, send

give

give	I **give** my mother a picture for her birthday.
present	They present an award to the winner.

OPPOSITES: get, take

go

go	**Go** to the library to find books.
depart	We depart for school in the morning.
leave	Buses leave for New York every hour.

OPPOSITES: halt, remain, stay, stop

good

good	Ripe, juicy apples taste **good**.
fine	Abraham Lincoln was a fine President.
great	When I woke up, I felt great.
nice	It is nice to know that you like me.
pleasant	We had a pleasant time at the park.

OPPOSITES: awful, bad, dreadful, terrible

happy — jump

H

happy — Sunshine makes me feel happy.
cheerful — I feel cheerful when I hear birds sing.
glad — Betty is glad that she won a prize.
merry — My aunt's eyes were merry as she told her favorite joke.
pleased — Trudy is pleased with her new puppy.

OPPOSITES: displeased, sad, unhappy

hard — Mom finds it hard to sleep when it is noisy.
difficult — It is difficult to put together the large puzzle.
tough — Learning to ski can be tough.

OPPOSITES: easy, simple

hit — Hit the nail with the hammer.
beat — The boy beat the drum.
kick — Kick the ball to me.
knock — Knock on the door before you come in.
slap — Beavers slap the water with their tails.
strike — Strike the ball with the bat.

house — We moved into a new house last summer.
cabin — We have a log cabin in the mountains.
cottage — The little cottage has only one bedroom.
home — Come to my home for dinner.

J

jump — The fish jump out of the water.
hop — The birds hop onto my window sill looking for seeds.
leap — The horses leap over the fence.
spring — The frogs spring into the pond.

kind   make

K

kind	A **kind** man took care of the stray cat.
gentle	Be **gentle** when you hold the puppy.
nice	Patty is **nice** to help me clean my room.
warm	Mom gives me a **warm** smile every morning.

OPPOSITES: cold, cruel, mean, unkind

L

lake	We went to the **lake** for a picnic.
pond	The ducks swim in the **pond**.
pool	There is a **pool** of water by the waterfall.

laugh	We always **laugh** at Tony's jokes.
chuckle	People **chuckle** at the funny movie.
giggle	I **giggle** when I am tickled.
guffaw	The men **guffaw** at the silly clowns.

OPPOSITES: cry, sob, weep

little	Large trees grow from **little** seeds.
short	The **short** person could not reach the top shelf.
small	A **small** child was going to school for the first time.
tiny	The **tiny** ant eats a bread crumb.

OPPOSITES: big, giant, huge, large, tall

M

mad	I got **mad** when I couldn't go skating.
angry	When Kate gets **angry**, she yells.
furious	Vera was **furious** when Jane took her crayons.

OPPOSITES: glad, happy, pleased

make	The campers **make** a bench out of wood.
build	The squirrels **build** their nests with leaves.
form	We **form** a circle to play the game.
shape	**Shape** the clay into a mountain.

OPPOSITES: break, destroy, ruin, wreck

mean	It is **mean** to hurt someone's feelings.	**plain**	She wore a **plain** white dress with her fancy new shoes.
cruel	It is cruel to tease the dog.	ordinary	The horse looked ordinary until it began to fly!
nasty	The nasty weather ended our picnic.	simple	The sign was simple and clear: "Don't Litter."
unkind	The man looked unkind because he never smiled.		

OPPOSITES: gentle, good, nice, kind **OPPOSITES: fancy, pretty**

N

nice	It was a **nice** day to go to the beach.	**pretty**	She wears a **pretty** dress to the party.
beautiful	It is a beautiful day for a picnic.	beautiful	The princess wore a beautiful golden crown.
fine	Lee did a fine job of cutting the grass.	lovely	We watched a lovely sunset.
lovely	We had a lovely time at the party.		
pleasant	The warm breeze feels pleasant.		

OPPOSITES: awful, bad, terrible, unpleasant **OPPOSITES: ordinary, plain, ugly**

P

part	The cat ate only **part** of the food in its bowl.	**pull**	I **pull** myself up with a rope.
piece	I ate a piece of bread.	drag	Ned and Tim drag the chair to the table because it is so heavy.
section	Who wants a section of my orange?	tug	The puppies tug at their mother's ears.

OPPOSITES: all, whole **OPPOSITES: push, shove**

push	The men **push** the big rock out of the way.	**R**	
move	Move your chair closer to the table.	road	Let's follow the old road to find out where it goes.
poke	I poke my finger into the sand.	highway	Many fast cars travel on the wide highway.
shove	Shove the packages into the bag.	street	This is the street where I live.
		way	This way leads to the park.

OPPOSITES: drag, pull, tug

put	**Put** the toys on the shelf.	**rock**	The waves rock our boat and make us all seasick.
lay	I lay my head on the pillow.	shake	Shake the paint to mix it.
place	Place the plates on the table.	sway	The trees sway when the wind blows.
set	They set the radio on the table.		

OPPOSITES: remove, take

run	We run as fast as we can in the race.
dash	Tina and John dash to the train.
gallop	The horses gallop toward the finish line.
hurry	They hurry to get there by five o'clock.
race	They race to get to school on time.

Q

quit	I **quit** playing the piano every day at 5:00 p.m.
stop	Stop making that awful noise.

OPPOSITES: begin, start

OPPOSITES: crawl, stroll, walk

S

sad	The bad news made Chris sad.
blue	I felt blue after our old dog died.
gloomy	The clouds make the day seem gloomy.
unhappy	Laurie was unhappy when her friend moved.

OPPOSITES: cheerful, glad, happy

said	I said that I would like some milk.
mumbled	We could not hear Rob's words when he mumbled.
told	He told an exciting story to our class.
whispered	Rosa whispered a secret in my ear.

save	I save some of my orange to eat later.
keep	I keep my pencils in a box in my desk.
store	Store your winter clothes in the empty closet.

see	They see the moon in the sky.
gaze	I gaze at the stars from my window.
notice	I notice you have a hole in your sock.
look	Look at the picture I painted.
peek	I peek around the tree and see my friends.
spot	Jenny and Tom spot the monkey in the picture.
stare	John and I stare at the huge rocket.
watch	We watch movies on television.

shine	The jewels in the king's crown shine.
gleam	Myra polishes the silver until you can see it gleam.
glow	Fireflies glow in the dark.
sparkle	Diamonds sparkle in the light.
twinkle	The stars in the sky twinkle at night.

smart

smart — A **smart** dog can learn new tricks.
intelligent — My dog learns quickly because he is intelligent.
clever — The clever boy thought of a way to escape from the giant.

OPPOSITES: dumb, silly

start — **Start** to run when you hear the whistle.
begin — The birds begin to sing before the sun comes up.

OPPOSITES: end, finish, quit, stop

stop — **Stop** the game after everyone has had a turn.
end — End the story now.
finish — I finish my homework before bedtime.
quit — They quit working at dinnertime.

OPPOSITES: begin, start

sudden

store — You can buy a doll in the **store**.
market — The corn in the market had just been picked.
shop — The shop on the corner sells gifts.

story — In the **story**, a duck and a goose fly around the world together.
report — Ben wrote a report about sharks.
tale — Phil told us a tale we found hard to believe.

strange — It was **strange** to see a squirrel eating from our cat's dish.
different — Grandpa looked different without his glasses.
odd — It is odd to see a cat and a dog playing together.
unusual — It was unusual for Tom to give me his favorite toy.

OPPOSITES: familiar, normal, ordinary

sudden — The car came to a **sudden** stop.
quick — The fox made a quick run for the woods.

OPPOSITES: expected

swim | | | want

swim	We swim in the lake in summer.	**throw**	Jim and Harry throw a ball back and forth.
paddle	I paddle across the pool with my arms.	pitch	Pitch the ball so that I can hit it.
splash	I splash around in the water.	toss	I toss a stick and my dog runs after it.

OPPOSITE: catch

T

turn	Please turn the radio dial to another station.
take	They take their coats from the closet.	spin	The tops spin so fast!
get	Get a seat now before they are all gone.	twist	I twist the lid to open the jar.

OPPOSITE: give

whirl	They whirl in a circle on the ice.
wind	Wind the yarn into a ball.

teach	The girls teach us swimming.
coach	Bill and Ann coach the swimming team.

W

walk	Kelly and Bryan walk to school every day.
march	The band members march in the parade.
step	Step around the hole in the ground.
stroll	Mom and Dad stroll together after dinner.

show	Show him how to set the table.
train	They train the monkeys to ride bikes.

terrific	I had a terrific time at the party.
fantastic	That was a fantastic movie!
great	It was great to see my old friends.
wonderful	Mom bakes wonderful muffins.

want	I want to go everywhere in our new car.
hope	I hope to see a funny movie on Saturday.
wish	The boys wish the rain would stop.

OPPOSITES: awful, bad, terrible

INDEX

EP = Extra Practice
G = Glossary
WB = Word Book
WH = Writer's Handbook

Adjectives. *See* Describing words.
Analyzing (studying) types of writing
    friendly letter, 114–115
    how-to paragraph, 266–267
    paragraph that describes, 160–161
    personal story, 60–61
    sentence about a picture, 10–11
    story, 214–216
Antonyms, 190, 193, 197, WH32
Art, 176, 232
Audience for writing, 2–5, 14, 65, 117, 164, 220, 270

Beginning, middle, ending of a story, 214–216, WH24
Book
    kinds of, 325
    parts of, 323

Capital letters, 284–301, WH10–11. *See also* Mechanics.
    in an address, 300–301, 309, EP48
    checking for, 22, 73, 126, 172, 228, 278, WH10–11
    in a friendly letter, 114, 298–299, 309, EP47, WH11
    I, 73, 96–97, 105, 109, 200, 286–287, 311, EP20, EP41, WH10
    recognition of, 283
    titles of books, stories, and poems, 296–297, 309, EP46, WH11
    using, 284–285, 305
Character. *See also* Glossary.
    definition, 214
Chart, 4, 162, 164–65, 250, 302
    using a, 328–329
Ciardi, John, 44
Cole, William, 191
Colorful words, using, 163, 194
Compare and contrast. *See* Paragraph.
Composition, WH16–31. *See also* Writing process.
    terms, G2–7
Compound words, 98, 105, WH32
Contractions, 248–249, 252, 257, 315, EP39, WH7, WH12
Cooperative learning, 11, 16, 19, 35, 46, 47, 98, 100, 117, 175, 192, 193, 231, 252, 282, 304
Cross-curriculum writing
    art, 176, 232
    health, 282
    mathematics, 76, 282

music, 26
physical education, 130
science, 26, 76
social studies, 130
Cumulative review, 106–109, 198–203, 310–315

de Regniers, Beatrice Schenk, 99, 303
Describing words, 178–189, 195, 202, 313, EP26–31, WH8
    connecting with writing, 193
    definition of, 178–179
    enrichment activities, language, 192–193
    with *er* and *est*, 188–189, 197, 203, 313, EP31, WH9
    for feelings, 186–187, 197, 203
    recognition of, 177
    for shape and color, 180–181, 196, EP27, WH8
    for size and number, 182–183, 196, EP28, WH8
    for taste, smell, feel, and sound, 184–185, 196, 202, EP29, WH9
Descriptive paragraph, 151–159, 173–174, 194, WH21
    analyzing (studying) a, 160–161
    writing a, 164–174
Details
    adding, 17, 120, 165, 221
    in order, 68
    paying attention to, 161, 162, 194
    taking out, 70–71
    thinking about, 118–119
    to tell about topic, 62, 102
    to tell the main idea, 12, 48
    using enough, 218–219, 255
Dictionary, 320, 321–322
Drafting, 4, 17–18, 68–69, 120–121, 167–168, 223–224, 272–273, G2, G3

Editor's marks. *See* Glossary.
End marks. *See* Punctuation.
Enrichment activities, language, 46, 47, 100, 101, 144, 145, 192, 193, 252, 253, 304, 305
Entertain, writing to, 151–159, 205–213, 220–230
Envelope, 300–301, 309, EP48, WH12, WH31
Exact words, using, 13, 49, 63, 102
Exclamations, 40–41, 42–43, 51, 284–285, EP9, WH3
Express, writing to, 112–113, 151–159
Extra practice, EP1–48

Foreman, Michael, 205–213
Forms, filling out, 239, 237
Friendly letter, 112–113, 146–147, 298–299, 309, EP47, WH28
    analyzing (studying) a, 114–115
    capital letters, 298–299, 309, EP47
    comma, 298–299, EP47–48
    parts of, 114, EP47, WH28
    writing a, 117–128

Glossary of composition and literary terms, G1–8
Grammar, 28–43, 78–97, 132–141, 178–189, 234–249, 284–301, WH3–9
Graph, bar, 330–331
Graphic organizer
    chart, 4, 63, 162, 165, 250, 302, 328–329, G3
    drawing, 120, 268, 270, G4
    list, 14, 62, 65, 164, 221, G4
    picture, 17, 118, 220
    story map, 214–215, 221, G5
    word map, G5

Health, 282
Helping verbs. *See* Usage; Verbs.
How-to paragraph, 259–265, 306, WH18
    analyzing (studying) a, 266–267
    writing a, 270–279
How-to sentences, 37
Hurd, Edith Thacher, 151–159

I, me, 73, 96–97, 105, 109, 200, 286–287, 307, 311, EP20, EP41, WH13
Index, using an, 324
Inform, writing to, 8–9, 54–59, 151–159, 259–265
Interview, 39
Invitation, 179, WH29

Journal entry, 29, 249, 285, WH22

Kinds of sentences, 42–43, 284–285

L

Listening. *See also* Listening and Speaking.
    to follow directions, 281
    to give reasons, 231
    for main idea, 25
Listening and speaking. *See also* Listening; Speaking.
    class talk, 16
    to follow directions, 281
    give an oral description, 175
    give directions, 280
    give reasons, 231

interview, 39
for main idea, 25
poetry, 45, 99, 143, 191, 251, 303
response group, 72
telephone, 129
tell about ideas in order, 67
Literary skills
choosing words, 13, 63, 67
Literary terms, G8
Literature, 232
Literature model
friendly letter, 112–113
how-to paragraph, 260–265
paragraph that describes, 152–159
personal story, 54–59
sentence about a picture, 8–9
story, 206–213

Main idea, 12, 17, 19–21, 25, 160
Map, 334–335
Mathematics, 76, 282
Mechanics, 284–301, WH10–12.
See also Capital letters; Punctuation.
apostrophe, 248–249, EP39, WH7, WH12
capital letters, 10, 22, 28, 73, 126, 172, 228, 284–301, WH10–11
comma, 114, 126, 298–299, 300–301, EP47–48, WH12
connecting with writing, 305
end marks, 28, 36, 38, 40, 284–285, 307, WH11–12
recognition of, 283
Merriam, Eve, 45
Message, telephone, 129, 336
Music, 26

Naming part of a sentence, 30–31, 50, 106, 198, 310, WH3
Naming words. See Nouns.
Nouns, 78–97, 310, EP11–20
connecting with writing, 101
enrichment activities, language, 100–101
more than one, 82–83, 84–85, 86–87, 104, 107, 108, 199, 311, EP13–15, WH4
people and animals, 78–79, 103, EP11, WH4
places and things, 80–81, 103, EP12, WH4
pronouns, 94–95, 96–97, 109, 200, 311, EP19–20, WH8, WH14
proper nouns
days, months, and holidays, 92–93, 105, 109, 199, 290–295, 308, EP18, EP43–45, WH5
names of people and animals, 88–89, 104, 108, 199, 286–287, 307, 311, EP41, WH5
names of places, 90–91,
105, 108, 199, 308, 311, EP42, WH5
titles of people, 286–287, 307, EP41, WH12
recognition of, 77
using, 101

Orleans, Ilo, 143, 251

Paragraph
that describes, 152–159, 173, 194, WH21
form of, 160, WH17
how-to, 260–265, WH18
that tells how things are alike, WH19
that tells how things are different, WH20
Personal story, 54–59, 102
analyzing (studying) a, 60–61
writing a, 64–75
Persuade, writing to, 293
Physical education, 130
Pictograph, 332–333
Picturing events, 116, 146
Poems, 44, 45, 99, 143, 190, 191, 251, 303
Poetry
rhymes, 44
writing, 47, 133, 237
Postcard, 91, 183
Predicate. See Telling part of a sentence.
Predicting outcomes, 217
Prefix, 250, 253, 257
Prewriting, 3, 14–15, 64–66, 118–119, 164–166, 220–222, 270–271, G3
Problem of a story, 214, 217
Pronouns. See also Usage.
He, she, it, they, 94–95, 105, 200, 311, EP19, WH8, WH14
I, me, 73, 96–97, 105, 109, 200, 307, 311, EP20, EP41, WH8, WH13
Proofreading, 5, 22, 73, 126, 172, 228, 278, G6
Publishing, 5, 23–24, 74–75, 127–128, 173–174, 229–230, 279, G5
Punctuation, 284–301. See also Mechanics.
apostrophe, 248–249, EP39, WH7, WH12
checking for, 22, 73, 126, 172, 228, 278
comma, 114, 126, 298–299, 300–301, EP47–48, WH12
exclamation point, 40–41, WH12
period, 36–37, WH11
question mark, 38–39, WH11
recognition of, 283
Purpose for reading, 8, 54, 112, 152, 206, 260
Purpose for writing, 2–5, 18, 69, 121, 168, 224, 273
to entertain, 151–159, 206–213
to express, 112–113, 151–159
to inform, 8–9, 54–59, 151–159, 259–265
to persuade, 293

Questions, 38–39, 51, 284–285, EP8, WH3

Ramsey, James, 54–59
Reader's interest, getting the, 269, 306–307
Reading model
friendly letter, 112–113
how-to paragraph, 260–265
paragraph that describes, 152–159
personal story, 54–59
sentence about a picture, 8–9
story, 206–213, WH24
Report
book, 326, WH27
dog, 189
about a picture, 87
about a play, 33
Responding, G6. See also Revising; Responding and revising.
Responding and revising, 4, 19–21, 70–71, 122–124, 125, 169–170, 171, 225–227, 274, 276, 277
Responding to literature, 9, 59, 113, 159, 213, 265
Response group, working in a, 72, G7
Revising, G7. See also Responding and revising.
combining sentences, 125, 277
Rhyming words, 44, 51, 187, 252, WH32, G8
Rosal, Lorenca, 259–265

Science, 26, 76
Sentence about a picture, 8–9, 10, 27, 48–49, WH16
analyzing (studying) a, 10–11
writing, 14–24
Sentences, 8–9, 27–43, 49, 60–61, 106, 284–285, 307, EP3–10, WH3, WH10–11
definition of, 10, 28–29, EP3, WH3
game, 243
how-to, 37
joining, 16, 123, 125, 277
kinds of, 36–37, 38–39, 40–41, 42–43, 51, 107, 198, EP10, EP40, WH3
movie script, 247
parts of, 30–33, 50, 106, 132, 198, 310, EP4–5, WH3
about a picture, analyzing (studying) a, 10, 48, WH16
recognition, 27

INDEX

INDEX

topic, 160, 167, 266, WH17–21
using, 47
word order in, 34–35, 50, 106, EP6
Sequence
checking for correct, 274
connecting ideas in, 67, 268–280, 306
time-order words, 60–61, 67, 266, 272, 280
writing in, 61–62
Setting, 214, G8
Social studies, 130, 176
Speaking. See also Listening and Speaking.
acting out sentences, 135, 252
game, 243
giving directions, 280
movie script, 247
to persuade, 293
poem, 133
puppets, using, 229
reading aloud, 46–47
report, 33
riddle, 141, 295
song, 187
telling a story, 235
Spelling, WH33–38
checking, 278
consonants, WH37
contractions, 248–249, 252, 257, 315, EP39, WH7, WH12
nouns that name more than one, 82–83, 84–85, 86–87, 104, 107–108, 199, 311, EP13–15, WH4
study steps, WH33
troublesome words, WH35
vowels, WH36
word list, WH34
Statements, 36–37, 51, 284–285, EP7, WH3
Story, 220–230, 254, WH24
analyzing (studying) a, 214–216
personal, 54–59, 74, 102
stacking, 101
structure of, 214–216
what might happen, 217, 254
writing a, 220–230
Story mapping, 214–215, 221, G5
Study skills, 317–337
ABC order, 319
chart, using a, 328–329
graph, bar, using a, 330–331
map, using a, 334–335
pictograph, 332–333
Studying types of writing. See Analyzing types of writing.
Subject. See Naming part of a sentence.
Suffix, 302, 305, 309, WH32
Synonyms, 63, 102, WH32

T

Task for writing, 17–18, 68–69, 120–121, 167–168, 223–224

Telling part of a sentence, 32–33, 50, 106, 132, 198, 310, WH3
Test, 327
Thank-you note, WH30
Thinking As a Writer 10–11, 12, 60–61, 62, 114–115, 116, 160–161, 162, 214–216, 217, 266–267, 268
Thinking processes and skills
analyzing, 10–11, 60–61, 114–115, 160–161, 214–216, 266–267
brainstorming, 14–15, 164–166, 220–222, 270–271
classifying, 62
connecting ideas, 12, 17, 61, 64
evaluating, 19–21, 70–71, 122–124, 169–170, 225–227, 274–276
observing, 162, 165, 194
synthesizing, 17–18, 68–69, 120–121, 167–168, 223–224, 272–273
visualizing, 116, 118, 146
Time-order words, 60–61, 67, 266, 272, 280
Title
of books, stories, and poems, 296–297, 309, EP46, WH11
definition, 215, 323
of people, 286–287, 307
Topic, 62, 102, 118, 160–161, 164, 266, 270, 272, G4, G7
Topic sentence, 160, 167, 266
Travel folder, 185

U

Unit checkup, 48–51, 102–105, 146–149, 194–197, 254–257, 306–309
Usage, WH13–15. See also Verbs.
he, she, it, they, 94–95, 105, 200, 311, EP19, WH14
I, me, 73, 96–97, 105, 109, 200, 307, EP20, EP41, WH13
subject/verb agreement, 134–135, 148, 234–247
words with *er* and *est,* 188

V

Verbs, 132–141, 145, 234–249. See also Usage.
action, 132–133, 147, 200, 312, EP21, WH6
come and *run,* 242–243, 256, 314, EP36, WH7, WH15
connecting with writing, 145, 253
enrichment activities, language, 144–145
go and *do,* 244–245, 257, 315, EP37, WH7, WH15
has, have, and *had,* 238–239, 256, 314, EP34, WH6, WH15
helping, 240–241, 256, EP35, WH7
is and *are,* 138–139, 148, 202, 236–237, 256, 313, EP24, EP33, WH6, WH14
recognition of, 131, 233
see and *give,* 246–247, 257, 315, EP38, WH7, WH14
subject/verb agreement, 134–135, 148, 234–247
that tell about now, 134–135, 148, 201, 234–235, 255, 312, EP22, EP32, WH6
that tell about the past, 136–137, 148, 201, 234–235, 255, 312, EP23, EP32, WH6
using, 233, 253
was and *were,* 140–141, 149, 202, 236–237, 256, 313, EP25, EP33, WH6, WH14
Vocabulary, WH32
antonyms, 190, 193, 197
compound words, 98, 105
prefix, 250, 253, 257
rhyming words, 44, 51, 187, 252, G8
suffix, 302–305, 309
synonyms, 63, 102
words with more than one meaning, 142, 149

W

Word Book, WB1–15
Word order in a sentence, 34–35, 50, 106, EP6
Words, choosing
antonyms, 190, 193, 197, WH32
colorful, 163, 194
descriptive, 171
synonyms, 63, 102
time-order, 60–61, 67, 266, 280
using exact, 13, 49, 102, 169
Words with more than one meaning, 142, 149, WH32
Writer's Handbook, WH1–38
composition, WH16–31
grammar, WH3–9
mechanics, WH10–12
spelling, WH33–38
usage, WH13–15
vocabulary, WH32
Writing, audience for. See Audience for writing.
Writing, purpose for. See Purpose for writing.
Writing, task for. See Task for writing.
Writing for your reader, 117
Writing process, 2–5, 14–24, 49, 64–75, 103, 118–128, 147, 164–170, 195, 220–230, 255, 270–276, 278–279, 307, G6–7